Environmental Politics
in Poland

Environmental Politics in Poland

A Social Movement Between Regime and Opposition

Barbara Hicks

Columbia University Press
New York

Columbia University Press
New York   Chichester, West Sussex
Copyright © 1996 Columbia University Press
All rights reserved
Library of Congress Cataloging-in-Publication Data

Hicks, Barbara (Barbara E.)
        Environmental politics in Poland : a social movement between regime and opposition / Barbara Hicks
                p. cm.
        Includes bibliographical references and index.
        ISBN 0-231-10540-1 (alk. paper) 0-231-10541-X (pbk.: alk paper)
        1. Political culture—Poland. 2. Green movement—Poland.
    3. Environmental policy—Poland. 4. Poland—Politics and government—1980–1989.
    5. Poland—Politics and government—1989–
        I. title.
        JN6766.H53   1996
        363.7'05'09438—dc20   96-19247
                                                                                          CIP

∞

Casebound editions of Columbia University Press books are printed on permanent and durable acid-free paper.
Printed in the United States of America
c 10 9 8 7 6 5 4 3 2 1
p 10 9 8 7 6 5 4 3 2 1

For Irek and Szymon

Contents

List of Tables and Diagrams

A map of Poland appears on page xix.

List of Abbreviations

BORE: Service Bureau for Environmental Movements
(*Biuro Obsługi Ruchów Ekologicznych*)

CBOS: Center for Public Opinion Research (*Centrum Badania Opinii Społecznej*)

ERS: Social Ecological Movement (*Społeczny Ruch Ekologiczny*)

GUS: Central Statistical Office (*Główny Urząd Statystyczny*)

KIK: Clubs of the Catholic Intelligentsia (*Kluby Inteligencji Katolickiej*)

KOR: Workers' Defense Committee (*Komitet Obrony Robotników*)

KOS: Committee for Social Resistance (*Komitet Oporu Społecznego*)

LOP: League for the Protection of Nature (*Liga Ochrony Przyrody*)

OBOP: Center for the Study of Public Opinion (*Ośrodek Badań Opinii Publicznej*)

PIOŚ:	State Inspectorate for Environmental Protection (*Państwowa Inspekcja Ochrony Środowiska*)
PKE:	Polish Ecological Club (*Polski Klub Ekologiczny*)
PRON:	Patriotic Movement for National Rebirth (*Patriotyczny Ruch Odrodzenia Narodowego*)
PROP:	State Council for Nature Protection (*Państwowa Rada Ochrony Przyrody*)
PROŚ:	State Council for Environmental Protection (*Państwowa Rada Ochrony Środowiska*)
PTTK:	Polish Society for Tourism and Knowledge of the Country (*Polskie Towarzystwo Turystyczno-Krajoznawcze*)
PUWP:	Polish United Workers' Party (*Polska Zjednoczona Partia Robotnicza*)
REFA:	Ecological Movement of St. Francis of Assisi (*Ruch Ekologiczny Św. Fanciszka z Asyżu*)
RS:	Statistical Yearbook (*Rocznik Statystyczny*)
TOT:	Society for the Protection of the Tatras (*Towarzystwo Ochrony Tatr*)
TWWP:	Society for a Free Polish University (*Towarzystwo Wolnej Wszechnicy Polskiej*)
WB:	"I Prefer to Be" (*Wolę Być*)
WiP:	Freedom and Peace (*Wolność i Pokój*)

Preface

Like the country it studies, this book has undergone several transitions. It started in 1986 as a study of the post-Solidarity "normalization" process, the attempt by communist leaders to reestablish a stable Soviet-type regime and control over society after a deep systemic crisis. By the end of that year it was clear to me that Poland was not "normalizing" and that the very policies the Jaruzelski regime adopted to achieve this goal actually were undermining it. First and foremost, this book describes this dynamic, tracing the growth of independent activism and the failure of "normalization."

A newer dimension of the study is my discussion of social movements. At the time of the original design, this was a secondary concern. Yet, when I returned from Poland in the fall of 1988, I realized that my analysis of the Polish ecological movement spoke to new ideas in social movement theory, especially the notions of political opportunity structure and national political context. This study's independent confirmation of these new trends is heartening, although I should say that the limitations one faces researching independent activism in a communist country do not always allow one the best possible sources of evidence for analyzing social movement development. I hope my findings suggest how a literature that has been focused on advanced capitalist societies in the West might be extended elsewhere. In any case, by 1989 this had become a book about a social movement.

Another new dimension of this study is a discussion of regime transition. I focus on one piece of the transition here—what is going on in society. By looking at the dynamics among societal actors I attempt to go beyond generalizations about "civil society" and "its" role in the transition. I do not reject the term "civil society"; indeed, I am interested in the roles of various actors in the project of building a civil society compatible with liberal democracy. However, in many discussions of democratic transitions and of the 1989 revolutions in Eastern Europe, "civil society" has become reified to the point that the use of that term masks—rather than reveals—the real dynamics in a society. With this study I want to shine a light into the shadows that surround those dynamics. Thus, the most recent purpose of the book is to analyze the role of social forces in the transition to democracy, particularly in the demise of communist rule.

A few technical notes to the reader are in order. As the study on which this book is based spans the communist and post-communist periods, several problems arose with verb tenses. Generally, I have placed the text into the past tense. Many of the actors and serials I discuss still exist, but since the context in which they function has changed so much, it is appropriate to consider their activities until the formation of the Solidarity government separately from the present. The original study ended with the beginning of regime transition. Follow-up research in the summer of 1993 allows reflection on the findings of the first study and leads me to discuss the current situation in chapter 8. Thus, in that chapter I have switched to the present tense.

I follow convention in calling the Polish United Workers' Party the "communist" party and referring to the 1945–1989 period as "communist." This does not mean that I agree that this label is a truly appropriate description; rather I recognize the political labels and the self-identification of the rulers during that period. Likewise, I use the terms "Eastern Europe" and "East European" in their political rather than geographic sense to denote the former European communist countries outside of Soviet borders. As the communist experience becomes less and less a defining feature of the present, applying the term "Eastern Europe" to this area is becoming more and more inappropriate. I am glad to see geography and pre-communist history reentering our discussion of the region, but in this book I maintain the post-World War II usage of "Eastern Europe" because it is a generally understood identifier for the period at the heart of my study. Finally, translations are given in the text for major offices and institutions, and the full reference for all laws and other sources are given at their first appearance in each chapter. Thereafter, I have used abbreviated forms.

Acknowledgments

This project has undergone many transformations since it was originally conceived. At each turn I have accrued a number of intellectual debts and benefitted from various grants and institutional support.

I would like, first of all, to thank my dissertation committee members Jack Bielasiak, Russell Hanson, Jeffrey Hart, Owen Johnson, and György Ránki. Agreeable as a group, as individuals each offered unique and valuable insights of their own. Jack Bielasiak has supported my work from the very beginning of my graduate career. His knowledge, insight and patience saw me through both graduate school and this project. Russ Hanson and Jeff Hart have always given me interesting things to think about and tolerated my amateur straying into unknown waters. On this project, they presented me with different perspectives and helped me to shape my own thoughts, at times quite differently, I am sure, than they expected. Thank you to Owen Johnson for agreeing to pick up the dissertation late and coming up with many great comments in the home stretch. György Ránki offered several insights and interesting comparisons in the early stages of this project. His untimely death came as a shock and tragedy to all of us who knew him as a teacher, scholar and friend.

A special debt of gratitude goes to Professor Zbigniew Wierzbicki in Poland, a great source of knowledge and contacts with movement participants. I was also lucky enough to have the guidance of Witold Morawski at Warsaw University and the organizers of the Nature-Man-Values seminar at the Polish Academy of Sciences. Many activists shared their time and experiences with me. Their work was not only one of the subjects of my study, but also the inspiration that kept it going. I would especially like to thank Piotr Gliński and Przemysław Czajkowski for information, printed materials, and introductions during the second phase of my research.

Several colleagues offered helpful comments on the manuscript at various stages of revisions. In particular, I would like to thank Steven Levine, Gary Marks, Gordon Whitaker, and the anonymous reviewers at Columbia University Press, who provided truly insightful suggestions. Michael Lienesch, James White, George Rabinowitz, Pete Andrews, Robert Hicks, Evelyne Huber, and Stephen Leonard also offered timely and sage advice on revisions to individual sections or the overarching framework of the book. Earlier versions of some chapters benefitted greatly from comments at conferences. In particular, I am grateful for the discussion of my work by participants in the Wilson Center's 1989 Junior Scholars' Training Seminar and by numerous colleagues at the 1991 and 1993 national meetings of the American Association for Advancement of Slavic Studies, as well as the Seventh International Conference of the Europeanists. Jan Kubik and Krzysztof Jasiewicz offered valuable insights on more than one of these occasions. Finally, I would like to thank those in my intellectual community who, in addition to the scholars cited above, helped to shape my broader understanding of Poland and politics of the time that I was most engaged in the research for this book—Michael Ausbrook, Angela Baker, Michael Bernhard, Lynn Berry, Carolyn Cooke, Keith Fitzgerald, Brendan Kiernan, Zenia Opuszko, Kristen Parris, Patricia Pauly, Mark Peterson, Tom Shaffer, Katarzyna Staszyńska and Ellie Valentine.

I have also accumulated a few debts for editorial, administrative and logistical help in the course of researching and writing this book. Kate Wittenberg and Leslie Bialler of Columbia University Press were resolute in their support and very adroit and cheerful in their handling of the manuscript. This is a better book for their input. Thanks are due to Amanda Quinby for the graphics and Roberta Engleman for the index. My appreciation also goes to Michael Ausbrook, Sharon LaRoche, Virginia Martin and Marian Żelazny for administrative and technical support, and to Ralph, Carolyn and Frank for the use of the farm.

This study was funded primarily by dissertation research grants from the International Research Exchanges Board (IREX), with funds provided by the National Endowment for the Humanities and the United States Information Agency, and the Fulbright-Hays program of the U.S. Department of Education. I discovered the topic of this study and developed my research plans while in Poland on the Indiana University-Warsaw University Exchange Program. During both that first stay and my research year I received institutional support from Warsaw University's Ośrodek Studiów Amerykańskich and Indiana University's Polish Studies Center. The staffs of these two centers offered invaluable advice and assistance with bureaucratic problems and legalities in both countries. Additional research funding was provided by Indiana University's Russian and East European Institute in the form of a Mellon Grant-in-Aid of Research to travel to the holdings of the Poland Watch Center in Washington, D.C. and by the Graduate School of Indiana University in the form of a dissertation fellowship while I was doing my preliminary library research. During the writing phase of this project, I received a dissertation write-up grant from the Joint Committee on Eastern Europe (JCEE) of the American Council of Learned Societies and the Social Science Research Council. The East European Program of the Woodrow Wilson Center International Center for Scholars also provided intellectual support by funding my participation in its Junior Scholars' Training Seminar. The Indiana Center on Global Change and World Peace at Indiana University allowed me a year of support for both writing and participation in its interdisciplinary MacArthur Scholars' program. Follow-up research in the summer of 1993 was made possible by funds provided by the JCEE as part of its support for creating a position in East European politics at the University of North Carolina. None of these organizations is responsible for the views expressed.

Despite all of these intellectual and financial contributions to this project, ultimate responsibility for its content and flaws is mine alone. Had I been able to incorporate more of the insights offered by my colleagues there might have been fewer of those flaws. As it is, I know the suggestions that I was able to act upon have improved the text.

When all of the preparation, travel and research was done and the arduous chore of writing and rewriting began, one person had to live through this task with me. Although I would not wish my worst enemy this fate, my husband Irek endured it with good humor and without flagging in his moral support.

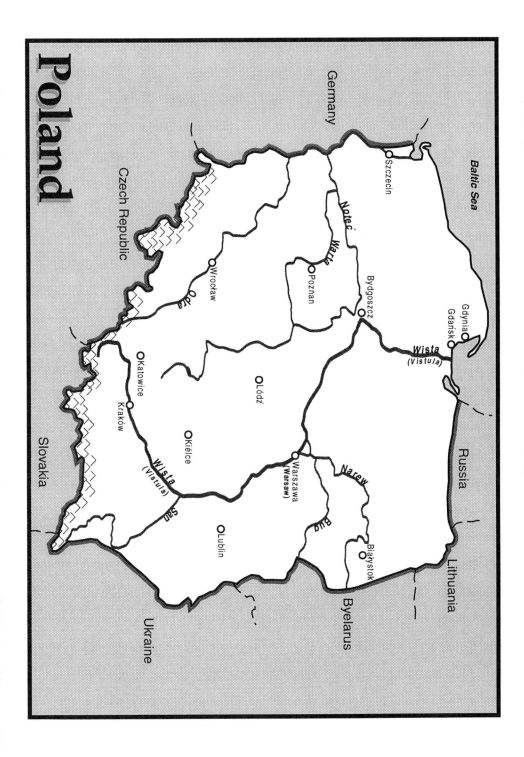

Environmental Politics
in Poland

Introduction

This book uses environmental politics as a window into the complexities of societal activism in the decade during which communist rule in Poland disintegrated. It then turns briefly to the reorganization of environmental activism during the regime transition of the early 1990s. I am interweaving four stories. The first story is that of a regime's failure to control social activism and, more precisely, the backfiring of its policies for doing so. That failure was the final crucial domestic element in the collapse of communist rule in Poland. In the midst of this overarching argument is the story of how an independent social movement emerged and developed in this Soviet-type system. Together these accounts give us an empirical case study of environmental politics in Poland, the third story. The fourth story—of how the environmental movement adjusts to its transforming context—is just beginning, but is worth telling for what it suggests both for politics and for ecology in the new era of Polish politics.

Poland's first partially free election in 1989 proved to be the final test that ended the "Brezhnev Doctrine" of limited sovereignty. After a non-communist government was installed in Poland without Soviet censure, other transformation processes in Eastern Europe quickly passed beyond the old barrier of maintaining communist rule. Those first Polish elections, in turn, resulted largely from the government's failure to "normalize" society after the 1980–81 Solidarity period. "Normalization" meant return to a functioning post-Stalinist system with a centrally administered economy and polity which guaranteed the leading role of the communist party and obedience to the Soviet Union.[1] Concerted attempts to reimpose these systemic features occurred in Eastern Europe after large portions of the citizenry had rejected them, or the policies resulting from them, in major political upheavals—including the East German workers' uprising (1953), Hungarian Revolution (1956), Czechoslovak "Prague Spring" (1968) and Polish "Solidarity" Period (1980–81). By repressing reform movements and atomizing society, linking economic welfare to political obedience and denying the chance for effective agency on the part of social groups, these regimes sought to create an acquiescent population of isolated individuals whose only hope for improvement of their situation was vested in carefully controlled "reform from above."

If Poland was indeed the critical case that opened the way for the overthrow of state socialism in Eastern Europe, then the question of how normalization failed in Poland is integral to understanding not only the Polish transition but also the process of system change throughout the bloc. This study focuses on the development of a social movement to examine the mechanism by which the regime's strategy for reasserting communist authority faltered. The failure of the government's strategy was linked directly to a key factor in the East European "revolutions"— the evolution and role of social forces. Studying a social movement that developed in the final decade of communist rule helps tease out the processes going on in society at large, a much more amorphous topic.

Beyond its usefulness as a window into state-society relations in Poland in the 1980s and thus into the system's disintegration, examination of the environmental movement in that country allows us to engage a few general questions that arise when studying social movements. Theorists have debated the sources of social movement activism, focusing among other things on individual psyches and decisionmaking processes, resources available to different groups and networks, changes in the nature of society or social structure, and the opportunities afforded by national political processes and institutions. Examining the evolution of a single movement in detail is one way to determine the major sources of and limitations on social movement development. Within the literature that looks at "new social movements," including environmentalism, the debate about the origins of activism centers on a search for the source of "newness." Do these new movements derive from post-industrial attitudes, the structure of advanced capitalism, or some other source? Identification of such a movement in a noncapitalist society helps to rule out or revise at least one of those arguments. Finally, an understudied aspect of social movements—their development under authoritarian systems—is also illuminated by looking at the experience of a movement under communist rule.

For those interested in environmental politics, this study provides empirical information about the governmental structures, laws, ideology, economic conditions, and social actors determining environmental policy in communist Poland. In so doing, it provides a baseline for studying current environmental politics and, more specifically, the fate of this issue area during regime transition. A preliminary look at the evolution of the ecological movement a few years into the transition suggests some tentative conclusions about new directions in environmental politics. For those interested in the quality of life in Poland—or, more broadly, in post-communist countries faced with severe ecological destruction of parts of their territories—the evolution of this issue area during political and economic transformation is of central importance.

Structure of This Study

The main task of this study is to examine two interrelated processes: the development of the Polish ecological movement and the failure of normalization. Together they form a case study in the development of "civil society" in Poland during the 1980s. Chapter 1 introduces the theoretical questions raised by this case. The following two chapters look at the economic, ideological, legal and administrative conditions that shaped the physical state of the environment and gave rise to social demands for change. The basic argument is that ideologically driven decisions about the nature of industrialization and about public debate predisposed the system to ecological degradation (chapter 2). Given these fundamental circumstances, Poland needed—but did not develop—an effective body of legislation and strong environmental administration to mitigate the damage caused by economic activity and rapid urbanization (chapter 3).

The focus then switches to the nature and development of the Polish ecological movement itself. A review of the forms of identity present in the ecological movement shows that it exhibits the traits characteristic of "new social movements" in the West (chapter 4). Western theory about the origin and role of these types of movements suggests that they both result from and seek change in society. These observations hold for the Polish environmental movement as well. The fifth chapter extends the "new social movement" argument by looking at the variety of organizational forms and the types of activism present in the movement. Not only do these characteristics provide further evidence of the movement's "fit" with new social movement patterns, they also demonstrate that the movement actively engaged in politics. In seeking institutional, procedural, and policy changes movement actors avoided the retreat from the political sphere into identity-seeking typical of some "new" and alternative social movements.

The third section of this study turns to the relations between the movement and the two main political actors in Poland in the 1980s—the regime and the Solidarity opposition. A review of opposition activism on environmental issues and the underground press shows that, although the opposition was instrumental in changing the Polish political arena for independent actors, including the ecology movement, it did not take the lead in pressing environmental issues onto the political agenda (chapter 6). The opposition did support some movement activities, but remained focused on broader political and economic issues. Still, the threat that the environment would become an "opposition issue" was a major force compelling the government to address the ecologists' and increasingly the public's concerns. Chapter 7 looks at the progression of the regime's normalization policies toward the movement. These policies and the growth of the movement were intertwined both temporally and substantively. Indeed, the government's policies led to wider press coverage and more critical analysis of environmental problems, both of which increased public awareness and support for ecology. In strengthening the base and appeal of the movement, these normalization policies actually undermined the general goal of normalization itself, that is the reassertion of regime control over society. Thus, of the competing explanations for how social movements arise this case supports those arguments that focus on opportunities provided by national political processes and institutions as the major factor shaping movement formation.

The eighth chapter is based on further research undertaken in 1993, four years after communist rule ended. The environmental movement has undergone some internal changes and has begun to function in its new political context. The internal changes have been shaped by the new political system and international influences, lending support to the view that the national political process is crucial to shaping social movements and their institutionalization as interest or pressure groups. Environmentalists' impact on domestic policy, however, remains quite weak because the policy agenda is crowded and the new political institutions and parties are too weak to serve as effective targets of interest activism.

In the end we come back to the question of what the development of this movement tells us about the development of "civil society" in Poland in the 1980s and its role in the transition to democracy. Also highlighted are some of the implications of this study for the general study of social movements.

1

Civil Society, Normalization and Transition

The formation and growth of an independent ecology movement in Poland in the 1980s was part of a much larger process of social and political change. The political dynamics of this period, taking place in the context of the failure of state socialism to meet the challenges of further economic modernization, can perhaps best be understood as an interaction between the regime's strategy for demobilizing social forces and what has been called the "reconstitution of civil society."

"Civil Society" in the Transition to Democracy

In discussions of the transitions in East Central Europe much attention has been focused on "civil society," on its constitution or reconstitution, inspired by democratic oppositions and carried out in contradistinction to the party-state and its officially controlled public sphere.[1] An independently constituted "civil society" has been proffered as one of the two primary forces explaining the downfall of communist rule in Eastern Europe, the other being Gorbachev's reforms and decision, when pressed, to retreat from empire. Moving back to the roots of these more immediate actors, we see two fundamental causes of the collapse. One was the economic failure of centrally planned economies to innovate in order to compete in the international economy and assure a continuing rise in the standard of living at home. The other was the growing pressure from a variety of groups—human rights activists, peace and ecology movements, national movements—as well as a plethora of socioeconomic interests for limits on authoritarian rule and an opening of the political process to interests outside the party-state elite. The rise of a civil society can thus be seen as both a fundamental and a proximate cause of the transition out of authoritarian rule.

A "civil society" is also seen by some as the greatest hope—or its lack the greatest fear—for the success of the second phase of transition, the building of democracy. Despite the complexities of employing a concept derived from discussions of political systems quite different from Eastern Europe's state socialism, the very use of the term "civil society" by participants in the East European revolutions, those involved in the praxis of evoking just such a civil society, compels its study by scholars of that area. Yet, there are other, more analytical reasons to use the term. Since one of the goals involved in democratization is the creation of a civil society comparable to those for which the term is used in Western democracies, analyzing progress toward the establishment of a democratic civil society becomes part of the study of these political transitions. More directly related to the term's use in describing the development of Western liberal democracy in an earlier period[2] are the projects underway to develop a democratic civil society. During the transition negotiations and the establishment of new political institutions, East Central European elites searched for ways to subordinate the state to control by civil society, to make the state society's instrument for self-government. There have also been more decentralized efforts by many groups to establish associations for a wide variety of purposes from the local to the national level. Finally, a few have tried to build more concerted interest associations to provide links between certain sectors of society and the policymaking process of the state. Thus, whatever one's definition of civil society, its development is very much on the agenda of East European transitions.

The conscious self-shaping of Polish civil society under communist rule has reflections in other epochs of Polish history, but its immediate roots are to be found in the new evolutionist strategy of the late 1970s. Espoused by Adam Michnik and other opposition intellectuals, "new evolutionism" advocated the creation of an unofficial public sphere from below as an alternative to officially delineated public life. Rather than attempting to reform the official sphere directly, members of society would develop their own public sphere alongside the official, eventually transforming the latter.[3] The reconstitution of a civil society not controlled by the state was thus a matter of building new identities and patterns of interaction from the "grass roots" of society.

In Poland, this strategy resulted in a flourishing of independent thought and culture in the late 1970s and eventually enabled Solidarity's explosive growth in 1980–81.[4] Social initiatives mushroomed and civil society grew strong and conscious during the first Solidarity period. Yet, the pluralism implicit in the new evolutionist strategy was somewhat eclipsed by the tendency of various social forces to unite under one umbrella against the party-state during both the Solidarity period and martial law.[5] Once martial law was lifted, the number and variety of social initiatives grew rapidly, this time with no attempt to unify, which made society as a whole much less readily controllable by the state or even by opinion-making elites within society itself. The existence of numerous groups, movements, and other social entities expanded the field for social action independent of both the official and opposition spheres, allowing many new actors to emerge whose concerns and identities were formulated on bases and philosophies other than participation in or opposition to the party-state.

This wide variety of social initiatives suggests that, despite its relevance as a *subject* of analysis, as a *unit* of analysis explaining regime transformation the term "civil society" may mask more than it clarifies. When used in and about Eastern Europe, the term came to mean the total of the unofficial public sphere—i.e. social activity not directly structured by the state—and all of the collective and individual actors engaged in this sphere. Although such an understanding of "civil society" had a normative use when confronting the party-state, it can muddle our understanding of politics in that period. Some authors have tried to break the term down or define it more narrowly in order to add more precision to their analyses. Driving the attempt to define civil society more precisely is not just the preoccupation of social scientists with taxonomy, but also the desire to understand what is at the heart of this phenomenon that makes it so central to democracy.

Narrowing the concept of civil society usually implies drawing boundaries along one of two dimensions. The first dimension, often portrayed as a "vertical" delineation of civil society's place between individuals and the state, could also be considered movement from the periphery of private life toward the core of the political system. Thus, binding the concept of civil society becomes asking how much of informal activity on one end and formal political organization on the other end we should include.[6] What types of actors do we include? Among the candidates might be: individuals speaking out or voting, study groups, choirs, social movements, pressure groups, organized interests and political parties. The concept of civil society cannot include all of social life or it would become synonymous with society. On the other hand, focusing only on well-established actors carries the danger of reifying civil society by leaving out some of the more fluid processes—those of norm formation and mobilization in a society—that actually produce these more formal collective actors and in so doing become the original vehicles for social influence in the polity, thus for democracy.

The second definitional dimension of civil society can be conceived of as "horizontal." How much of the economy, an important shaper of political actors, do we include?[7] Likewise, should we include state-initiated social organizations? Hegelian and Marxian conceptions of civil society are rooted in the economy, yet many contemporary theorists tend to counterpose civil society to both the state and the market. The creation of a public space, emphasized above, is not only fundamental to the development and continuance of civil society, it is also a process of resisting penetration by the market and the state. However, the economy clearly has a strong influence in defining social groups and generating many of the collective actors who engage in social and political processes, e.g. class, regional, and sectoral interests. These actors are an important part of civil society, even if economic organization itself is left outside the bounds of the concept.

One's overall definition of civil society blends decisions taken on both of these dimensions. Many authors define the space. If we conceive of civil society as a public space for social organization free from the direct control of the state, we still need to delineate who occupies this space. I favor including a broad range of actors from intellectual currents to institutionalized interest groups, as long as their actions are directed toward public life. This last requirement derives from the fact that the referent for my definition is the political system. Thus, I would not include choirs in civil society but I would include charities and social movements. The reason I include such a range of actors is that I feel that the normative content of "civil society" when it is used in reference to democracy depends on the notion that the norms of society shape the political system and public policy. To capture this essence, we have to include the processes of norm formation and initial informal mobilization to forward those norms in our definition of civil society. Although slightly narrower than a conception of civil society as all of the unofficial public sphere, this definition is still too broad to use as an explanatory variable. To understand the political dynamics leading to the fall of communist rule, then, we have to look more individually at the collective actors of civil society. My focus here will be on one type of collective actor—on social movements and their relationship to the state as well as to change in the broader civil society.

In the Polish context, where much has been made of the "us-them"[8] perspective that united society against the party-state, it is also useful to make a further distinction among the collective actors of civil society. Some political actors cannot be classified as belonging to the "us" of the political opposition or the "them" of the party-state. Indeed some deliberately superseded that split to define their identities on their own terms. The Roman Catholic Church is perhaps the clearest and earliest example of an independent actor, one that was important enough to influence the political framework for other collective actors, including Solidarity. The Church, however, is a unique case in Poland of a historically embedded and powerful institution. The collective actors to which I refer here are a host of small movements and associations—for example, ecology and peace movements, alternative youth and culture movements, consumer associations.[9] Although they functioned in a political context largely defined by the conflict between the state and Solidarity, these other actors must be considered "independent." Now, when the party-state has been broken down and the unity of the opposition and of the "civil society" that resisted the party-state's control has also disintegrated, the societal actors that formed their identities differently may be better suited to adapt to the new situation, to maintain collective identities or at least values around which interests in society can organize and become the more conventionally understood civil society of democratic systems.

The environmental movement in Poland during the 1980s sought to influence norms and lifestyles in society, other collective actors, and the state. Moreover, it included groups that could be considered oppositional, independent, and even official. These disparate environmental groups united in a movement through those common elements of their identities which focused on the way society lived and on the values and programs of political actors. The disparity in participants' political and social backgrounds reinforced the tendency of the movement to supersede the "us-them" conflict in Polish politics and to define itself as independent of both the political opposition and the party-state. This "independence," of course, was made possible by the existence of a strong political opposition which both opened up an arena of social activity that was not controlled by the state and expanded the regime's tolerance of activity that fell short of hardcore underground political opposition. Yet, independent movements also strengthened the political opposition by adding a heterogeneity to the civil society the opposition sought to create, a heterogeneity that rendered it impossible for the party-state to control all collective actors in society.

To understand the process by which this heterogeneous independent society emerged in the 1980s, we must turn to the other half of state-society interaction: the government's ultimately ineffective strategy for reasserting control over society—for breaking the wave of activism that started in the late 1970s, produced Solidarity, and rebuilt after martial law to bring Poland to the 1989 elections.

Environmentalism, Normalization and Communist Rule

Normalization failed in Poland. Profound economic and legitimacy crises were compounded by the refusal of many in society to believe in and cooperate with government reforms. General Jaruzelski's attempts to restore central control over society after the 1980–81 Solidarity period could not combat the persistence and proliferation of a wide variety of social initiatives. The environmental movement's development illustrates this process. Not only was that movement a specific target of normalization policies, but those policies also failed to coopt the ecological groundswell and even contributed to the reach and force of the movement by inadvertently encouraging the creation and activism of independent groups.

The failure of normalization, in turn, was the failure of the regime's last strategy for maintaining the system. After a series of crises throughout the period of communist rule, the party had exhausted the range of feasible crisis-management strategies that would achieve social peace and reassert the authority of the regime.[10] This dearth of strategies resulted from a history of political, economic, and social crises in Poland and was reflected in the unusual nature of the Polish normalization process. First, the military—the official institution which enjoyed the most respect among the people—was compelled to step in not only to implement martial law but also to rule afterward. One could argue that the military was the party in uniform, but, whether or not this argument holds, Poland in the early 1980s was notably the first case in the Soviet bloc where the military occupied most of the major positions in the government. Second, the Jaruzelski normalization process was much more open and legalistic than had been the case in Hungary in 1956 and in Czechoslovakia in 1968. The Polish regime was forced by the nature of the Solidarity challenge, persistent economic crisis and the history of political crises to seek a further-reaching accommodation with society than had been required to achieve stable control in the other states. Such accommodation and the measures necessary to achieve it carried, in turn, more risks for losing or changing the nature of regime control over society.

As the Polish government struggled to achieve an elusive "normalization" the burgeoning environmental movement presented a challenge to the reestablishment of social peace by means of return to a modified *status quo ante* Solidarity. The challenge was both similar to that of other social initiatives and distinct. Like several other groups and movements, environmentalism was a threat to "classical" East European normalization in that it evoked collective actors engaged in activities outside the control of the state and made demands critical of state institutions and policies precisely during the period when the party-state was trying to reassert control over society and build a new legitimating rationale. It is this similarity with other social initiatives that makes the environmental movement such an instructive case study of the politics of normalization. The environmental challenge was (and remains) distinctive, however, because it addressed an issue that was as fundamental as the economy but virtually ignored by the state and not of primary importance to Solidarity.[11] Moreover, the physical measurability of ecological destruction rendered purely political solutions to environmental demands ineffective and assured a constant source for renewed activism and critique, one that continues under the new political system. Thus, as an issue to be dealt with during normalization, the environment was particularly persistent, matched only by the failure of the economic system.

Accordingly, the independence of the environmental movement and the salience of its critique of state policies made the movement an early and clear target for the Jaruzelski regime's efforts to normalize through inclusion and cooptation. However, attempts to coopt the movement failed. These efforts failed because the goals and identity of the movement superseded the primary political cleavage in Poland, because the regime could not offer effective environmental policies as an incentive to become politically quiescent, and because resistance to inclusion had been rendered less frightening by the existence of a more radical political opposition. Despite its critical nature, the Polish ecological movement grew larger and more active in a period during which, according to the pattern established in earlier cases of East European normalization, the government should have repressed all independent initiatives.

The Normalization Quandary

Although normalization was the expressed goal of the Jaruzelski government, it was not altogether clear that Poland would go through this period without profound changes that would take the system in a new direction. Theorizing about Soviet-type systems held that such normalization was based on a few key principles, some of which were stretched, if not broken, in the Polish case. The most developed model of post-crisis normalization in these countries divides normalization into three stages, each with essential tasks to be performed. The first stage is to stop unrest and crush the "cause" of the crisis. Defeat should be swift and complete. All social initiatives and reform activity must be repressed. During the second stage the population is atomized by dismantling any remaining social groups of suspect character, including purging official organizations that have become "corrupted" during the unrest. Only once people have given up hope of bringing about any changes from below and recognized defeat as irreversible is it possible to move on to the last stage. In the third stage the regime links economic rewards to political obedience and might introduce some small changes as long as citizens continue to acknowledge that all change or "reform" comes through official channels (Mlynar 1982, 3–4). In Poland, the continued existence of a well-organized opposition meant that resistance and hope had not been fully crushed. Economic crisis—both in the country and in the bloc as a whole—also limited the government's room for maneuver in linking economic rewards to political quiescence.

In the case of the Polish environmental movement, serious ecological problems were first raised in public discussion by independent actors. Physical conditions demanded action. Poland's water, air, and soil were so polluted that in some regions the damage to human health was severe. If the government were to continue to put off effective action, the situation would only have become worse and stronger civil action was likely to be combined with growing involvement of the political opposition. This was exactly what East European communist-ruled governments did not want to see. Normalization would then be threatened or, at most, supplanted by the use of force. Another possible scenario was that the government's resolve not to acknowledge social demands from outside official political institutions would produce a general sense of resignation in an already tired and increasingly atomized society. This might have been the case, especially if ecological activism had been coopted by the creation of ineffective official groups and organizations. Still, resignation would likely have been only temporary, because the problems would have continued to worsen, in many cases exponentially. It would only have been a matter of time before groups in society, which were already looking at serious health problems, renewed their efforts toward effective action on the part of the government, the owner and operator of the polluting factories.

On the other hand, if the government acted to address concerns raised by ecologists, independent collective action would then have been successful in pressing upon the government demands which were inherently critical of past and present official policy, even of ideology. Thus, a sense of agency based on independent activism would be returned to groups in civil society. This, in turn, was a threat to normalization as commonly understood to involve societal atomization and the explicit recognition that change can only come from above and that any demands must be forwarded through official channels. The logical conclusion was either that normalization in Poland was threatened by the types of activism in which the environmental movement was engaging or that existing theory regarding normalization must be changed.

From the imposition of martial law, the Polish case presented a challenge for would-be theorists of normalization. At first there was a general disbelief that normalization would even be achieved for a number of political and economic reasons.[12] Then analysts began to see a general normalizing trend, but one that had a number of peculiarities and implied further-reaching political change than in the other cases (Kolankiewicz 1988, 180–83). This study follows the latter trend, suggesting that to reduce the political onus of and begin to resolve ecological problems, the government not only had to allow social forces access to policy agendas at various levels of government but also had to give ecologically minded experts a fair amount of true power in policy formulation and implementation at the heart of the most important sectors of the economy. These changes, however, go well beyond the scope of "normalization."

We have now come back to a conceptual quandary never clarified either by those implementing normalization policies or by those studying this process. In order to achieve long-term stability, these policies could not simply return the country to the *status quo ante*, as the original sources of discontent and mobilization would remain. The question remained open as to what sorts and how much modification of the *status quo ante* could fall within the bounds of the concept.

Inclusion: Normalization Revised

George Kolankiewicz expanded the understanding of normalization, stressing the need of the normalizing regime to exercise more inclusionary policies to validate its rule (1988, 153–54).[13] Indeed, in East European communist systems inclusion of extra-systemic demands into the system had long been a method of mobilizing support for the regime (Jowitt 1975). However, the government had always defined the terms of such cooperation. "Inclusion" meant bringing the demands or groups in question under the limitations imposed by participation in the system, implicitly reinforcing the polity as it existed while diffusing societal criticism and at most adding or changing some policies. As such, the term "inclusion" was synonymous with the term "cooptation." Yet, theoretically, inclusion could also result in more of an incorporation that imparted change to all parties concerned, including the system itself.

Kolankiewicz goes on to demonstrate that the Jaruzelski government in fact applied an inclusionary strategy, which allowed for the development of social groups, organizations and institutions, "the growth of rule-boundedness," and the cooptation of opinion-makers outside of the official sphere (1988, 155–57). Claiming that normalization cannot occur without authentic discussion between autonomous actors, Kolankiewicz concludes that "the political limits of normalization must extend far enough to accept these preconditions" (p. 176). In other words, if the included social forces are so thoroughly coopted into the existing system that they lose their autonomy to act as they deem necessary to secure their interests, they cannot speak on behalf of those interests and thus cannot contribute to normalization. By losing social support, these groups lose their usefulness to the government as instruments of social control.[14]

Kolankiewicz's discussion of inclusionary policies provides for an extension of the amount of change tolerable in normalization, allowing us to reexamine whether the environmental movement indeed fits within the confines of normalization policies. Much of the regime's response to the new political issue of the environment was along the lines Kolankiewicz described. Environmentalists became a significant enough force in society to become a target of inclusion politics only in the mid-1980s. Yet, they were a difficult target, because they came from all socio-economic groups (even though well-educated white-collar workers and students predominated), spanned the age spectrum from schoolchildren to retirees, and organized themselves into several different sorts of associations with different goals. The tenacity of environmental problems and their physical measurability made cooptation, muddling-through policies, and redefinitions of abstract concepts like political participation ineffective political strategies for government officials who wanted to control ecological groups. In the case of ecology, inclusion had to bring policy change. And, as experience had taught many in Polish society, there are no guarantees of policy change and its implementation without changes in the procedures of policymaking and institutional changes to assure those procedural changes.[15] Thus, both the process of inclusion and the guarantee of policy changes required to keep these social forces "included" implied changes in economic priorities, planning, policymaking, related institutions, oversight authority, and ultimately power. Taken together, these changes represented systemic changes and indicated the likely direction of political development in Poland—before the revolutions of 1989 brought down the entire bloc system—toward decentralization, depoliticization of expert and social participation in policymaking, and reorientation of economic priorities.

For the success of normalization, however, a couple of problems proved intractable. First, a number of independent initiatives remained just that, independent, beyond the control of the government. Furthermore, the determination of ecologists who allowed themselves to be included into the political process was such that, had government measures continued to be insufficient, they would have continued to press ecological issues in any forum and form necessary, even at the price of exclusion. This determination was most visible in the fact that many individual ecologists engaged simultaneously in official, independent and even opposition initiatives. Ironically, inclusion had not coopted the majority of ecologists but it had made them and their cause more visible to the general public. If the government intended to keep at least this group of ecologists included sufficiently to control environmental activism, it would have to accept regular social influences and changes hitherto unseen. Meaningful inclusion in this case represented a change of the old system—political evolution, not just normalization of the political situation so as to uphold the old system.

Major factors determining the outcome of inclusion are the nature of the issues involved, the strength and determination of the social forces to be included, and the dynamics of the interaction between these forces and the government. With growing environmental activism on the part of various social groups and the government's belated realization that something had to be done at least to slow the degradation of the environment, all sides were confronted with the imperative of cooperation. The Polish government—in part fearing opposition involvement—did engage in discussions of ecology, and the process of its engagement as well as the discussions themselves had an irreversible effect on public awareness of the issues. From a political point of view, this strategy was dangerous, as any analysis of ecological problems in Poland was a critique of many aspects of the system: official ideology with respect to industrialization, official policies in a number of domains, the policy agenda and its creation, the structure and conduct of parts of the political, economic, and judicial system, information policies, the development and use of technology, and the role of social forces in the political system. In other words, ecologists' critiques, even restrained, were radical.

Social Movements

As I examine the growth of environmental activism, I am not only describing normalization's failure. I am also analyzing the development of a social movement. The term "social movement" is a theoretical construct. "Scholars infer their [social movements'] presence from selected combinations of ideas and actions, and they do not otherwise exist as separate or distinct social realities" (Sklar 1988, 4; cf. Melucci 1980, 202; Kitschelt 1985, 275). A social movement is the product of actions taken by many concrete actors. Yet, once used in a particular context, the term and the entities it embraces reinforce each other. These actors themselves may use the term "social movement" for strategic reasons having to do with the formation of an identity and its recognition by other actors in the same political context. Conversely, the use of this label by others outside the movement can contribute to the development of the movement and self-awareness of its participants. The growth of the movement and the sharpening of its identity, in turn, confirm the relevance of the theoretical construct used to describe those phenomena.

This study will use the following working definition of a social movement: a number of actors—groups and individuals—united by their communication, actions and goals around a certain set of issues or vision, a principal element of which is change in society itself.[16] The unifying theme of a social movement is the change sought by or inherent in the actions and goals of actors in the movement. What defines it as *a* movement is the network of direct and indirect communications among its component actors. What makes a movement "social" is a matter of some debate. Confusion results from the use of "social" to mean (1) action that is undertaken by members of society and/or (2) action that targets society itself for change. Since almost all movements are comprised of actors from society, the first criterion is of little value in distinguishing "social movements" from other movements. That leaves the second criterion. As distinct from movements which seek only specific benefits or discrete policy changes, social movements seek to change some aspect(s) of the organization or norms of civil society, either directly or through the state. That is, they strive in at least some respect to be transformative by affecting everyday life or values as well as collective decisionmaking processes, and they focus particularly on the connections between these two spheres. This focus on societal change, of course, does not preclude a movement from targeting other sectors of the political, economic and cultural context. Indeed, most social movements do aim at changes in policies or political processes.

Resources, Identity and the National Political Process

For some time western theorizing about social movements was divided roughly into two "camps," both of which were reacting to the classical tradition of collective behavior that proffered largely psychological explanations for participation in social movements.[17] The "resource mobilization" school studied movement organizations and networks, strategies and action repertoires, types of incentives for participation, and the resources that individuals and groups were able to mobilize both to sustain collective action and to pursue their goals.[18] Scholars of the second school, responding in part to what they saw as a gap in both the collective behavior and the resource mobilization literatures—i.e. the question of how movements get started in the first place—and in part to the proliferation of what they saw as different types of movements in the 1960s and 1970s, sought the roots of movements in macro-level changes in social structure and culture.[19] Although both schools addressed important parts of the social movement process, their focuses and research agendas generally remained separate, if not antagonistic. Taken alone, neither adequately explained why social movements arise when and where they do. Even taken together, the growing wealth of survey data, organizational studies, and social theory still could not make the link between attitudes or social structure and the emergence of social movements. Moreover, little was said about the connections between social movements and political systems. In the 1980s, theorists began to bridge the gap between these studies with a focus on political process models and "political opportunity structures."[20] Their general argument is that changes in certain conditions—openings of the political process or opportunities—make it more advantageous for people to join together in collective action, easier to mobilize the resources necessary to engage in such action, and/or more feasible to challenge certain institutions, procedures, or cultural norms. To understand why movements get started and how they develop, we must therefore look at the institutions and ongoing political processes that shape these opportunities.

Following from the political opportunity perspective, Sidney Tarrow has argued that the study of social movements must focus on *national* political processes in order to synthesize "the 'big' processes of state theorists and the microprocesses and individual and group variables of the collective behavior tradition" (1988, 436). A growing body of empirical research in American and West European politics supports this argument.[21] Analysis of unofficial collective action, especially of social movements, in communist Eastern Europe must necessarily center on national politics as well. There are several reasons for this link. In part, the centralized political system and media made most political issues national issues. At the same time, official control of public activity, discussion and the political agenda in the Soviet-type system rendered collective action not organized by the state as "opposition" and meant that certain issues could be brought up only by individual and collective action in this opposition sphere. Opposition and its repression were, in turn, central to national politics in these countries. Even where social movement participants avowedly denied political intentions, the very existence of grassroots social movements was "political" in countries where regimes deliberately (dis)organized and controlled society.

A number of elements of the national political process in Poland facilitated the rise of the ecological movement. Predominant among them was the emergence and persistence of a strong political opposition and that opposition's resistance to state control. Among other things, the existence and activity of this opposition changed the areas of and limits on public dialogue. As the substantive content of the public dialogue expanded, a greater space opened up for views and activities that were "unofficial" yet not branded as "opposition." The environmental movement grew up in this "unofficial" space. That the movement first formed during the wave of social mobilization associated with Solidarity also fits the pattern of "waves" or "cycles" of mobilization found by social scientists studying Western Europe and the United States.[22] The legal existence of Solidarity and its later continuation as a strong opposition can be seen as having changed the political opportunity structure for other social movements.[23] Solidarity performed a double role. It was both a political opposition whose conflict with the government served as a foil for other movements and the anchor of a "movement sector" that extended far beyond the boundaries of political opposition.[24] Central to this anchoring role was Solidarity's contribution to building and maintaining an alternative press.

A more institutional look at the national political process shows us both the sources of environmental destruction and a number of venues where ecologists could affect agendas and policies. Traditionally, environmentalists in Soviet-type societies focused on internal—often informal—policymaking circles within the system. With strong controls on social activism, these access points were the most effective means for influencing both the policy agenda and the content of policy.[25] In Poland, the attention given to institutional reform in the aftermath of the 1980–81 crisis broadened these avenues of influence. The Jaruzelski regime restructured parts of the state administration in an attempt to both break old patterns of interest and make administrative units more effective in their own policy areas. As environmental protection became the purview of a separate ministerial level office (1983) and then of an entire ministry (1986), activists were able to focus their lobbying efforts more directly on the state administration. The other new avenue of influence was comprised of research institutes and public opinion polls set up to gauge attitudes and concerns in society in order to prevent issues from becoming the sources of future crises. Experts consulted by these institutes were often sympathetic to the movement; some were directly involved in it. Alliances between those working in official institutions and environmentalists outside of the established political system became more numerous and more visible. Yet, the predominant concerns and power relations of the communist system continued to restrict the impact of these groups. Even when they did manage to inspire or shape new laws and standards, the power to enforce them—almost always against state-sponsored actors—was never developed.

Despite our focus on the level of national politics and political opportunities, it is at times useful to look at the other approaches to analyzing social movements. The different nature of organizational resources in communist systems and lack of organizational records, membership lists, written communication among movement actors, and systematic survey data about individual attitudes limit the ability to apply Western-based resource mobilization theory to this case. Still, consciousness of the resources available to ecologists, e.g. the use of advisory positions in the state administration to place the environment on the regime's political agenda and hence in the mass-circulation press (a resource in itself), pierces some of the riddles about the growth of the movement. New social movement theorists' work on identity and the characteristics of "new movements" is also quite useful for examining the nature of the Polish environmental movement. Not only does it help us understand the self-perceptions of those individual and collective actors involved in the movement, but the new social movement perspective also suggests ways in which the movement may derive from and spur changes in the broader civil society. Indeed, we can intertwine the processes with which new social movement theorists are concerned with an approach focused on political opportunity structures. While the impetus toward forming new identities and challenging social norms may derive from broad—often evolutionary—changes in society, the ability and incentives to form collective actors that further new identities, norms, and institutional or policy changes is shaped by the structure of political opportunities in the system. This structure is itself fluid and often influenced by the same broad changes affecting society (for example, shifting material or human resources). At the same time, as political opportunities shape the formation of movements, these new actors are changing the norms, practices, and, possibly, institutions that comprise the political opportunity structure for the movement itself and for others, including state authorities.

New Social Movements and Civil Society

"New social movement" theories were developed primarily to explain the proliferation of social movements in Western Europe and the United States in the 1960s and 1970s. Some debate has arisen as to whether the features these thinkers describe are in fact "new" phenomena in social movements or whether "new" really refers to temporal difference.[26] New social movement theorists, however, claim that the temporal difference accounts for part of the different quality of the movements they examine.[27] These movements are invoked by features of modern (post)industrial society. The theorizing of those focusing on new social movements is therefore oriented toward explaining movements by examining change in the nature of society as a whole. Although the new social movement theorists generally study change in advanced capitalism, their focus on changes in social structure and life is a useful approach for understanding both the evolution of the Polish ecological movement and its role in the broader societal changes taking place in the 1980s.

Leaving aside the empirical question of historical precedent for the features of so-called new social movements, the argument can be made not only that the Polish environmental movement fits their criteria but also that these criteria indeed define the most important features of that movement. Environmental movements are among those social movements most frequently labeled "new" by theorists working in what Jean Cohen (1985) calls the "identity paradigm." In her review article of the literature on contemporary social movements, Cohen finds the following criteria for "newness" or, as she specifies, "the new identity in contemporary movements":

> . . . a self-understanding that abandons revolutionary dreams in favor of the idea of structural reform, along with a defense of civil society that does not seek to abolish the autonomous functioning of political and economic systems—in a phrase, self-limiting radicalism.
>
> . . . heterogeneity. The old patterns of collective action may certainly continue to exist. . . . *some* identities, implying specific forms of organization and struggle within contemporary movements, are new . . .
>
> . . . actors involved in contemporary movements do not view themselves in terms of socioeconomic class. . . . they focus on grass-roots politics and create horizontal, directly democratic associations that are loosely federated on national levels. Moreover, they target the social domain of "civil society" rather than the economy or state, raising issues concerned with the democratization of structures of everyday life and focusing on forms of communication and collective identity (pp. 664–67, emphasis in the original).

Whereas older social movements usually took their identities from their places in the social structure (class, stratum, occupation, region, minority status, etc.), new movements engage in a conscious process of identity formation that cuts across or is independent of social structure.[28] The establishment of this identity becomes a primary goal of such movements. Other goals include changes in the patterns of interaction within society and then change in political or economic structure or policy (depending on the specific focus of the movement). Older movements held change in the political or economic system or in policy as primary; consciousness of one's identity was necessary to articulate and pursue that primary goal. Strategies for achieving goals also differ. Though all movements employ a variety of strategies, the strategies of new movements are consistent with their identities and act simultaneously on identity formation, patterns of interaction within society and relevant policy, political or economic processes, institutions, or structures. In new social movements the means and ends cannot be separated.

More important than the particular labels assigned various movements are the explanations these authors offer for "newness." For Cohen, newness is rooted in "the emergence and transformations of civil society" (1985, 664). By change in civil society, Cohen is not referring to a new stage of historical development. In fact, she explicitly eschews such arguments (pp. 664–65). The change in civil society which Cohen sees as instrumental in analyzing contemporary social movements is the penetration of the market (increasingly corporate) economy and the administered state into (already modern) everyday life. These social movements, then, are the self-defense of society as it more and more consciously seeks to "expand and defend social spaces in which collective identities form."[29]

Rooting new social movement formation in the penetration of the private by the public suggests an interesting comparison between advanced capitalism and state socialism. While this extension of state and market control was going on in Western societies, reformers in communist societies were trying to reverse the process of penetration after the height of Stalinism. According to Ekiert's interpretation of the process, the post-Stalinist pact between the state and society was aimed at removing state attempts to penetrate "domestic society" (private life organized around meeting one's material needs) in exchange for citizens' withdrawal from attempts to build a political society (collective actors engaged in an active political community). The resulting expansion of domestic society colonized and weakened the state, which helped break the ground for the reconstitution of political society (1991, 301–305). In effect, social movements in both types of societies attempt(ed) to create a buffer zone between the private and the state by taking back part of the public for civil society itself. They thus try to expand the field left to civil society for nonofficial public interaction and to make value formation and identity formation conscious social processes outside the coercion of state and economic structures.

Another argument explaining the appearance of new social movements has focused more on the change in individual values and capabilities over time. These scholars detect a "post-materialist" shift in values in advanced industrial societies, specifically developed capitalist systems of the West (Inglehart 1977, 1990; Inglehart and Rabier 1986). Material security and higher education levels of the generation born after World War II predispose them to emphasize nonmaterial and social values. These stronger educations and the skills they develop in complex jobs entailing more face-to-face interaction with others also give this new generation the capability of organizing and developing new forms of political action (Kitschelt 1985, Dalton and Kuechler, eds. 1990). In a similar vein, Touraine attributes the expanded scope of social movement activity over time to human society's growing capacity for self-transformation, rather than reliance on "metasocial principles" (e.g. the notion of modernity) to guide its actions and identities (1985, 778). The type of survey evidence used to assess post-materialism in the West is lacking for the communist period in the East, so we can only offer some conjectures about the argument's plausibility in that setting. East European societies underwent similar changes in material security and education. Thus the postwar generation could be expected to show a similar shift in values and skills. The East's lower standard of living and stronger controls on individual initiative in the workplace, however, might have mitigated these effects. On the other hand, working for the development of more socially oriented values were ideology, socialization, and perhaps certain cultural factors. It is quite likely, then, that this generation in Eastern Europe exhibited a different mix of material and "post-material" values.[30] Neither the links between generational experience and values, nor those between value change and activism, can be assumed to parallel the West.

If we locate the source of "newness" in social movements in "the emergence and transformations of civil society," the question arises as to why societies that are different in historical experience and in their recent development under different types of states and economic systems might be producing similar movements. If the same types of movements appeared in East and West, did they have roots in the same sort of fundamental changes in society? Similarity in the degree if not the type of penetration by the state and economy is one potential root. Another phenomenon common in both societies might be, as Touraine suggests, the disappearance of "metasocial principles," such as natural law and modernization, able to both mobilize and limit collective action (1985, 778–79). Still another explanation may lie in the new tolerance for pluralism during the 1980s in some Soviet-type societies. Touraine's focus on the role of social movements as a "bridge between the observation of new technologies and the idea of new forms of political life (1985, 781–82)." suggests a fourth common cause: changes in developed industrial societies irrespective of their political systems. This factor seems particularly relevant in explaining why similar environmental movements have developed in various types of societies. A final plausible explanation for similar movements in different types of polities may be the diffusion or spread of movements across national borders. This phenomenon did influence individual actors in the Polish environmental movement and international opinion may have made it less attractive for the Polish regime to repress ecologists. However, international influences alone cannot explain the original commitment of movement activists and their sustained efforts in the face of various difficulties and threats before the systemic change of 1989. Although post-1989 transformation of the movement has seen a real increase in the influence of transnational groups and models (see chapter 8), movement development under communist rule was rooted mainly in domestic conditions and politics.

If some directions of inquiry are suggested by the application of Western-based theory to East European societies, so are some warnings. Cohen warns against the assumption that "society vs. the state" *per se* is something new (1985, 665). This point should be noted lest the "us-them" perception of citizens and opposition movements toward the communist regimes in Poland and other East European countries be misconstrued as evidence of new social movements. In addition to the danger of taking old as evidence of new, another problem arises with a "society vs. the state" perspective. Returning to Touraine's terminology, such a perspective confounds social movements with anti-state movements. Although a movement may be both social and anti-state, the connection between the two is not necessary.

Social movements in these two different types of polities also share the risk of moving more and more into the cultural sphere and further and further onto the political margin. They "can easily be segmented, transform themselves into defense of minorities or search for identity, while public life becomes dominated by pro- or anti-State movements (Touraine 1985, 780)." Yet this fate is not inevitable. A look at "new social movements," especially environmental, feminist, and some alternative culture movements, shows that in focusing on value change and the expansion of the unofficial public spheres they are *not* retreating either from politics or from public life. In fact, the possibility of individual or private solutions is antithetical both to the nature of the problems addressed by the movements and the nature of the movements themselves. New social movements seeking changes in the organization and norms of society are simultaneously seeking change in social, political, and economic interaction. The Polish case shows not only that social movements can be political in their own right, but also that they can play an important political role in the interaction between the state and anti-state movements. There independent social movements broadened and diversified the sociopolitical field, making use of and changing the political dynamics between the state and anti-state opposition. This proliferation of independent social movements and initiatives, heterogeneous organizational forms and new identities, in turn, made "normalization" after martial law impossible, forcing the Polish regime to seek social cooperation through systemic political change.

Another danger of some Western theory lies in treating civil society as an undifferentiated whole and assuming that political actors in the countries under examination do the same.[31] This point is crucial for understanding the Polish party-state's policies toward the environmental movement and other social initiatives during the second half of the 1980s. The Jaruzelski-Messner government clearly distinguished among and targeted different segments of civil society with its normalization policies. Aside from the many cleavages present in any society, Polish society in the 1980s could be divided into four major components regarding activism *vis-a-vis* the state. The first obvious but often overlooked section was comprised of those who were members of the state, party, and economic bureaucracies and therefore obligated to support and implement policy decisions but who, as members of civil society, sought to influence the political agenda, decisionmaking and implementation. Perhaps the bulk of society fell into the next category of those who refrained from any public or collective activism. Of those who were publicly active outside the party-state there were two major groups: those (including the Roman Catholic Church) acting independently of the state-controlled public spheres and those working in opposition to state policies and the leadership of the communist party.

The government perceived these differences. Moreover, it attempted to prevent the inactive parts of society from becoming active and those independently active from becoming part of the opposition. In the meantime, the policies designed to do this were influenced by some members of the leadership and advisory structures who were sympathetic to various social initiatives. These policies eventually contributed to the growth of the environmental movement and, more generally, to the failure of normalization that led Poland into its transition away from authoritarian rule.

The Environmental Movement After Communist Rule

The context for the development of social movements and civil society has changed dramatically since 1989. The change in context gives us an unexpected opportunity to look at the influence of national political processes on movements and their transformations, to see how a movement changes when its environment does and which internal features of a movement tend to persist.

The approach taken here to understanding movement development under communist rule can be carried into the post-communist period. Extension of this framework produces a number of expectations. First, the claim that the fundamental identity of the ecology movement was independent of the two main political camps and the persistence of environmental degradation suggest that the movement should continue to exist in the new system. Second, an opportunity-based understanding of activism suggests that the strategies of the movement's participants would include expanding influence in several directions opened up by the change of the regime. Thus, we should see new types of movement actors. Moreover, groups might be expected to increase their participation in governmental processes such as legislation and ministerial decisionmaking, given the relatively greater openness of policymaking. Part of this effort would be establishing beneficial relationships with other actors, especially political parties. As decentralization gives voivodship (county) and local governments more true decisionmaking power, activists should also increase their participation at these levels. With the freer flow of financial and other resources, ecologists could also be expected to attempt to raise or attract domestic and foreign resources, as well as direct their use. (Given the increased availability of foreign resources and the domestic economic crisis of the early transition, the focus—as one might expect—has been clearly on foreign funding and technological assistance.) With respect to movement growth, activists should be taking advantage of freer and more varied mass media, as well as expanded political rights, to encourage group formation and activism.

Finally, the extent to which ecologists engage in all of these activities should be "weighted" by the difficulty of acting and the potential effectiveness of particular channels. Difficulties of all sorts may raise the threshold for participation even as the political system appears to become more open to social participation. Among these difficulties could be lack of individual time and financial resources, departure of prominent activists from the movement, breakdown or uncertainty of central decisionmaking procedures and the centralized media, and the need to develop new strategies. Even when activists can overcome these difficulties, the incentive to do so will not be there if individuals and groups do not feel that their actions will have any effect. In the post-communist transitions a lack of a feeling of efficacy could derive from the crowded policy agenda, the weakness of new institutions, strained government budgets, and uncertainty about jurisdictions and procedures that accompany rapid change.

The fate of the Polish ecology movement since the end of communist rule confirms some of the findings of the pre-transition study. Above all, the continued existence of the movement and the participation of some of its leaders in various post-communist governments suggest that the movement was never "normalized" by the communist regime or absorbed by the political opposition. It remained independent: the ecological critique continues despite political and economic transformation, reaffirming its fundamental challenge to both types of political systems.

Also coming out of this temporal comparison are two tentative conclusions about the more durable aspects of social movements. The political identities that were important in delimiting the activities of various ecological groups in the communist period—i.e., relationships to the government and opposition—have shaped post-communist activism less than the nature of the groups' activism in the earlier period. Key organizations within the social movement have maintained their centrality and their predominant characteristics, while the interpersonal network built among pivotal activists in the 1980s has stayed pretty much intact. Moreover, experts remain experts, radical activists remain radical, and those working through the systems' institutions continue to do so, even when the political spectrum rotates 180 degrees. This phenomenon suggests that the type of activism a group engages in may have a more enduring appeal than its political coalitions and even its allegiance to a specific political ideology.

The second conclusion concerns the sources of a social movement and explanations for social movement development. National political processes and institutions, albeit very different from those that shaped the origin and evolution of the movement under communism, remain the dominant source of the Polish ecological movement's transformation. Other factors, especially international influences, are more visible than they were before the transition began, but at the root of change in the movement are the attempts of its individual groups and networks to adapt to the new political and economic institutions and processes, as well as the new realities of change in mass media, that shape the context of their activism.

2

Industrial Development, Ideology and Ecological Destruction

The roots of environmental degradation in Poland (and other centrally planned economies) are similar to those in capitalist countries. Most citizens and political authorities of both systems subscribe to a general ideology of unlimited economic growth. Moreover, the ideologies that govern economic activity and its political regulation in both capitalism and state socialism stress human ability to conquer and tame nature for human purposes, as well as a belief in technological solutions to almost all problems, especially those created by technology itself. These fundamental beliefs girding industrialized social, economic, and political systems are reflected in economic accounting systems that leave destruction of the environment largely as an externality. Both these accounting practices and the short-term anthropocentric perspectives they reflect are maintained through the political power of certain producer interests and through a growth in consumerism without a concomitant growth in ecological awareness. The industrialization and urbanization of human society that have both derived from and reinforced these "roots" have been the primary causes of ecological degradation.

Although ecological degradation and the threats it poses to human society as well as to natural processes derive from the same roots in both capitalism and state socialism, the abilities of these political and economic systems to deal with such degradation vary. Neither system has been terribly successful, but they face different limitations. Whereas capitalist systems suffer a tension between governmental ability to regulate ownership rights in order to assure collective goods and the rights of individuals to the free use of private property, at least on the surface state socialist systems with centrally planned economies provide an ideal situation for developing a rational, overarching approach to environmental protection. The danger in state socialist systems, however, stems precisely from this identity of owner and regulator. Even if there is an administrative division between those charged with developing the level of industrial production and those responsible for protecting the natural environment, the government as a whole is much more directly accountable for economic performance than in capitalist countries. Raising the level of industrialization and the standard of living are essential to claims of political legitimacy in these systems. Unless popular values place ecology ahead of such economic indicators, legitimacy concerns will continue to place production ahead of ecology among the priorities of the government that is directly responsible for both.

Ideology also differentiates capitalist and state socialist approaches to environmental protection, often interacting with the differences just discussed. Ideology in the Soviet-type system was much more inclusive than Western liberalism when it came to delineating how much of social and economic life was considered "political" or should be subject to political decisions. Ecological degradation did not merely raise questions about policymaking in these systems. Rather, environmental problems were linked to ideological concepts, such as the mode of production, and thus to ideological claims about the exercise of political authority. These questions about ideology and the environment in state socialism are complex and will be taken up in more detail below. First, however, we need to note another political difference affecting the handling of environmental degradation in these two types of systems.

Fundamental differences in the nature of public discussion between liberal democratic and state socialist countries influenced not only what was said about the environment but also what was known and done about it. Although government restriction of public debate may not necessarily be inherent to state socialism, it was a feature of the Soviet-type system. Such restriction, stemming from political concerns, was justified with ideological arguments. Regarding the environment, limits on public discussion meant that criticism of government policies and practices was generally absent until the last couple of decades of communist rule, and in the 1970s it was at best partial and muted. The dearth of public discussion made ecological awareness a rarity among the populations of these countries, thus virtually assuring that environmental protection would never become enough of a priority to be considered a legitimate control on productive processes. Available information about the state of the environment also suffered from the lack of extensive monitoring and still more from the lack of alternatives to self-monitoring by the polluters. Without information and awareness, even the best attempts to devise effective environmental regulations and policies fell to a lack of understanding of what was required. Still, there was some discussion about environmental problems in these countries before the changes of the 1980s. Generally carried out in the academic sphere and within state institutions, these debates were sometimes centered on ideological arguments, but more often ideology entered the fray merely through its overall role in determining the limits of public discussion.

Activists continually pressed against the limitations on public debate, incrementally broadening the range of issues discussed in the press and taking full advantage of the opportunity whenever restrictions were unclear or relaxed. On the side of extending discussion were also deteriorating ecological conditions and rising public concern about the health effects of pollution.

Environmental Destruction

Poland's post-World War II industrialization and urbanization campaign resulted in a rapid and extensive deterioration of the natural environment. Communist development policy placed a priority on producer-goods industries (the "heavy" industries of metallurgy, machine-building, chemical production, and military production) and resource extraction, both of which take a great toll on surrounding ecosystems. These priorities compounded the usual destruction accompanying industrialization. Dramatic increases in the use of artificial fertilizers and pesticides, combined with poor or nonexistent regulation of industrial waste disposal, served to contaminate soil and water. The smokestack became the icon of progress. Inefficient use of resources resulted not only in the waste of those resources but also in further ecological degradation.

Preoccupied in the earlier decades with transformation of the socio-economic system along Soviet lines, the Polish authorities were slow to recognize the extent of the ecological damage such industrialization was causing. In the 1970s, legitimacy concerns led the Gierek regime to place a higher priority on the types of production necessary for raising the standard of living. Again, environmental concerns were subordinated to production and consumption. Administrative bodies charged with enforcing environmental regulations were subordinated either to territorial authorities charged with responsibility for a given region's economic development as well or, in the case of national environmental agencies, to the

Council of Ministers, which was dominated by the industrial and economic ministries. Although environmental and economic interests do not necessarily have to be contradictory, the economic accounting systems used in the centrally planned economies did not internalize environmental "externalities." As a result, these two sets of interests remained in conflict. Shortages of air filters, delays in building water-treatment facilities for both municipal and industrial wastes, and a lack of innovation in production technology as well as in environmental protection all contributed to the problem.

Almost all environmental indicators show the state of Poland's natural environment declining and pollution rising steadily throughout the communist era (table 2.1). Some governmental efforts from the mid-1980s on slowed the downward spiral of ecological degradation, but the country's major environmental problems were not really tackled.

The one area where investment was visibly successful was the effort to cut dust emissions into the air. The extent of this success, however, is difficult to determine, since most emissions data both before and after these investments were supplied by the polluters themselves. Moreover, some of the change should be attributed to slowed production during the economic recession of the 1980s. Despite the relative success in limiting dust emissions, gas emissions remained at high levels, contributing significantly to forest damage. By the end of 1988 and the beginning of regime transition, 73.6 percent of Poland's forests were damaged. An estimated 65 percent of the total forest area was damaged to varying degrees by industrial emissions, 8.1 percent of it severely.[1] The quality of surface water declined steadily, unabated by the slowly increasing percentage of cities with treatment facilities. Industrial emissions, untreated municipal sewage, and agricultural run-off rendered *all* of Poland's rivers biologically unfit for human consumption and nearly 65 percent of them unsuitable even for industrial use by the end of the 1980s. River pollution, in turn, contributed directly to the ecological degradation of the Baltic Sea. Despite the alarming situation in the quality of air and surface water, several environmental scientists considered chemical contamination of the soil and ground water to be the gravest of Poland's ecological time bombs (Pawłowski and Kozak 1984). Industrial plants, mining and construction sites, military units and agricultural enterprises had dumped untold amounts of concentrated chemicals directly into the soil. One result was contamination of foodstuffs (Nikorow 1985), while well water in several parts of the country was unfit for consumption due largely to heavy metal content and, especially in agricultural regions, biological contaminants.[2]

Table 2.1 *Selected Environmental Indicators*

Indicator	1950	1955	1960	1965	1970	1975	1980	1985	1988
Dust Emissions (1,000 m. tons)	—	—	—	—	—	2226[a]	2338	1788	1615
% retained in air filters	—	—	—	—	—	89.0[a]	91.7	93.8	94.7
Gas Emissions (1,000 m. tons)	—	—	—	—	—	3040[a]	5135	4932	5193
% retained in air filters	—	—	—	—	—	14.4[a]	11.4	12.7	15.0
SO2 Emissions (1,000 m. tons)	—	—	—	—	—	2081[a]	2755	2652	2827
Rivers: % polluted beyond all use[b]	—	—	—	22.8	23.4	30.8	34.9	39.4	40.4[c] [64.7]
Rivers: % fit for human consumption[b]	—	—	—	33.0	24.9	9.7	6.8	4.2	4.7[c] [0]
% of Cities with Mechanical Sewage Plants	—	—	—	—	—	18.4[d]	19.7[e]	21.7[e]	20.9[e]
% of Cities with Mechanical & Biological Sewage Plants	—	—	—	—	—	20.0[d]	24.8[e]	23.7[e]	33.3[e]
Artificial fertilizer use (kg per ha)	17.7[f]	26.7[f]	36.5[g]	56.4[g]	123.6[g]	181.9[g]	192.9[h]	175.2[h]	176.4[h]
Pesticide supply to agriculture (1000 m. tons)	—	—	45.0[i]	65.7[i]	53.7[i]	60.0[i]	29.3[k]	36.5[k]	56.3[k]
Energy intensity of gross material product TOE/1000USD[l]	1.49	1.40	1.24	1.02	0.96	0.75	0.88	0.89	—

SOURCE: GUS, Rocznik Statystyczny, 1990, p.26 unless otherwise noted.

Note: For the first two decades of communist rule, the Polish statistical yearbook did not report environmental data

[a] *RS 1981, 21.* [b] Measures recorded here are for non-campaign seasons, taken every 3–5 years by the ministry responsible for environmental protection at the time. See *RS 1989*, p.18, for the exact dates. (This table disappeared from the statistical yearbooks from 1982 to 1988. The figures in the 1985 column are for 1986 as reported in Ministerstwo Ochrony Środowiska i Zasobów Naturalnych 1988, 96.) [c] Data for the year 1987. First number reflects physical and chemical criteria only. Number in brackets reflects biological criteria as well. [d] *RS 1984, 19.* [e] *RS 1990, 25.* [f] *RS 1971, 319.* [g] *RS 1976, 282.* [h] *RS 1989, 445.* [i] *RS 1981, 360.* [j] *RS 1971, 320.* [k] *RS 1989, 444.* [l] Olszewski, Bielański and Kamińska 1987, 23. Data is reported in tons of oil equivalent per 1000 1980 US dollars. Comparative data presented by the authors indicate that Poland was second only to Romania in energy inefficiency among the East European countries, which as a group were energy intensive economies. (Note: the figure in the 1985 column is actually for 1984.)

The stress on Poland's natural environment led even the government that imposed martial law to map out 27 areas of severe ecological degradation in the 1983–85 national economic plan.[3] Designation as an "area of ecological threat" (*obszar ekologicznego zagrożenia*) was intended to prevent further ecology-destroying investment in the region and to provide it priority status in cleanup efforts. The program continues to this day, but by the beginning of the regime transition little progress had been made. Few resources existed for cleanup efforts and there had been cases of further investment in damaging enterprises in these regions. Areas of ecological threat were characterized by concentrations of air, water, and soil pollution surpassing allowable limits and the breakdown of the self-regulating processes of nature, resulting in the death of certain ecosystems (Kozłowski 1985, 106–107). When they were set up they comprised much of the industrial plant of the country, covered 10.3% of its surface area, and included 12.3 million residents, approximately one-third of Poland's population (p. 108). Perhaps the greatest political concern with these areas, however, arose from their correlations with significant effects on human health and their mobilizing potential among citizens who were increasingly linking their health problems to environmental contamination despite the censorship of official data on this topic. Taken together, these areas had lower live birth rates and higher cancer rates than the rest of the country and the differences were growing (pp. 107–108). Individual areas showed even more marked contrasts to the Polish health norms, with the nature of the illnesses varying according to type of industrial production. Among these region-specific health effects were birth defects, mental and physical underdevelopment, severe respiratory illnesses, several particular cancers, higher miscarriage rates, higher infant mortality rates, lead poisoning, and lower life expectancies for adults.[4]

From even the partial data available, it is clear that efforts to protect Poland's environment were not keeping pace with its destruction. At the root of the problem was the nature of the industrialization process, which had created a structure of production particularly burdensome to the environment. Administrative subordination of environmental protection to economic development and low levels of investment in environmental protection compounded the problem. Reduction of industrial emissions would certainly have helped the ecological situation in Poland, but even administrative reform and more investment in pollution control would not have changed the energy-intensive, resource-demanding character of the economy.

Industrialization and Urbanization

Poland began to industrialize in the nineteenth century under a native capitalism peppered with elements of foreign ownership and restrictions imposed by foreign political domination. Because Poland was partitioned among three neighboring powers, the development of a unified market and a national industrial base was severely hampered. Railroads were built toward the dominating capitals; tariff walls were erected between partitions; taxes were high; and ownership rights were restricted. Thus, as Poles started to build industries, they were not developing an integrated infrastructure or even the types of production necessary for what would become a national economy after 1918.[5]

After Poland regained its independence in World War I, capitalist enterprises flourished, but state investments in infrastructure, banking, and key industries were the predominant modernizing force. This state-led development was seen as necessary to overcome the economic legacies of partition, as well as to protect Poland from the vagaries of the international economy between the wars. However, the worldwide depression and a policy of maintaining exchange rates at all costs led the state to cut investment dramatically between 1929 and 1932, intensifying the negative effects of the depression and leaving the rate of development investment below the 1929 level for the remainder of the interwar period (Wereszycki 1979, 586–87). World War II left much of Polish industry and infrastructure destroyed or plundered.[6] The rebuilding campaign of the late 1940s, capped off by the 3-year Plan of National Reconstruction for 1949–51, gave way to the intensive industrialization and urbanization campaign of Stalinism. By 1973, Polish industrial production had reached a level 20 times the 1938 level, rising in essentially 25 years from destruction of an already underdeveloped economy to an industrial capacity that ranked it among the world's more industrialized countries (Topolski 1986, 272). Although Silesian air has contained coal dust for over a century, it is to this post-World War II industrialization that most of Poland's ecological degradation can be attributed.

Poland's post-war industrialization drive resulted in a rapid transformation of the economy beginning in 1946 and peaking in 1978, just before an economic crisis that would continue through most of the 1980s stagnated growth. The negative growth rates of the early 1980s gave way to a very slow recovery. By the end of 1988, national income in constant prices had almost, but not quite, reached the 1978 level. The next year saw the beginning of the fundamental changes in both the political and economic systems that followed the 1989 Round-Table Agreement. Several indicators reflect the pace of economic transformation during the

Table 2.2 *National Income During the Communist Period*
(in constant 1970 prices)

Year	1970 = 100	Previous Year 100	% created in industry[a]	% created in construction[a]	% created in agriculture[a]
1947	15.2	NA	22.0	4.6	70.0
1950	26.8	115.1	24.3	8.2	60.3
1955	40.4	108.4	28.6	9.2	42.3
1960	55.5	104.3	34.5	10.3	34.5
1965	74.9	107.0	38.9	10.2	29.7
1970	100.0	105.2	44.0	11.7	22.7
1975	159.4	109.0	47.5	13.6	15.4
1978	184.1	103.0	49.5	12.6	14.6
1979	179.9	97.7	49.8	11.9	14.1
1980	169.1	94.0	50.2/50.9	13.3/10.0	12.9/12.7
1981	148.8	88.0	48.7	11.3	14.9
1982	140.6	94.5	49.2	11.0	16.5
1983	149.0	106.0	49.1	11.1	16.4
1984	157.3	105.6	49.0	11.4	16.3
1985	162.6	103.4	48.6/49.2	12.0/11.5	14.4/15.8
1986	170.6	104.9	48.4	11.9	14.6
1987	174.0	101.9	49.1	12.0	13.0
1988	182.4	104.9	49.1	12.1	12.6

SOURCE: GUS, Rocznik Statystyczny, 1989, pp. xxxii—xxxiii.
[a]Data for 1946—1979 and the numerator of 1980 are calculated in constant prices from January 1, 1977. Data for 1980 denominator, 1981—84, and 1985 numerator are calculated in constant prices from 1982. From the 1985 denominator on, calculations are based on 1984 constant prices.

first three decades of the centrally planned economy. While agriculture's share of national income dropped from 70% to 14.6%, industry's share rose from 22% to 49.5% (table 2.2). Employment statistics mark this transformation as well (table 2.3). Although Poland's agricultural sector remains overpopulated relative to the developed economies of the West, the percentage of the work force engaged in agriculture had almost halved by the end of communist rule. The industrial work force increased steadily until the late 1970s, when economic growth stagnated at the same time that Poland's small service sector started to develop. By 1988 the percentage of labor force engaged in industry in Poland had peaked and subsided to roughly the same level as Germany's and slightly higher than those of the United States and Japan.[7] Another indicator of industrialization, electric energy use by industry, also increased continuously with the exception of a drop in 1981 and 1982, when shortages and strikes idled factories (table 2.3). Finally, as may be expected, the country's industrialization drive was accompanied by migration to the cities and rapid urbanization. The number and size of cities grew steadily as surplus labor in the rural areas migrated to new industrial jobs in the cities (table 2.4).

Table 2.3 *Employment by Economic Sector and Industrial Energy Use*

Year	% Population Working in Industry	% Population Working in Construction	% Population Working in Agriculture	Electricity Used in Industry[a] (billion KW-h)
1946	NA	NA	NA	4.3
1950	20.7	5.0	53.6	6.9
1955	24.4	6.4	48.2	13.2
1960	25.5	6.5	43.3	19.9
1965	27.6	6.7	39.1	30.3
1970	29.3	7.1	34.3	43.4
1975	31.1	8.5	29.3	62.9
1978	30.6	8.1	29.5	73.9
1980	30.3	7.7	29.7	73.7
1985	28.5/29.2[b]	7.5	28.9	75.2
1988	28.6	7.9	27.6	80.2

SOURCE: GUS, Rocznik Statystyczny, 1989, pp.xxxii-xxxiii, xxxvi-xxxvii.
[a]Although electric energy use may indicate change over time within Poland, it is not a reliable indicator for comparing levels of industrial development with other countries as production in the Polish and other CMEA countries was particularly energy-intensive.[b]Manner of calculaton changed on January 1, 1986. the numerator was calculated by the new method, the denominator by the old.

The very pace of this industrialization and urbanization drive had strong negative consequences for environmental protection as there were few resources and little time for exigency planning, infrastructure development, and adjustment to local conditions along the way. However, Poland's high level of ecological degradation was also a result of the *nature* of the country's economic modernization. At the end of the 1940s, the Polish communist leadership adopted the Stalinist model of economic development. This model favored extensive development of the industries considered to form the "base" of an industrial economy: iron, steel, machine-building. Investment, production, and distribution of goods were controlled by the State Commission for Economic Planning. The planners were thus in a position to squeeze resources necessary to build and run such an economy from nationalized enterprises, collectivization of agriculture (largely unachieved in the Polish case), and extensive exploitation of mineral and other natural resources. Central control of wages and enterprise earnings also assured a net flow of resources into the central budget, especially during the early phases of socialist development. The "Stalinization" of the Polish economy was achieved largely through the six-year plan adopted in 1950.

The type of industry favored by the Stalinist development model was also quite energy-intensive. This was in part a legacy of its pedigree, since the Soviet Union had rich energy resources and thus did not prioritize energy efficiency. Artificially low administrative prices for energy in cen-

Table 2.4 *Urbanization*

Year	% Population[a] Living in Cities	% Population Living in Cities of over 100,000	No. of Cities Registered	No. of Cities over 100,000
1946	33.9	10.1[b]	703[b]	11[b]
1950	36.8	16.4[c]	706[d]	16[d]
1955	43.8	18.6[c]	729[d]	19[d]
1960	48.3	20.8[c]	889[e]	22[e]
1965	49.7	21.4[c]	891[f]	23[f]
1970	52.3	22.6[g]	889[h]	24[h]
1975	55.6	25.8[i]	810[g]	29[g]
1978	57.5	27.7[j]	803[g]	33[g]
1980	58.8	29.2	804[k]	37[k]
1985	60.3	30.1[l]	812[k]	40[k]
1988	61.2	30.4	822[k]	41[k]

SOURCE: GUS, Rocznik Statystyczny, 1989, pp. xxxii-xxxxiii, unless otherwise noted.
[a] Percentages calculated on the basis of the information presented in Ibid. [b] Calculated on the basis of information presented in RS 1947, 13–14 and 21–27. [c] RS 1966, 24.[d] RS 1956, 56.[e] RS 1981, 41.[f] RS 1976, 34.[g] RS 1983, 38.[h] RS 1984, 40.[i] Calculated on the basis of information presented in RS 1983, 32, 38.[j] Calculated on the basis of information presented in RS 1984, 35,40.[k] RS 1989.[l] Calculated on the basis of information presented in RS 1984, 43, 49

trally planned economies and CMEA trade until after the oil shocks of the 1970s reinforced the tendency to pay little attention to this particular factor of the production process. The energy-intensiveness of centrally planned economies burdened the environment with three types of costs.First, extracting, transporting and storing large amounts of energy in any form was ecologically damaging; second, high amounts of harmful emissions resulted from the use of energy, especially Poland's primary domestic energy source of high-sulfur coal; finally, not having to focus on energy efficiency probably prevented or postponed technological innovations that might have reduced other detrimental effects of the production process. When the energy crunch came in the 1980s, the structure of the economy was already well established and there were no resources for investment in technological innovation even as energy costs became prohibitive.

Compounding the ecological effects of a strong focus on "heavy" industry was another feature of Stalinism: an emphasis on building massive industrial plants and conglomerations of enterprises and coal-burning power facilities. Concentrating heavily polluting enterprises in relatively small areas meant that nature's mechanisms for dealing with contaminants would certainly be overloaded. Often housing for workers was built in the immediate vicinity of these large enterprises. Many of these industrial and housing projects were built with insufficient infrastructural development to assure water supply and sewage treatment, and little attention was paid to the environmental effects of construction processes themselves or to maintaining green spaces. In the early 1970s, the Gierek regime launched a campaign to raise the level of technology and develop consumer industries. Many more medium-sized and small enterprises were built, but the huge heavy industry combines of the 1950s and 1960s continued operation.

In sum, Poland's industrial development after World War II was rapid, intense, and governed by ideologically determined economic priorities. In four decades, almost a third of the society moved to the cities and half of the population working in agriculture left for industrial jobs. Not only did the industrial plant develop quickly, but it was also energy-intensive and concentrated in several urban centers or large conglomerates, creating areas of severe multi-source pollution. The provisions for environmental protection were very few in the first decades of industrialization, when the real base of the economy was established. New regulations introduced starting in the late 1960s were often circumvented in the interest of raising production and in the face of an inadequate supply of environmental technology.

Ideology: Marxism-Leninism and the Environment

The basic tenets of communist ideology have very little to say about the environment.[8] Neither Marx nor Lenin seems to have foreseen the extent of the threat industrialized society would pose to the natural environment on either the local or global scale. Thus, neither effectively integrated the problem into his theories about the development of human society. However, "the term 'Marxism-Leninism' (as used here and by the Soviets themselves) actually refers to the Soviet interpretation of Marx and Lenin at any given point in time" (DeBardeleben 1985, 6–7). Marxism-Leninism was an ideology in power, which served to legitimate the rule of the communist party. To maintain that ideology as a basis for legitimation of the regime, its keepers had to allow it to evolve to meet new exigencies that arose in the process of governing. Political exigencies had suppressed the rich history of conservation and ecological science in the Soviet Union after the debates of the late 1920s and early 1930s (Weiner 1988). In the 1970s, however, communist ideology had to begin addressing the problem of rapidly increasing environmental destruction and its political ramifications.

As Joan DeBardeleben (1985, 10) rightly points out, our concern should not be with what the classics say about the environment, but with how ideology defined, incorporated, and limited the debate on the environment.[9] Her comparative study of the Soviet Union and the German Democratic Republic argues that:

> . . . while official Marxism-Leninism has (sometimes subtly) constrained Soviet and East German responses to the environmental challenge, at the same time the real dilemmas posed by environmental deterioration have also stimulated reevaluation of some basic assumptions in these countries, at times even reflected in official party doctrine. Marxism-Leninism may, in some ways, help shape policy-thinking, but at the same time it may be molded to legitimize policies adopted for other reasons. Furthermore, ideology may affect the *manner* in which political and economic factors influence environmental debate and policy, acting as a sort of mediating variable (1985, 5, emphasis in the original).

These same relationships between ideology and environmental debate and policy apply to the Polish case, although Poland generally was not as conservative in the restriction of policy debates to ideological precepts as were the two countries in DeBardeleben's study (particularly after Gomułka's removal from the leadership in 1970). For the period of this study, the limitations on debate in Poland stemmed from more direct political concerns. Ultimately, however, both ideological limitations and limitations imposed out of what the authorities perceive to be immediate political necessity derive from concerns about the political legitimation of the existing regime.

The pursuit of political legitimacy, so central to Marxism-Leninism's evolution, was also the Polish government's major concern in limiting not only public debate on the topic of ecology but also the amount of basic information about environmental degradation and access to that information. Environmental destruction could be de-legitimizing in several ways. Some of these legitimation problems were seen through the prism of ideology; some were not. Moreover, what the authorities perceived as ideologically based and nonideological political threats to the regime's claims to legitimacy were layered and interwoven.

DeBardeleben's analysis of the interaction of ideological and nonideological explanations for environmental destruction in the Soviet and East German mass and scholarly press remains the most penetrating treatment to date of the relationship between communist ideology and environmental policy debates in Soviet-type societies. A brief synopsis of her argument will demonstrate the complexity of that relationship.[10] From a review of environmental discussions in her two case studies, DeBardeleben detects three levels of explanation and debate. "The interaction of these various levels of explanation accounts for the existence of environmental deterioration in state socialist societies, asserts the superiority of socialism over capitalism, and allows leeway for specialists to debate policy responses" (p. 46).

The first set of arguments is overtly ideological and takes place on the general level of what DeBardeleben labels as "relations of production": environmental destruction is linked to the private ownership of the means of production and their utilization for individual gain, which results in the use of natural resources for private profit rather than with general social goals in mind (pp. 47–48). Problems with this explanation arose as wide-scale ecological destruction became readily apparent in the Soviet Union and Eastern Europe, i.e. countries whose social ownership of the means of production was to guarantee that the use of productive and natural resources would be in the interest of the whole society (p. 50). Furthermore, denying the possibility of such problems under socialism would not resolve them (p. 51). They would remain sources for social dissatisfaction with the existing regime.

DeBardeleben's second layer of explanation also occurs on the general level, but is not essentially ideological. It focuses on the "forces of production" or technology of modern industrial production (pp. 45–46). Careful to avoid the ideologically proscribed argument of convergence, authors using "forces of production" analyses—mostly scholars—are able to study and discuss actual processes by which the environment is eroded and the means necessary for its protection and reclamation (pp. 54–55). This debate is essential if the problems are to be resolved. Ideologically, the admission of some of the same problems that result from capitalist production is covered by the recognition that socialism is capable of overcoming them, but that this accomplishment does not come automatically with change in the relations of production (p. 51). Rather, the ecological vagaries of modern industrial production can be countered only by a concerted effort at technological development and policy innovation (pp. 51–53). This argument has the added benefit of averting any challenge to the regime's claims that socialism can provide for continuous improvement in the standard of living, a question that arises if industrial production is linked to ecological degradation regardless of ownership and social structure (pp. 38–39). By the same token, other fundamental questions that could arise to threaten the political legitimacy of the communist system once its leaders acknowledge the existence of "capitalist" problems are also headed off at the pass. These challenges include questioning the superiority of socialism's social policy, e.g. health care, its strategy of growth based on extensive development of heavy industry, and the efficacy of central planning (pp. 39–41), which, theoretically, should be able to implement a more consistent approach to ecology than is achieved through individual decisions under capitalism.

The final layer of debate and explanation detected by DeBardeleben, the micro-level of specific policy decisions, enterprise performance, or ministerial behavior, can also serve to legitimize the regime (p. 56). Analysis of specific problems or criticism of specific actions is necessary to remedy the adversities likely to cause dissatisfaction with the regime's performance. Meanwhile, targeting certain actors or decisions can reinforce faith in the system's ability to deal with flaws, at the same time that it distances responsibility for environmental destruction from the basic structure of socialism and modern technological development.

Having discerned these levels of argument and their connections to Marxism-Leninism, the author proceeds to examine their occurrence in the public debate about ecology. She finds that the overall ideological argument is never contradicted, though at times it is ignored (p. 46). The mass-circulation press is more likely than the scholarly press to repeat the general position on capitalism and socialism, whereas the scholarly press is more likely to delve into the "forces of production" arguments (pp. 46, 48–49). Micro-level discussions appear in both with some variation depending on the type of micro-level argument (pp. 48–49). These patterns differ somewhat according to the particular legitimation needs of the country and those needs define limits on individual topics (for example, East German authorities were especially vigilant against "convergence" arguments), but the overall give and take among the levels of explanation is fairly consistent (p. 53).

In the Polish case, DeBardeleben's analysis seems to be relevant to the limited public discussion of the environment in the 1960s and 1970s. From the mid-1970s, however, the terms of public debate in Poland and the limitations imposed upon it by ideology began to change substantially. This was especially true once Solidarity emerged in August 1980. The opposition press provided an alternative public forum and in doing so changed the content of the official press. Ideology was less of a constricting force than it was in the Soviet Union and the German Democratic Republic, indeed than anywhere else in the Soviet bloc, not the least because it carried little currency in the general public and even among many party members. This does not mean, however, that there was a free and open public debate about the unfortunate state of Poland's natural environment and its causes.

The government was acutely sensitive to public opinion about particular policy issues during the 1980s, when a strong, organized political opposition existed and the communist regime, if it ever had gained any fundamental legitimacy after its imposition from abroad, had lost that legitimacy by the 1980–81 Solidarity period and the subsequent declaration of martial law. The very belief that any ideology or a substantive claim could legitimate governmental rule without democratic process had already died.[11] The regime's only hope for gaining social adherence to its rule, beyond that extracted by the use of force, was to win acceptance for its policies, especially its attempts to increase the standard of living or, more generally, social well-being. Thus, a wide and accurate public discussion of the environment was one more political threat to be countered. When at last such a discussion could not be silenced, the government had to shift to a position of apparent activism on the ecological front in order to neutralize the political impact of the ecological critique. Even after the government had joined the debate, ideology did not enter the official discussion of the environment during the 1980s. On the occasions where Marxism-Leninism was mentioned it was as the object of criticism by ecologists or opposition activists.[12]

Historically, however, ideology has greatly affected Poland's natural environment, the public discussion of ecological problems, and environmental policy (or the lack thereof). It was upon this historical base of development and ideologically inspired selective blindness that the current physical conditions for environmental politics were shaped. Likewise, past policy performance and past limitations on public discussion still shaped the debate in the second half of the 1980s, even if only partially or indirectly. Much of what was written about ecology focused on the results of past performance or past limitations, often adopting the dominant values and approaches to refute them. A good example of an area where this trend was particularly visible is the appearance of a whole group of economic analyses of the costs of pollution.[13] A lot of effort was also spent on criticizing previous information policies and censorship. In many ways, Polish ecologists were still devoting more time in the 1980s to breaking down the old barriers or justifying having broken them down than to improving the actual ecological situation.

Environmentalism: the Birth of a Social Movement

It was not until the second half of the 1970s that environmental issues became recognized as a topic of politics, although differences in the environment were noticed by the beginning of the 1960s. One preliminary sign of the developing interest in ecology was an increase in professional publications on this topic, especially in the scientific journals and the field of administrative law. Even though the 1970s were a period of international mobilization in environmental protection, starting with the Club of Rome report *The Limits to Growth* and the United Nations' Conference in Stockholm, and including the political success of the West German Greens, in Poland environmental destruction was still a censored topic.[14] Thus independent ecological initiatives generally took the form of letters to the editors in various publications—a classic form for expressing officially tolerated "alternative" views in Soviet-type systems—and involvement of professionally trained scientists and social scientists in drafting legislative proposals and in "scientific councils" to various administrative bodies. Often environmental demands were channeled through the official League for the Protection of Nature.

With the formation and legalization of Solidarity in 1980, censorship was broken in almost all areas, including environmental protection. During that heady period social activism flourished in every area. Press coverage of issues not only increased, but also encompassed alternative perspectives to those which had dominated the official press until then. The precedent established by Solidarity's official recognition cleared the way for the creation of other independent groups. One of these groups, the Polish Ecological Club, became the heart of a new environmental movement. A number of Polish Ecological Club initiatives, some joined by Solidarity, drew attention to the environment and resulted in some specific concessions by the government. Martial law, however, soon brought an end to this activism and the environmental movement lost momentum. The electronic and print media were carefully orchestrated to achieve society's resignation to repression. Issues that implied criticism of the regime were nowhere to be found. As soon as martial law was lifted, however, the movement began to stir. The Polish Ecological Club, taking stock of itself at its first national congress in 1983, opted for a nonpolitical "expert"-based identity and enterprising journalists began to write environmental features.

By the end of 1985 the martial law moratorium had been broken by the reactivation of the Polish Ecological Club and numerous press reports. Public controversy over two government-sponsored reports and a West German institute's assessment that Poland might be Europe's most ecologically destroyed country sparked a sharp increase in press coverage of environmental problems.[15] Yet, while journalists became more aggressive and citizens began to raise environmental questions at campaign meetings with *Sejm* (parliamentary) candidates in Fall 1985, government publications and officials were making contradictory statements, ranging from recognition of the gravity of the ecological situation to denial of any serious problems beyond those of any industrially developed country. This inconsistency testifies to the lack of a clear government stance or "line" on discussion of the environment. Activists at all levels began to form small ecological groups in response to the rapidly declining quality of the environment and to the failure of official regulations and administration to halt the decline.

Just as the Polish ecological movement was beginning to develop a broader popular base, the nuclear accident at Chernobyl provided a chilling reminder of human dependence on the environment. With the exception of a slight increase in Poland's small anti-nuclear movement, the boost in consciousness caused by contamination from Chernobyl did not produce an immediate growth in environmental activism. In fact, a sense of helplessness and resignation followed the initial anger and panic.[16] On the other hand, society as a whole became more receptive to environmental activism. With each person realizing his or her own susceptibility to seemingly undetectable contamination, willingness to consider ecology seriously increased.

Coming on top of the already escalating discontent with the state of the country's natural environment, public anger at the regime's delayed and equivocating response to the Chernobyl catastrophe compelled the party leaders to adjust and clarify their stance on the recognition and discussion of environmental problems. Such a clarification came two months later in June 1986 at the Tenth Congress of the ruling communist party, the Polish United Workers' Party. In his main speech to the Congress, General Secretary Wojciech Jaruzelski mentioned environmental protection as one of the serious challenges facing the nation, thus signifying official acceptance of ecology as a topic for public discussion. (See chapter 7.) The result was even greater and more critical press coverage of all facets of environmental politics, problems, and decisionmaking. Increased official press coverage of these dilemmas reinforced the growth in ecological consciousness of the general public, especially among the youth for whom the achievement of industrialization was a given. From 1986, the number and types of groups engaged in environmental activism in Poland simply mushroomed.

Thus, the Polish ecological movement was not only established but also varied and growing well before the systemic transformation begun by the strikes in 1988. Although the movement closely resembled those found in advanced capitalist states in Western Europe, it arose under Soviet-type state socialism. More specifically, the Polish ecological movement developed in the context of Solidarity and post-Solidarity Polish politics. It was constricted by and utilized basic features of the system as well as the peculiarities of that context to foster an ecological identity in society and promote environmental activism by any and all actors.

Conclusion

Awareness of the ecological consequences of its industrialization process came later to Polish authorities and society than it did to the West. While this is logical given the country's later development and the intensity of its industrialization campaign, delayed awareness was also the result of ideological limitation of the first attempts to raise public awareness and the government's pragmatic underestimation of the importance of Poland's ecological degradation when faced with economic crises and rising economic expectations. Yet, despite tightly controlling public discussion of environmental problems, the regime did make some attempts to slow ecological degradation. Long before environmental activism began to take the form of a social movement, scientists and other "experts" had pressed the government to protect the environment. Most of this pressure came through internal channels—advisory councils, commissioned reports, legislative committees, and the government's own administrations. Still, these forces amounted to very little in the face of the regime's development policy even while the corpus of legislation and number of administrative offices dealing with the environment increased. As in other countries, measures to protect the environment in Poland (including setting up proper administration) were reactions to worsening environmental conditions rather than the results of foresight and rational planning. The problems pulled attempts at abatement behind them. The primary legacies of this pattern of development were incongruous and uncoordinated sets of administrative bodies and laws concerning the environment, most of which did not have their intended effects. It is to these administrative and legislative measures that we now turn.

3

The Structure of Environmental Protection: Legal Provisions and Administration

Faced with rapid industrialization based on heavy industry, Poland needed effective environmental legislation and administration to avoid serious ecological destruction. Yet, a belated realization of these needs combined with the power of various economic interests to retard the development of environmental protection. Although the parliament passed a number of laws and ministerial regulation increased in the 1970s and 1980s, environmental destruction continued largely unabated. Often the laws were simply not enforceable. In some cases, the standards were unrealistically high. Usually, however, no administrative body was capable of implementing them. Though far from unified and coherent itself, environmental law in communist Poland was hamstrung most by splintered administration and subordination to economic interests.

This chapter looks at the development of Poland's environmental administration and law to elucidate the framework in and around which the environmental politics examined in the rest of the study developed. For most of the communist era, administration of environmental protection evolved on the basis of piecemeal adjustments to historically rooted institutions rather than according to an overall plan. Even the establishment of communist rule had brought no significant revamping of environmental institutions. Likewise, although pieces of environmental legislation were generally reactions to new problems, they were usually *ad hoc* revisions of old laws. To understand, therefore, how environmental law and administration actually functioned and how they were perceived by actors in Polish politics, it is best to take a historical approach to their development.

Especially important for understanding the different nature of actions taken to protect the environment and for assessing the political connotations of these actions are three terms used in the recent Polish literature on ecology. To some extent these concepts represent the historical progression of environmental consciousness and policy, but they also delineate the different concerns still held by various activists. Under communist rule, as these concerns became increasingly inclusive in scope, they also became increasingly threatening from an ideological point of view.

The first is the term "conservation" (*konserwacja*), or "the keeping of something in good condition, taking care of something for the purpose of insuring against its quick use, destruction, or spoilage. (*Słownik języka polskiego* 1981, 1:993)" As applied to ecology, conservation refers to action to protect individual creations of nature, the goal being to "insure the protected objects against destruction or any sort of violation of their natural state" (Szczęsny 1982, 10). Conservation measures may also be taken to protect buildings and other monuments created by humans, but such activity is not considered to be nature conservation. In Polish the term is often used in reference to the conservation movement whose beginnings date back to the nineteenth century.

A more inclusive term is "protection of nature" (*ochrona przyrody*). "Nature" (*przyroda*) in this context is understood to be "the whole of things and phenomena creating the universe, the world (without the creations of human work); land, water and air along with the flora and fauna living in and on them."[1] Protection of nature has thus generally focused on the creation and defense of areas where human activity is not allowed to alter nature in any significant way—in the Polish case, national parks, landscape parks, and nature reserves (Zarzycki 1988, 7–9; Szczęsny 1982, 10). Although some Polish authors have continued to use this term "in a broad sense" to refer to all efforts in environmental protection, most have followed the general trend toward distinguishing between the "natural environment" and the "environment" (implying "human environment") as a whole, including areas where nature has been transformed drastically.

"Protection of the environment" (*ochrona środowiska*) involves even more extensive action. Simply defined, the environment (*środowisko*) is "all of nature with its living and non-living components, including humans and their technical activities" (Wojciechowski 1987, 49). Thus, Wojciechowski, the author of a Polish textbook on the ecological basis of shaping the environment, understands the object of action to be "an area settled by an organism or arrangements of organisms with everything, which found in that area comprises, either directly or indirectly, the surroundings of the organism, and that which is connected with these organisms through direct action or indirect effects (1987, 49)." This definition coincides with that of the dictionary (*Słownik języka polskiego* 1981, 3:456) and the legal definition of environment adopted in the 1980 "Law on the Protection and Shaping of the Environment." The latter specifies the object of protection as "the whole of natural elements, in particular the earth's surface along with (including) the soil, minerals, water, atmospheric air, the world of flora and fauna, and also the landscape, which are either in their natural states or transformed by human activity."[2] Most environmental activists share this understanding of the term.

Conservation—which has generally been the first stage of human attempts to limit ecological degradation—delineates rather limited action vis-a-vis isolated objects. Protection of nature carries a more complex understanding of the tasks involved in stopping degradation of the natural environment. Proponents realize that whole groups of interlocking processes which occur naturally have to be safeguarded. Environmental protection is a broader and more complex task. Here ecologists are dealing not only with nature, but also with changed nature and human-created conditions. When activism reaches this level, measures become much more controversial, pitting different political, economic, and social interests directly against each other.

From the point of view of communist ideology and politics, conservation and nature protection have not been particularly controversial goals. They both imply a politics concerned with promoting general social good; and it was to these goals that most official environmental organizations directed their activism. Problems with conservation and protection of nature arose only when economic planning entailed the use of territories or resources slated for defense. Generally, the economic ministries won out in these conflicts and demands for the protection of nature, to the extent that they became a political "issue," were contained within the normal institutional channels of the system. Questions about transforming nature during the development process or (partially) restoring it afterward were generally discussed in terms of a fourth concept, the "shaping" (*kształtowanie*) of nature or the environment. This term with its anthropocentric and technocratic focus on controlling nature predominated in the literature on economic and spatial planning. While its use could and often did serve as a euphemism for the transformation of the natural environment, some planners and activists used it as an acceptable means of introducing environmental controls into the official discussion of development processes.

"Environmental protection," however, presented a more formidable challenge to both official ideology and official politics. No matter how shaded the "mode of production" arguments became in the 1970s and 1980s, the growing "issue" of ecology was a political threat to ruling elites from at least three angles. First, the critique of existing conditions not only implicated the behavior of certain officials but also reached to the very heart of the economic planning system and its politically set priorities. Second, the issues of industrial pollution and its regulation tended to set various state institutions (economic ministries, state agencies charged with environmental protection, and local administrators) against one another, increasing bureaucratic politics and undermining the rationality of centralized administration. Finally, increasing popular attention to this "issue" and growing environmental activism challenged the institutional procedures of the political system and with them the mechanisms by which the regime controlled society and politics. Thus, it was when "environmental protection," understood as protecting nature *and* environments transformed by human activity, began to enter the political agenda that Soviet-type regimes became concerned by the ecological critique.

Before an ecological critique developed in Poland, however, a number of factors shaped the actual physical conditions and political interaction surrounding environmental protection. One of these factors was the rapid industrialization process summarized in the previous chapter. Two other factors were the legislative and administrative history of environmental protection in Poland.

The Development of Environmental Protection in Poland

The history of environmental protection in Poland is not exceptional, either for its vigilance or for its negligence. From 1795 until 1918 the lands that now comprise Poland were under the occupation and administration of three neighboring powers, Austria-Hungary (Austria until 1867), Prussia, and Russia, so there was no possibility of any coordinated environmental or even conservationist program before the twentieth century. Instead, each Polish partition followed the nominal beginnings of conservation in the empire to which it was subject.[3] When Poland regained its independence the new government faced the task of pulling together territories developed under disparate sets of policies. In environ-

mental affairs the first step was taken in 1919, when the government created the Temporary State Commission for the Protection of Nature
(*Tymczasowa Państwowa Komisja Ochrony Przyrody*) (Garścia 1988,
2). Although some Poles cite a few isolated conservation measures dating
back to the Middle Ages as evidence of a Polish ecological tradition,[4] the
first popular organization to concern itself with nature conservation, the
League for the Protection of Nature (*Liga Ochrony Przyrody*, or LOP),
was founded only in 1928.[5] The first modern legal measures concerning
the environment, laws on the protection of certain animal species,
appeared in 1932.[6]

There were some important initiatives in the interwar period, especially concerning the creation of national parks, but the more salient
issues of environmental protection did not arise until the post-World War
II period of intensive industrial development under the new communist
regime. While the increase in pollution and other forms of ecological
destruction far outpaced the increase in legislation regarding environmental protection during the 1950s and 1960s, the few maverick voices
of ecological conscience found little resonance in public consciousness
and even less responsiveness from the government. Throughout the
1970s, the heyday of green politics in the West, the state of the environment in Poland was a carefully controlled topic. It took the break in censorship of the Solidarity period to open the way for the growth of a popular, critical environmental movement. Until then, citizen participation in
environmental activism was in most cases limited to membership in the
LOP.

Liga Ochrony Przyrody

Certainly one of the most important forces in the history of conservation
in Poland has been the League for the Protection of Nature. Its main initiator, Władysław Szafer, a nationally acclaimed botanist, was the first
leader of the Temporary State Commission for the Protection of Nature
(later, still under Szafer's leadership, renamed the State Council for the
Protection of Nature) (Garścia 1988, 2). In 1932 the League was admit-
ted to the International Bureau for the Protection of Nature. During its
earlier years the League dedicated itself to building a base of societal support, conservation of certain types of flora and fauna, protection of the
Tatra Mountain region, creation of national parks and nature reserves,
and fund-raising (Komitet Obchodów 1988, 4). Although the Second
World War forced suspension of the League's activities, its organizational
basis and the beginnings of the park system had already been established.

Reactivated in Łódź following the war, the League for the Protection of Nature experienced numerous organizational and financial difficulties, particularly upon moving its headquarters to Warsaw in 1953. After the Polish October of 1956, the League was able to launch a number of its more notable efforts. In 1957 it was the major initiator behind the creation of the Nature Protection Guards (*Straż Ochrony Przyrody*), which by the end of the communist era numbered almost 40,000 members, recruited largely from the League's overall membership (Komitet Obchodów 1988, 5). That year also saw the creation of the Division of Tree Plantation and Greenery (*Zakład Zadrzewień i Zieleni*), whose original task was to reclaim devastated areas, largely through the planting and protection of trees and other greenery. In the next three decades, this unit grew to 12 Divisions of Tree Plantation, Greenery, and Recultivation (*Zakłady Zadrzewień, Zieleni i Rekultywacji*) whose services expanded to efforts on the behalf of local economies and industrial units, generating a major portion of the League's income (Komitet Obchodów 1988, 4–5). The League also established its own press and began to publish a popular monthly, *Polish Nature* (*Przyroda Polska*), and an organizational bulletin. By the last year of communist rule, *Polish Nature* was in its thirty-second year with a circulation of 50,000 and recommended by the Ministry of National Education for use in the schools. It was a colorful publication with short pieces on current national and international issues, information about the League as well as other groups and activities, and nature specials with several quality photographs. This magazine, combined with readings, films, exhibitions, competitions and other efforts to popularize nature conservation, sparked a rapid growth in the League's membership from the mid-1950s on. With growth came the development of a network of chapters that spread throughout the entire country. By 1988 the League boasted a membership of 1.7 million (about 4% of the total population) and 13,000 units in schools, youth organizations, industry, universities and its territorial structures at the voivodship (*województwo*), city, and village (*gmina*) levels.[7]

As an officially sanctioned and controlled "social organization"—the sixth largest such organization in the country throughout the 1980s[8]—the League for the Protection of Nature was well integrated into the official political system. For many years it was the only significant channel for environmental activism and undoubtedly played the key role in establishing nature conservation programs and developing popular consciousness of the need for conservation in Poland. Recognized by the Council of Ministers in 1968 as an "Association of Higher Merit"[9] and awarded the Officers' Cross of the Order of Poland's Rebirth by the Council of

State in 1985, the League continued to serve as the backbone of environmental protection even after the independent ecological movement developed. It created and promoted environmental funds, organized environmentally inclined people in various circles, including journalists in its "*Ekos*" group, suggested new laws and regulations, backed efforts initiated by smaller groups, and published extensively. Some of its members ran for and were elected to People's Councils (*Rady Narodowe*) at the local and voivodship levels.

Its long association with official institutions and programs earned the League an only partially deserved reputation for being coopted. Although it is true that the League did not challenge the foundations of the existing system and its programs, members never lost sight of their goals for the protection of nature. A more accurate criticism often expressed among environmentalists is that the age, size, and diversity of the organization left it bogged down in bureaucracy—unwieldy, inert, slow to react to immediate problems, and somewhat superficial and formalistic in its activism. Moreover, the League tended to retain a conservationist approach, expanded to encompass the more complex natural networks protected in parks. Many felt that, while resulting in worthy efforts, this approach was dated and only partial. In the Poland of the 1970s and 1980s the pressing questions of environmental protection applied as much or more to human-influenced environment as they did to "wild" nature.

Legislation

Both the legal measures and administrative structures concerned with environmental protection in Poland have developed alongside the League in a rather piecemeal fashion, leaving overlaps and gaps.

The more comprehensive laws on nature and the environment were passed in 1934, 1949, 1974, and 1980 (summarized in table 3.1, below). Newly independent Poland's first laws on the protection of nature came in 1932.[10] In accordance with a 1902 international convention on the protection of birds useful for agriculture, ratified by Poland thirty years later, the Polish government adopted its own law on the protection of endangered animal species. The first general law on protection of nature was passed in 1934.[11] Of a conservationist character, the law focused on individual natural objects and places, rights and responsibilities of their owners, and the financial obligations of the state in the upkeep of these objects. Thus it introduced legal recognition that certain natural objects or areas are "societal" despite private ownership. The 1934 law was also important in that it specified administrative procedures and responsibility in decisionmaking regarding nature and created the Nature Protection Fund. In addition, it introduced the legal groundwork for the creation of nature reserves and national parks.

Although the 1934 law was a significant step forward in the legal protection of nature and Polish scholars' contributions to international organizations and conventions in this field during the interwar period were several, in practice, there was little change in the protection of nature in Poland. Respect for the prerogatives of private ownership, upheld in several articles of the 1934 law, was firmly entrenched in both government and society. Moreover, there was little time for people to change their attitudes about nature and ownership as World War II broke out on Polish territory five years later. Six years of war and occupation brought untold destruction to Poland's environment. After the war, reconstruction, a new administrative system, nationalization, and the introduction of a planned economy changed the socioeconomic and legal bases for environmental protection.

Until 1980, the legal foundation for environmental protection was the 1949 law on the protection of nature. Comprehensive for its time, the new law widened somewhat the legal scope for protection of nature.[12] First and foremost, this law established new and more extensive administrative procedures for decisionmaking regarding the protection of nature. Advisory councils of experts were set up, as were formal procedures for their use. This did not mean, however, that they were given any power. Officials could circumvent them by appealing to a higher administrative level. Nature protection still took a predominantly conservationist form, namely the declaration of natural monuments (*pomniki przyrody*), nature reserves (*rezerwaty przyrody*), national parks (*parki narodowe*), and protected wildlife and plant species. The measures that could be taken to protect these objects and the penalties for violating these measures (fines, confiscation of equipment used to violate the law and imprisonment for up to three months—art.28–32) were also spelled out in the law.

Like its predecessor, the 1949 law left many holes to be filled by later administrative decisions. It also followed the 1934 law in placing serious limitations on the power of authorities, councils, and organizations involved in the protection of nature. For example, the Council of Ministers, which had a heavy representation of forces favoring the development of industry, could approve projects rejected by the State Council for the Protection of Nature (art. 9, para. 3). Another limitation was the explicit condition that the Nature Protection Guards not receive funds from the state treasury (art. 8, para. 11). Finally, there were no clear distinctions between the rights and responsibilities of the administrative structures of the Ministry of Forestry and the organs set up specifically for the protection of nature, except that the latter could issue and collect fines (art. 7, para. 1,2). Moreover, the penalties specified were not severe enough to deter state firms (the major polluters) from breaking the law.

More than thirty years passed before a new law on environmental protection was promulgated, but a number of other measures supplemented the 1949 law. It is symptomatic of Poland's approach to environmental protection during this period that legal measures concerning the environment were scattered across various fields of activity and that responsibility was equally diffused.[13] Usually the decisions that most affected the environment (investments, construction, industry, etc.) were made by one set of authorities, while another set was held responsible for the protection of the environment. Although similar divisions of responsibility are fairly common across political systems, the position of environmental administrators in Poland was particularly weak for two reasons. First, there were few provisions for their participation in the decisionmaking processes of the industrial, mining, and construction sectors. Second, both the environmental "controllers" and the "controlled" were subordinated at various levels of government to the same governing authorities, where development interests dominated, leaving the environmental administrations with virtually no independent base of power. Moreover, the dominant concept in this period was still "nature protection," interpreted as conservation of remarkable natural elements and ecosystems in unique areas considered to have retained their natural value. Other elements of the environment, especially those most transformed by human activity, were treated separately.

Subsequent laws most directly related to environmental protection were the 1966 law on air pollution and the 1974 water law. The 1966 law on air pollution demonstrates very well the partial and splintered character of environmental protection in Poland. According to its provisions, firms were responsible for taking and reporting measurements of their own emissions. The State Sanitation Inspectorate (*Państwowa Inspekcja Sanitarna*) and the voivodship commission for air protection (which is a committee of the voivodship's people's council, or legislature—i.e. part of an entirely different and weaker administrative structure) were to oversee the validity of these measurements and take their own when they deemed it necessary (art. 8). Above these two organs of control was the Central Office for Water Economy (art. 10). The president of that office and the Minister of Health and Social Welfare would determine acceptable emissions norms and the data required to check them.[14] Aside from setting up overlapping authority, all of these provisions were weakened by the low penalties to be assessed for violating the law (and for state enterprises fines could be taken out of the state budget as costs of production); additional fines and how they would be paid were left up to the decision of the Council of Ministers, on which heavy industry was overrepresented. Also, the laws did not apply to air inside buildings (for example, factory air) or to radioactive substances, the latter of which were to be controlled by separate regulations.

The 1974 water law is a general piece of legislation covering the ownership, management, extraction, pollution, and treatment of surface, ground and coastal water. It brings together measures contained in three earlier bills and other administrative decrees. In most instances the law relegates principal administrative responsibilities in water regulation to "territorial authorities" or to future decisions to be made by central authorities, often the Council of Ministers. In addition to an extensive discussion of water use permits and the obligations associated with them, the law contains sections on conflict resolution, general and specific uses of water, protection against pollution, flood control, construction and melioration, the water supply system, water management firms, record keeping, and penalties.[15] The water law was seen as an accomplishment because it collected and codified many previously dispersed issues in one bill and related the new regulations to the new administrative system (Surowiec, Tarasiewicz, and Zwięglińska 1981, 3). However, the pollution provisions are few and general. Article 63 states that every firm, service, etc. must treat their wastes before dumping them into water or into the ground. They are obligated to build, maintain, and use equipment for this purpose. In fact, they are not allowed to operate without using it (art. 63, par. 3). To this day many firms and cities lack the necessary equipment. So, protection of water from pollution remained largely on paper. As in the case of air pollution, the penalties for violation of these laws were not prohibitive, even in the relatively few cases where the laws were enforced.

Both the air pollution law and the water law were attempts to deal with problems not foreseen by the 1949 law on the protection of nature. Among other measures adopted during this period to address new problems was the section on environmental protection in the 1974 construction law. This law contained some general principles for investment and planning procedures, as well as for the actual construction process, that were meant to safeguard the environment.[16] Moreover, buildings such as factories were to be certified for use only when the accompanying equipment to protect the environment was in place and operative (art. 15). In practice, this was the exception rather than the rule and construction plans were changed, generally expanded, without reconsideration of the environmental effects and the measures necessary to limit them.

These laws and supplementary decisions made by the Council of Ministers and authorities from the central to the local level and grafted onto a dated law on protection of nature were the only shields that existed to protect the environment from the effects of rapid, extensive industrialization until 1980. Judging by the statistics on air and water pollution and soil contamination (see table 2.1), they were not at all successful. The 1980 law was the first major coordinated attempt to control destruction of the environment, not only as nature had created it but also as humans had transformed it. Still shaped by the laws that had come before it, the new law, along with subsequent supplementary measures, formed the basis of environmental protection in Poland throughout the period analyzed in this study and we will return to it in the section of this chapter focusing on environmental protection in the 1980s.

The history of environmental legislation in Poland contains a few persistent patterns. One was the trend of a slow evolution from conservation through protection of nature and to environmental protection. Although the trend itself was positive, the partial and "amending" nature of most legislation and its belated enactment reflect lack of both environmental priorities and a comprehensive perspective on the part of the Polish government. Another tendency was to introduce overlapping authority not only in environmental policy in general, but also in specific policy areas. Furthermore, too much was left to interpretation by further laws and executive directives. Law was also weakened by the fact that expert involvement—indeed even official environmental assessment—as foreseen in most measures, was only "advisory." Finally, in many cases "wishful thinking" about the capabilities for environmental protection incorporated into laws and regulations effectively nullified them, as no one could achieve or therefore expect full implementation. Despite these problems, however, the actual texts of Poland's environmental legislation were in many cases no more disjointed and *post hoc* than those of many other countries during that period.

Laws on the books can be only a first step toward environmental protection. To be effective, they must be implemented and enforced. Three weaknesses plagued Polish environmentalists' attempts to move beyond legislation to effective enforcement. The first weakness was a loophole sometimes included in the legislation itself and usually included in the specific regulations developed to implement the legislation: an appropriate authority had the discretion to suspend certain measures or to free certain enterprises from requirements to install antipollution devices for

Table 3.1 *Major Environmental Laws Prior to 1989*

Year	Legislation	Main Features for Environmental Protection
1934	Law on Nature Protection[a]	-conservationist -focused on individual objects and places in nature -rights and responsibilities of private owners, financial obligation of state for upkeep -specified administrative responsibility in decision-making regarding nature -set up Nature Protection Fund -legal groundwork for national parks and nature reserves
1949	Law on Nature Protection[b]	-conservationist -established more extensive decision-making procedures regarding nature -established natural monuments, nature reserves, national parks and protected plant and wildlife species -set penalties for violation of these provisions
1966	Law on the Protection of the Atmosphere from Pollution[c]	- firms responsible for measuring and reporter their own emissions - State Sanitation Inspectorate and voivodship commissions for air protection to oversee validity of these measurements - President of Central Office for Water Economy and Minister of health and social Welfare to determine norms
1974	Water Law[d]	- general water law covering use of surface, ground and coastal waters - water use permits - administrative responsibilities to "territorial authorities" - every enterprise must treat wastes before dumping them - an enterprise is obligated to build and use equipment for this purpose and is not allowed to operate without such equipment
1974	Construction Law[e]	- investment and planning procedures to include environmental considerations - guidelines for construction process to safeguard the environment - new buildings to be given over to use only when environmental protection equipment is operative
1980	Law on the Protection and Shaping of the Environment[f]	- fairly comprehensive - updated, expanded and codified environmental provisions of other laws - included non-economic criteria in definition of "rational utilization" [of resources] - invalidated decisions of any administrative body that violated environmental law - created State Inspectorate for Environmental Protection - created State Council for Environmental Protection

Notes:
[a]Dz.U.1934, nr 31, poz.274
[b]Dz.U.1949, nr 25, poz.180
[c]Dz.U.1966, nr 14, poz.87
[d]Dz.U.1974, nr 38, poz.230
[e]Dz.U.1974, nr 38, poz.229
[f]Dz.U.1980, nr 3, poz.6

"important" reasons. Often fulfillment of the economic plan was a sufficient reason. The second pitfall had to do with the power of sanctions. In the case of state enterprises, fines were not incentives to change behavior as they were too low, rarely imposed, and paid from (and calculated into) the enterprises' state-supplied budget. Even when fines and other sanctions were imposed, prosecutors were known to dismiss them, declaring that the imperative of fulfilling the economic plan took precedence over environmental regulations. Perhaps most important, though, effective implementation of environmental legislation requires coordinated administration and clearly defined spheres of responsibility. Here, Polish law was clearly weak.

Administration

The history of Polish governmental administration in the area of environmental protection can be broken down into periods more or less corresponding to the major laws discussed above.[17] The first administrative body created for this purpose after Poland regained independence was the Temporary State Commission for the Protection of Nature. Created in December 1919 by the Minister of Religious Faiths and Public Enlightenment, this commission had an advisory, "opinion-giving" nature (Jastrzębski 1983, 10). The idea of setting up a state institution to introduce nature protection was developed ten days before the commission's creation at a meeting of naturalists in Warsaw (Szafer et al. 1973, 19). The commission developed a program for a permanent institution and founded its main bureau in Kraków and curators in Lwów, Poznań and Warsaw. From 1919 until the Warsaw committee helped establish the League for the Protection of Nature in 1928, the council and its committees devoted most of their efforts to publication. Once the League took over this burden these institutions could devote more time to legislation and the issues of the day.

These provisional beginnings were institutionalized in 1925. The temporary commission was renamed the State Council for the Protection of Nature (*Państwowa Rada Ochrony Przyrody* or PROP). The curators became Committees for the Protection of Nature (*Komitety Ochrony Przyrody*) (Szafer *et al.* 1973, 20). The council could propose delegates to act as its territorial organs. The Minister of Religious Faiths had the formal power to appoint these delegates, as well as members of the committees, and could also found new committees.[18] All of these organs were advisory and "opinion-giving." In addition to the delegates, this administration was comprised of officials from other state organs and territorial self-government organs, representatives of different associations and activists in nature protection (Jastrzębski 1983, 10–11). The work of PROP and its network of committees relied heavily on the academic communities in major university cities and was unpaid (Szafer et al. 1973, 20). Another major change introduced in 1925 was the establishment of an Office of the Delegate of the Minister of Religious Faiths and Public Enlightenment for Nature Protection (*Urząd Delegata Ministra Wyznań Religijnych i Oświecenia Publicznego do Spraw Ochrony Przyrody*). This was the ministry's office for cooperation with and oversight of the council and its network of committees. Administration of nature protection maintained this form until 1934, when the first general law on the protection of nature was passed.

The 1934 law confirmed PROP's advisory nature. Decisionmaking authority remained in the hands of ministers and voivodship officials.[19] The Minister of Religious Faiths and Public Enlightenment, who was also PROP's chairman, continued to hold the central role in decisions regarding the protection of nature, often in consultation with other ministers. Article 12 gave the Minister general control over nature protection measures and designated Nature Conservators (*Konserwatorowie Przyrody*) appointed by the Minister in consultation with the Minister of Agriculture and Agricultural Reform as the administration's specialists in these matters. A conservator was part of the Voivodship Office (*Urząd Wojewódzki*) and could fulfill that function in several voivodships at once. Article 15 provided for the establishment of a Nature Protection Fund (*Fundusz Ochrony Przyrody*) administered by the same minister in consultation with both the Minister of Internal Affairs and the Treasury. The only other important organizational measure was the provision empowering the Minister of Religious Faiths and Public Enlightenment together with the agriculture minister to create special Nature Protection Guards (art. 16).

The administration of nature remained the same until the occupation of Poland in 1939. One crisis did occur in this administration, however. In 1936, the members of PROP unanimously resigned in protest against the government for breaking the conditions of the 1934 law and destroying nature under the pretext of opening the beauty of the Tatra Mountains to tourists and sports enthusiasts.[20] This incident was indicative of the powerlessness of the country's highest expert authority in the area of nature protection. Unable to reverse the decision of the central authorities regarding what it saw as the devastation of the Tatras, the only thing the Council could do was resign. The conflict was not resolved before the outbreak of World War II.

After the war, the new government reestablished the State Council for the Protection of Nature, calling together all members of the 1936 council who had survived the war and occupation (Szafer et al. 1973, 25). During the 1945–48 period, a completely new state system was created. The 1949 law on the protection of nature adjusted nature administration accordingly. The main responsibility for the protection of nature fell on the shoulders of the Minister of Forestry.[21] In addition to the forestry administration itself, the Minister of Forestry had three smaller organizational hierarchies to aid in the protection of the nature. One of these was the set of advisory and consultative bodies headed by PROP and consisting of the Voivodship Committees for the Protection of Nature (*Wojewódzkie Komitety Ochrony Przyrody*), in other words a slightly more regularized version of the academic consultative structure set up in the interwar period (art. 3–4, 6). The conservators comprised the second set of officials. Starting with the Chief Nature Conservator (*Naczelny Konserwator Przyrody*), the Minister's expert, and extending through the Nature Conservators at the voivodship level to the Directors of National Parks and the State Chief Foresters at the local level, these officials were the executive branch's own specialists. Their duties and authority were defined by the Minister of Forestry in consultation with the Minister of Public Administration. Below the ministerial level these officials were part of the territorial authorities. Thus, the ultimate authority in protection of nature at the local level was the "*starosta*" (equivalent to a mayor), at the voivodship level the "*wojewoda*" (Chairman of the Voivodship Council in the communist state structure, the equivalent to a governor) (art. 5). These territorial officials were overseers of their districts in every area, responsible for economic development, public services, etc. The third set of organs—hypothetical until 1957—were the Nature Protection Guards, which were to be defined and appointed by the same two ministers but were to rely on funding from social organizations and to coordinate their activities with those organizations (art. 8).[22]

The outcome of these measures was a fragmented administration of nature, an administration that was also subverted by industrial interests. The forestry ministry was not only in charge of protecting Poland's forests, but also responsible for the forest products industry, in other words the exploitation of these forests. The expert councils had no independent authority. The conservators were small voices in voivodship offices which were trying to attract investment and direct the economic development of their regions. In fact, these offices were full of contradictions since they were territorial authorities subject to the decisions of several national-level ministries at once. Moreover, the role of the conservators vis-a-vis the forestry administration was left in the hands of the forestry minister. Finally, the guards were hybrid bodies limited by administrative controls from one side and subject to the uncertainties of social support from the other side.

The environmental administration resulting from the 1949 law was essentially the same as that from 1934, even 1925, regularized and grafted onto the new governmental structure of the Polish People's Republic. Some of its basic elements—and its shortcomings—remained the same throughout the communist period. However, several modifications were made in this administration during the 1960s and 1970s—even before the changes effected by the 1980 law on the protection and shaping of the environment. (See table 3.2 for an overview of national-level institutions responsible for environmental protection during the communist period.) Until 1972, primary responsibility for nature protection remained with the Ministry of Forestry, renamed the Ministry of Forestry and Wood Industry in 1956. However, other ministries and offices held responsibility for some facets of environmental protection. Among these other administrations were the Central Office for Water Economy, the Central Office for Geology, and the Ministry of Agriculture.

The Central Office for Water Economy (*Centralny Urząd Gospodarki Wodnej*) represents one of the earliest attempts to rationalize control over the environment. Created in mid-1960, this administration was directly responsible to the Chairman of the Council of Ministers, not to another ministry. (The president of the office was appointed by the Chairman of the Council of Ministers.)[23] As the foremost water authority this office aggregated a number of the responsibilities that had been scattered throughout the system. The scope of its activities included, among other things, navigation and transportation, water resource use and supply infrastructure, oversight of pollution control and the sewage system, waterway maintenance, flood protection, and hydrological and meteorological services.[24] The Central Office for Water Economy also had oversight of the organs concerned with water in the people's council system and its own advisory council of experts.[25] With the passage of the 1966 law on air pollution, this office was even given joint responsibility along with the Ministry of Health and Social Welfare and that ministry's State Sanitation Inspectorate for regulating and controlling emissions of air pollutants.[26] The Central Office for Water Economy ceased to exist in 1972, when its functions were split among the Ministry of Agriculture, the Ministry of Water Transportation, and the new Ministry of Territorial Economy and Environmental Protection.

During that same time period, control over various aspects of the environment was shared by still other administrations. The Central Office for Geology (*Centralny Urząd Geologii*) was created in 1961 to study and control the use of ground water and mine beds. This office also set the standards for mining and other geological work. And, finally, the Ministry of Agriculture[27] governed the use of agricultural lands, irrigation projects, soil conservation projects, water supply to the villages, and the use of the sewage system for agricultural chemical substances—fertilizers, pesticides, and herbicides.

In 1972, the Gierek government introduced a major set of administrative changes in central ministries. Taking power after the violent repression of workers' demonstrations in December 1970, Gierek introduced a campaign to reinvigorate the Polish economy and shift politics onto a more "pragmatic" and less ideological basis. Included in this strategy was the technocratic rationalization of political and economic administration. Primary responsibility for environmental protection was shifted to the newly created Ministry of Territorial Economy and Environmental Protection. Although this was the first time environmental protection had made it into the title of a ministry, the change did not result in much more attention to ecology. As created in 1972, this ministry had a number of responsibilities of which environmental protection was only one. In the environmental field it took over responsibility for greenery on public property from its predecessor, control of water pollution from the now defunct Central Office for Water Economy, and responsibility for air pollution from both the Central Office for Water Economy and the Minister of Health and Social Welfare. Forests, national parks, and nature reserves remained under the jurisdiction of the Ministry of Forestry and the Wood Industry, and agricultural soil and irrigation remained the province of the Ministry of Agriculture and Food Economy.

One important feature of Gierek's administrative changes was that they united some of the major responsibilities for the environment with powers over territorial planning and zoning. For ecology this was a double-edged sword. Depending on the proclivities and interests of those who occupied the offices of the ministry, the environment had either gained proponents with power over important areas of spatial planning or it had been left in the hands of its destroyers. The record of industrial development, other building construction, and ecological destruction in the 1970s suggests that either the less-ecologically minded had the upper hand or the decisions made at the ministerial level were revised in the field. The specific duties of the new ministry included: programming and spatial zoning of cities, neighborhood settlements and villages; land usage in cities and settlements; the housing economy and municipal infrastructure; surveying and cartography; property ownership; state control over general construction and over specific municipal construction; establishing norms for the abovementioned construction; protection of the natural environment, specifically water, greenery and air.[28]

Three months later the Council of Ministers defined exactly what the Ministry of Territorial Economy's environmental responsibilities entailed. They included general responsibility for developing and popularizing environmental protection, as well as extensive duties in water management and pollution control. The latter involved assessing environmental quality, setting norms and fines, balancing sources of harmful pollutants, and sponsoring research and development of environmental technologies. The ministry was also to issue opinions on the localization of investment and to coordinate the activities of the several agencies involved in protecting the environment.[29]

The following year the Council of Ministers created the Institute for Environmental Protection (*Instytut Ochrony Środowiska*) as the new ministry's own source of expertise. Centered in Warsaw with affiliates in Kraków and Wrocław, its purpose is to conduct academic studies and scientific tests.[30] Despite its subordinate position, the Institute for Environmental Protection has become influential over the years. It groups together some of Poland's highly respected experts in ecology and most of its members have appointments at other academic institutions and are active either in actual protection of the environment or in environmental politics. These are some of the same people to whom we can trace initiatives within the system that helped put the environment on the political agenda (see chapter 7 for further discussion).

Another set of administrative and personnel changes occurred in central organs and in the system of People's Councils in 1975–76. At this time the Ministry of Territorial Economy and Environmental Protection gained a number of responsibilities for state administration from the Ministry for Internal Affairs and became the Ministry of Administration, Territorial Economy, and Environmental Protection.[31] Again, the Council of Ministers later delineated the more specific responsibilities in each area. Except for wording there were very few changes in the responsibilities for environmental protection. The measures concerning control over construction and equipment for environmental purposes were worded more precisely. The new laws added soil pollution and environmental damage due to vibration to the ministry's jurisdiction. However, the specific provision empowering the ministry to impose fines on water polluters was left out. Responsibility for informing the public about and popularizing

Table 3.2 *Major National-Level Institutions in Environmental Protection*

	1945–49	1950–54	1955–59	1960–64	1965–69	1970–74	1975–79	1980–84	1985–89	1990–95
Advisory Councils and Research Institutes	State Council for the Protection of Nature [PROP] (reconstituted in 1946) →					Institute for Environmental Protection (1973) →		State Council for Environmental Protection [PROS] (1980) →		
Forests and Parks	Ministry of Forestry (1949)		Ministry of Forestry and Wood Industry (1956)						Ministry of Agriculture, Forestry and Food Economy (1985)	Ministry of Environmental Protection, Natural Resources and Forestry
Environmental Protection						Ministry of Territorial Economy and Environmental Protection (1972)	Ministry of Administration, Territorial Economy and Environmental Protection (1975)	Office of Environmental Protection and Water Economy (1983)	Ministry of Environmental Protection and Natural Resources (effective 1/1/86)	
							State Inspectorate for Environmental Protection [PIOS] (1980, under ministry) →			
Water and Mineral Resources				Central Office for Water Economy (1960)						
				Central Office for Geology (1961)						

ecology was changed to cooperation with social organizations involved in environmental protection. Curiously, the new law omitted the clause "issuing opinions on the localization of investment from the point of view of environmental protection."[32] In its functions dealing with "territorial economy" the ministry would obviously maintain control over zoning and other activities that affect local investment decisions; perhaps it was assumed that in making such decisions and reviewing specific investment plans for compatibility with ministerial guidelines, ministerial personnel would automatically incorporate environmental concerns.

Environmental protection maintained this administrative form until 1983. Even the comprehensive 1980 law did not introduce changes in institutions; rather, new legal measures were grafted onto the old structure. It was not until the new set of administrative changes, enacted at the end of martial law to rebuild the political system and achieve "normalization" after the first Solidarity period, that most environmental responsibilities were pulled together under one office charged primarily with protecting the environment.

The administrative history of environmental protection in Poland reinforces the pattern of fragmented and partial responses to problems seen in the legislative record. Indeed, even after the 1980 law, the system of advisory councils from the interwar period and the ill-defined overlapping jurisdiction between specialized central institutions (ministries) and general territorial authorities (especially the Voivodship Office), seen at least from 1949, persisted. These jurisdiction problems occurred even within policy areas, such as water economy, where more comprehensive legislation was passed and attempts were made to establish one central office. Although the number of offices charged with responsibilities for protecting the environment grew with the increasing complexity of both the economy and the state administration after World War II, their activities were not coordinated and in many cases their primary areas of responsibility produced interests that were at odds with environmental protection. Finally, no authority commanded power to sanction actors for violating laws sufficiently to deter such transgressions.

Parks and Reserves

The most visible benefit of all the legislation, administrative changes, and activism of the League for the Protection of Nature over the years was the creation and development of Poland's national park and nature reserve systems. By the end of communist rule Poland had 14 national parks and close to 1,000 nature reserves. In addition there were landscape parks,

Table 3.3 National Parks

Estab-lished	Name	Area (ha.)	Area Protected (ha.)	% of Park Protected	Threatened Area[a] (ha.)	Change in Area after 1988 (ha.)
1947	Białowieski	5,317	4,747	89.3	na	31
1950	Świętokrzyski	5,906	1,741	29.5	na	4
1954	Babiogórski	1,734	1,061	61.2	958 (55.0%)	—
	Pieniński	2,329	804	34.5	na	-98
	Tatrzański	21,164	11,514	54.5	na	—
1956	Ojcowski	1,592	338	21.5	na	—
1957	Wielkopolski	5,198	221	4.3	254 (4.9%)	140
1959	Kampinoski	35,486	4,303	12.1	na	169
	Karkonoski	5,563	1,717	30.9	3,769 (67.8%)	-1
1960	Woliński	4,844	162	3.3	na	157
1966	Słowiński	18,247	5,935	32.5	na	550
1973	Bieszczadzki	5,587	4,489	80.4	na	21,477
1974	Roztoczański	6,857	518	7.6	na	1,028
1980	Gorczański	6,750	2,968	44.0	na	13
Total	communist era	126,574	40,518	32.0	4,981 (4.0%)	—
1990	Drawieński	8,735	368	4.2	na	8,735
1990	Poleski	4,907	428	8.7	na	4,907
1990	Wigierski	15,113	1343	8.9	na	15,113
1993	Biebrzański	59,223	2569	4.3	na	59,223
1993	Gór Stołowych	6,280	39	0.6	na	6,280
Total		244,302	59,941	24.5	—	117,728

SOURCES: Dziennik Ustaw; RS 1989, 28; RS 1990, 31; RS 1994, 39. Protected means under strict (ścisły) protection.

[a] These are forest areas threatened by gas and particle emissions according to a special study carried out in 1983. Comparable figures are not available for the other parks.

areas of protected landscape, and natural monuments. Despite some of their beginnings in the creation of parks during the interwar period, all national parks gained their legal status after World War II. They are the fruit of the conservation movement begun in the nineteenth century and of the "nature protection" emphasis during the interwar and immediate post-WWII periods.

National Parks.

Poland's national parks are large areas (at least 500 hectares) of extraordinary natural value or splendor. They can include areas that have seen limited development for tourism or other purposes (some people live and farm within the boundaries of these parks), areas where development is prohibited, and areas where any human intrusion is forbidden. The latter are designated as "strict reserves" (rezerwaty ścisłe), which are parts of the nature reserve system. Since national parks can contain a number of reserves and monuments, the total area of protected nature in Poland amounts to less than the sum of areas covered under each category. Together national parks comprised 0.4 percent of Poland's territory by the end of communist rule. Ten of the national parks were created between 1947 and 1960; four were created in the next two decades (see table 3.3). Under consideration in 1989 was the creation of a fifteenth national park in the Northeastern lake region (*Mazury*). This area, however, was included in the Green Lungs of Poland (*Zielone Płuca Polski*) project, an initiative begun by environmental activists and adopted by the state in the late 1980s to create an extensive network of parks and wilderness in Poland's relatively undeveloped eastern region. Five new national parks have also been created since the beginning of 1990, while others (especially Bieszczadzki) have been expanded, bringing the total area of national parks to 0.8 percent of Polish territory.

Some of these parks have longer histories than their establishment dates suggest. Six have beginnings that can be traced to the activism of PROP during the interwar period. The earliest efforts to create a national park came in the Tatra region near the end of the nineteenth century. Polish conservationists tried from 1888 on to create a national park in the Tatras (Szafer et al. 1973, 687), but their efforts were frustrated by the imperial rulers in Vienna. Partial success finally came in 1939 with the creation of the Nature Park in the Tatras (*Park Przyrody w Tatrach*).[33] What was later to become the national park in Białowieża was formed in 1932 with the first measures taken as early as 1921. This unique, very old forest, almost 90% of which is a strict reserve, is the last home of a number of nearly extinct animal species (Szafer et al. 1973, 22, 685). It is also at the center of the Green Lungs of Poland project. The Wielkopolski and Pieniński parks were created in the 1930s, as was a national park in Czarnohora, which is on territory lost to the Soviet Union in World War II. Part of what became the Babiogórski National Park also came under protection during the interwar period (Szafer et al. 1973, 22, 685–87).

As with national parks in other countries, hikers and tourists have taken their toll on the parts of these parks that are not controlled as "strict reserves." The biggest challenge facing some of these parks, however, comes from industrial pollution, especially sulfur dioxide and its concomitant acid rain. The figures given in the next to last column of table 3.3 are official calculations of the areas of national parks which overlap with the 27 areas of severe ecological degradation declared in the 1983–1985 national plan. Both official and unofficial estimates of damage to national parks exceed these figures.

Nature Reserves.

Though a few are bigger than the smallest national parks, Poland's nature reserves are usually smaller areas of great value to plant and animal life or of particular aesthetic value. If natural development changes their fundamental characteristics, destroying their uniqueness, they can be (and have been) dissolved. There are two categories of reserves: strict (*ścisły*) and partial (*częściowy*). Earlier on, naturalists had more success in founding reserves than they did national parks. By the time World War II broke out, Poland had 180 nature reserves and proposals had been introduced for as many more (Szafer et al. 1973, 22). As of the end of 1988 the Ministry of Environmental Protection and Natural Resources reported 988 nature reserves with a total area of 113,897 hectares (less than 0.4% of Polish territory). Of this total 7,349 hectares (or 6.5% of the area designated for nature reserves) was in strict reserves, where no human interference was allowed (*RS 1989*, 30). (Often the only people allowed to enter these areas are nature-reserve personnel.) The rest of the nature-reserve territory is designated "partial." There visitors and scientists are allowed and restrictions are more individualized (Szczęsny 1982, 150).[34] Nature reserves can be located within the boundaries of both national parks and landscape parks.

Natural Monuments.

Natural monuments or landmarks are individual creations of nature, e.g., cliffs, caves, a stand of trees, waterfalls. Early conservationists started lists of Poland's most remarkable natural landmarks in the nineteenth century when Poland was still in partitions. By 1939, they had already designated about 4,500 natural monuments (Szafer et al. 1973, 22). At the end of 1988, 17,167 of these *pomniki przyrody* were protected against human destruction (*RS 1989*, 30).

National parks, nature reserves, and natural monuments all have their roots in the pre-World War I and interwar periods. There are, however, newer forms of nature protection: landscape parks and areas of protected landscape. These new forms, covering 13.5 percent of the country, resulted from the development by PROP of a comprehensive program of landscape protection. The conceptualization and working out of this program lasted from 1964 until 1974 (Szczęsny 1982, 118).

Landscape Parks.

A second part of the park system (after national parks) focuses on broad territories, whose landscape is protected. These areas are a functional part of economic development. Their resources may be used as long as that use does not cause environmental degradation. All investments in enterprises that pollute, drain, or otherwise burden the environment are forbidden. Naturalists carry out studies in landscape parks and there are several trails and facilities to meet social needs for aesthetic enjoyment of nature (Szczęsny 1982, 119–20). By the end of 1988 Poland had 43 landscape parks amounting to 1,013,449 hectares or a little over 3.2 percent of Polish territory (*RS 1989*, 29).

Areas of Protected Landscape.

These areas are designated for vacation and recreational use. In the communist period, they had priority in all such investments. Although their development is not as restricted as the development of landscape parks, the same prohibition exists on investments that would result in the degradation of the environment (Szczęsny 1982, 121–22). At the end of 1988 there were 155 such areas covering 3,209,422 hectares, 10.3% of Polish territory (*RS 1989*, 29).

In the face of largely ineffective environmental policies, these various forms of nature protection provided the main bulwark against ecological destruction in communist Poland. The park and reserve system grew substantially and the "landscape" system was developed during that period. Indeed, until the 1980s, most environmental activism was of a conservationist nature and took the form of pressing authorities to declare certain regions parts of the park and reserve system. Here the League for the Protection of Nature and various scientific and advisory councils played major roles. This strategy made little headway in controlling the real sources of destruction—industrial pollution and municipal waste—but it did salvage some of Poland's unique lands and animal habitats. Unfortunately, some of the parks themselves were damaged, in a few cases severely, by unabated air and water pollution originating outside their boundaries. Still, the development of the park and reserve system during the communist period is a legacy ecologists have continued to utilize rather effectively during the transition period. The total area of national parks has nearly doubled since 1989 and almost a quarter of Polish territory now falls under one of these forms of legal protection (*RS 1994*, 38).

Environmental Protection in the 1980s

Clearly, the most important factors affecting Polish environmental politics in the 1980s were the changed political situation after the formation of Solidarity in August 1980 and the increasingly visible effects of pollution on the environment and human health. Before turning to the study of those politics, however, it is necessary to examine the form in which administrative and legislative developments left environmental protection at the beginning of the decade and what changes were made throughout the decade as environmental politics became more heated.

The 1980 law on environmental protection was the first major legislation that attempted to treat the environment as a whole. (The 1934 and 1949 laws concerned mostly the protection of *nature* and did not include human-made environments.) Passed by the parliament on January 31, 1980 and effective as of September 1 of that year, the "Law on the Protection and Shaping of the Environment" did not replace the 1949 law on nature protection as much as it addressed a new concern.[35] Since the new law was passed *before* the formation of Solidarity, to the extent that it can be viewed as the result of social pressure on the government, its passage must be credited to ecologists working in the legal field, official environmental organizations, and various government administrations. (Legal scholars had been particularly active in this area in the 1970s.) In other words, it was members of society, in their capacities as part of the state administration or academia that had influenced the government agenda from within.

Above all, the 1980 law pulled together measures contained in the legal acts dealing with environmental protection that had preceded it (discussed earlier in this chapter). Supplanted entirely were laws on zoos, city green spaces, and air pollution. The main environmental points of the 1974 water law were reaffirmed; and relevant parts of mining and construction laws were also reiterated. The 1949 law on the protection of nature remained in force. Some of its measures, however, were updated and some new matters were addressed. In particular, sections on vibration, noise pollution, radiation, investment procedures, and penalties were expanded.

In codifying previous legislation, the new law defined "rational utilization" of the environment to include noneconomic criteria, maintenance of the natural balance, and use such that the state of the environment is not worsened.[36] Moreover, decisions of administrative organs were not allowed to violate the demands of environmental protection and any decisions doing so were legally invalid.[37] This attempt to thwart continuing ecological destruction by planners and industries proved not to be very effective in everyday decisionmaking, but it did provide environmental activists with an additional weapon for working within the system. Indeed, in the 1980s several firms found themselves in court for violation of environmental laws.

In terms of administration, the new law created a State Inspectorate for Environmental Protection (*Państwowa Inspekcja Ochrony Środowiska* or PIOŚ), headed by a Chief Inspector for Environmental Protection. It also created a State Council for Environmental Protection (*Państwowa Rada Ochrony Środowiska* or PROŚ), which must be distinguished from the old State Council for the Protection of Nature (PROP). The new council did not replace PROP; rather its sphere of activity was defined more broadly. PROŚ was concerned with all aspects of the environment, including industrial emissions, etc. This left PROP more narrowly defined as a council for overseeing the protection of *nature*, as opposed to the whole environment. The new inspectorate was placed under the Minister of Administration, Territorial Economy, and Environmental Protection, while the new council was made directly responsible to the Council of Ministers. PROP remained under the Minister of Forestry and Wood Industry.

In a package of supportive legislation passed later in 1980, the duties and powers of the Ministry of Administration, Terroritorial Economy, and Environmental Protection, with its new inspectorate, were expanded significantly and more clearly specified. To aid in its longstanding responsibility for general coordination of environmental protection, the ministry was given explicit power over environmental activities and functions in a number of different organizations, including cooperatives, productive and service enterprises, trade unions, and other central administrations.[38] New regulations spelled out the areas of coordination between the ministry and 16 central government organs, including the planning commission, 12 ministries, two central offices at ministerial level, and two central government committees.[39]

The State Inspectorate for Environmental Protection was established to ensure that the growing body of legislation was implemented. It became responsible for supervising compliance with environmental regulations and carrying out any tests necessary to do this. Incorporated in this calling were the following duties:

- establishing testing methods;
- activities that would help prevent or reverse pollution;
- monitoring the execution of the plan for territorial use in terms of environmental protection;
- preparing norms;
- proposing projects;
- cooperation with other organizations;
- guidance and instruction of environmental services connected with individual organizations;

- developing and introducing an observation system;
- control over territorial environmental services;
- reviewing complaints;
- preventing production and import of machinery and products whose use would harm the environment;
- recovery measures;
- prohibition of fuel-burning and/or certain technologies when and where they would contaminate the environment to the point of threat ening human health;
- and any other task the Minister assigned.[40]

These duties made the Inspectorate the ministry's technical arm and main vehicle for affecting the actual state of the environment.

The State Council for Environmental Protection (PROŚ) was created as an extra-ministerial advisory organ to the Council of the Ministers in order to introduce an ecology-minded voice into decisions taken above the level of the ministry charged with environmental protection. Its chairman and members were appointed directly by the Chairman of the Council of Ministers. In general, PROŚ's responsibilities included preparing opinion statements on environmental matters for the Council of Ministers, the Government Presidium, and the Chairman of the Council of Ministers, as well as introducing proposals and requests to these organs concerning the creation of conditions for promoting environmental protection and maintaining or improving the current state of the environment.[41] Later a more specific delineation of PROŚ's duties and powers concentrated on the steps to be taken in order to fulfill these obligations. Included were the right to issue opinions about the national plan, actions of ministries and other central organs, and investment, and the right to comment on proposed legislation and use of the national Fund for Environmental Protection as well as other environmental funds. PROŚ was also to cooperate with other national and international advisory organs.[42] Of particular interest was the provision that all state administrative organs and socialized enterprises must provide information necessary for the council to complete these tasks.[43] This proviso tackled (but did not solve) a problem that had long plagued environmental research in Poland: the lack of complete and reliable information. In terms of organization, PROŚ was to consist of 30–50 members from academia, professional spheres, and social organizations. Its chairman, together with a deputy and a secretary formed the presidium; office work was to be performed by a secretariat. To ensure the council's independence of any particular ministry, its expenses were to be met from the budget of the Council of Ministers.[44] In sum, PROŚ had a strong basis for forming independent positions—depending on who was actually appointed to this council—and having them heard at the highest levels of government. However, these positions were just that—opinions and advice. As the decade of the 1980s progressed, the "expert" base from which PROŚ's membership was culled became more involved in the environmental movement and the press grew freer; in turn, the council's profile increased and its opinions became more critical of various government decisions. Nevertheless, PROŚ remained an official body whose critique was contained within the parameters of the existing system.

With the lifting of martial law in July 1983 came a number of administrative changes. In the area of environmental protection the old ministry was reorganized into a Ministry of Administration and Spatial Economy (*Ministerstwo Administracji i Gospodarki Przestrzennej*). Although this ministry maintained the powers of control over the environment that are implicit in authority over spatial planning, most of the environmental responsibilities of the old ministry were handed over to a newly created Office of Environmental Protection and Water Economy (*Urząd Ochrony Środowiska i Gospodarki Wodnej*). Created as an independent unit at the level of the Council of Ministers, the office was effectively a junior ministry. Along with the environmental duties of the old ministry the new office also received jurisdiction over the State Inspectorate for Environmental Protection.[45] The more specific list of its tasks shows a detailed explanation of responsibilities connected with water; the other areas of environmental protection are incorporated with control over the inspectorate. Two important provisions appear concerning the environment as a whole. First, the office was responsible for establishing the principles upon which an area could be declared as an "area of special protection" (*obszar szczególnej ochrony*). Second, the office took over the responsibility formerly held by the Council of Ministers for establishing the principles for creating and managing protected areas (*strefy ochronne*).[46] In order to carry out its tasks, the Office of Environmental Protection and Water Economy received the power to evaluate payments for economic use of the environment and the system of fines for not following environmental regulations. In addition, it enjoyed the already traditional rights to cooperate in the drafting of the socioeconomic plans and monitor their implementation, draft legislation, conduct tests, request studies, publish, coordinate activities of other organizations involved in ecology, work with the Central Statistical Office, use environmental funds, and cooperate with international efforts.[47]

The 1983 changes proved to be the first of two steps in a general restructuring that culminated after the Sejm elections in the last quarter of 1985. On January 1, 1986 the environment got a ministry of its own—the Ministry of Environmental Protection and Natural Resources (*Ministerstwo Ochrony Środowiska i Zasobów Naturalnych*). This new ministry replaced the former Office of Environmental Protection and Water Economy and the Central Office of Geology. The rest of the old ministry was renamed and focused on spatial planning and building. Another relevant administrative change was the combination of the Ministry of Forestry and Wood Industry and the Ministry of Agriculture and Food Economy into one Ministry of Agriculture, Forestry, and Food Economy. With these changes the Jaruzelski regime sought administrative rationalization. However, the new arrangements were also part of a general institutional reshuffling that entailed personnel changes and verifications, broke down old power bases, and attempted to gain some legitimacy by showing decisive action toward overhauling the discredited old system.[48]

Despite the moves in the 1980s toward rationalizing environmental law and administration, unclear jurisdiction and limited power to sanction continued to hamper effective implementation of environmental protection. For example, the new minister had the power to close down an enterprise violating the law, but no recourse was given should the manager refuse to close. Economic factors and the lack of information about the environment also hampered protection. The new Fund for Environmental Protection and planned increases in investment were not sufficient to meet the challenges. Monitoring systems were woefully inadequate. (Indeed, they became a priority item in Western environmental aid after communist rule.) Even when various government organs had information, it was often not publicized and therefore could not serve as an impetus for change from outside "knowledgeable circles."

Conclusion

Historically, Polish environmentalists have focused on and succeeded more in the traditional areas of conservation and nature protection than in controlling modern sources of environmental destruction. Although legislation protecting nature and the rest of the environment was more or less on the level of that in other developed countries through 1949, it fell off the pace during Poland's period of intense industrialization and urbanization, i.e. precisely when innovation was needed. Now, despite increased efforts to protect the environment since 1980, the accomplishments in conservation are threatened by the failure to control industrial pollution. Until 1985 environmental administration was more the result of patchwork than of an overall design for dealing with the problems at hand. Although ignorance and a lack of foresight certainly contributed to the shortcomings in administrative and legislative development, the main sources of these shortcomings were conflicts of interests between pro-ecology forces and more powerful industrial and economic forces, especially at the national and *województwo* (voivodship) levels. Ministries with environmental responsibilities often contained these conflicts within their own jurisdictions. Even where they did press for environmental protection at the national level, they were overpowered by the industrial interests that enjoyed a preponderance of strength in the Council of Ministers. Likewise, the environmental departments of the voivodship offices were single departments in offices dominated by economic interests. Without effective sanctioning powers and independent courts, the environmental agencies were unable to counter the power of polluting interests. The centrally planned economy and centrally controlled administration, which might theoretically afford a rational and coherent approach to environmental protection, actually coalesced the forces against regulation and control of environmental destruction.

4

The Independent Ecological Movement: Building New Identities

Worsening environmental conditions and the new political situation introduced by Solidarity's formation in 1980 inspired the modest collective actions that became the beginnings of a social movement. The ecological movement, however, did not develop significantly until the mid-1980s. Movement formation involved many factors including changes in individual consciousness, identity and group formation, activism, and networking. Although the impetus to action may ultimately have been concrete conditions resulting from environmental mismanagement, participation in the movement—and thus in the processes just mentioned—was shaped by the political context. In particular, new opportunities for expression, organization, and influence were afforded by the underground press, opposition networks, and the independence of the Roman Catholic Church, on the one hand, and, on the other, the loosening official media, normalization strategies, growing body of legislation, and institutional expansion in the area of environmental protection.

To understand how environmentalism in Poland took the shape of a social movement it is necessary to examine major actors' senses of identity, organization, and types of activism. Once the actors are sorted out, we can begin to see how the events that form the history of the movement guided certain groups, inspired the creation of others, and redirected the activities of yet others. The coalescing of heterogeneous actors into a whole, perceived by participants and observers but having no organizational expression, can then be seen in the networking among groups. Parts of this networking were avowedly voluntaristic and conscious;

other parts were initiated in the very course of political processes at the national and local levels. This chapter focuses only on the types of identities in the movement and the development of an overall movement identity. More detailed discussion of the organizational features of the groups mentioned here and of the types of activism in the movement is reserved for the following chapter. (See table 5.1 for an overview of selected groups' political identities, organization, and activism.)

Identity in Poland's Ecological Movement

Building an identity is part of the development of all social movements, old or new. Various actors within a movement and different types of movements may place dissimilar degrees of importance on this process, but it is to some extent essential for the networking and public action in which all social movements engage. For theorists of new social movements the formulation and development of identity is the focus of a new type of social interaction. Indeed it is the main process in, and purpose of, collective action that takes the form of new social movements. The development of such movements and new identities, in turn, constitutes change in the nature of civil society. The Polish ecological movement in the 1980s did have a very strong focus on identity; it also brought together several different identities, new and old.

The Old Identity

Arising out of the conservationist movement of the late nineteenth and early twentieth century, the League for the Protection of Nature (LOP) had been the carrier of environmentalism in Poland from the interwar period. Over the years the League underwent a transformation from a movement among scientists and naturalists to an interest group and then from an interest group to a large, bureaucratic organization.

Polish conservationism in the nineteenth century, in concerning itself with the defense of certain natural landmarks and resources, tapped the potent symbol of the nature and land of the fatherland. This was one of the main symbols of Polish national identity during the period when Poland was partitioned and ruled by its neighbors (1795–1918). From these roots, League activists had a strong sense of being a social ("societal") force (Drewniak 1988, 3). The League's primary goal was always the protection of Poland's natural landscape, a goal that allowed it to fit into the official system without causing controversy as long as "nature" was segmented into parks, recreation areas, etc., and not applied to industrially developed areas. What changed in the 1980s was the definition and understanding of nature. Common understanding of the term "nature protection" was expanded to include anthropogenic effects and environments. The League maintained its title and its orientation toward "nature protection," claiming that the use of the term "environment" to mean more than just the natural world was an artificial distinction. Although League activists did delve into the 1980s debates on emissions regulation, administrative reform, fines and sanctions, etc., the main body of the League for the Protection of Nature was still seen as oriented primarily toward defense and creation of parks and conservation of other green areas.

While League members felt themselves to be expressing a social concern, they were also conscious of the fact that the League itself was a large, hierarchical, formal organization. This organization was at once an instrument and a quagmire for environmental activists and for the social movement of which they were a part. The part of the League's activism that was most directly social was its promotion of education about the environment. In this endeavor, the size of the organization and its penetration into the country's educational and socio-occupational structures, as well as its publications and other promotional efforts, slowly raised Polish society's level of knowledge about the environment over the decades of communist rule. This education, however, did not tend to question fundamental values of material development as pursued by the communist regime or official perspectives on human society and its ability to conquer environmental problems through technology.

The New Identity

The new identity in the Polish ecological movement was carried by a number of new groups and movements. Although these groups focused on the development of their own identity as expressing an alternative to the dominant cultural norms regarding the environment, they also sought to change the rest of society's understanding and evaluation of what is essential, of what human society's role is in the environment, and therefore of society's own identity.

The first of these movements, the Polish Ecological Club (*Polski Klub Ekologiczny* or PKE) was founded in 1981 and saw itself as " . . . a social movement of people conscious of the dangers associated with the unsettling of biological balance by technical civilization and by the consumptionist model of life, acting for the good of the Nation in the fields of nature protection and protection of the environment in which man lives" (PKE 1989a, para.1).

The club based its activism on the Constitution of the Polish People's Republic, the 1972 Stockholm Declaration of the United Nations' Conference on the Human Environment, the Universal Declaration of Human Rights, the Geneva Convention, and the Global Declaration of Animal Rights (paras 3, 4). It embraced people from different segments of society and emphasized the variety of roles to be played in environmental activism: "A member of the PKE should be characterized by high ethical qualities, and the basic principle of PKE work is the cooperation of enthusiasts (passion for activism), experts (knowledge) and publicists (social consciousness), possessing the support of recognized and valued scientific authorities" (para. 8).

The Polish Ecological Club's first programmatic principle concerned activism targeted at raising awareness and changing attitudes in the general society. "The PKE aim[ed] at the shaping of a *moral responsibility* on the part of the people for the state of the environment for current and future generations. Therefore it [sought] a radical *transformation of their way of thinking.*" The club wanted to foster a holistic perspective where growth and development "must take into consideration primary ecological requirements." "People, *conscious of the limits of the environment's tolerance* . . . must accept a moderate state of possession of material goods, negating the model of a *consumer civilization.*" They have to aim for a *radical elimination of waste*, learn a symbiosis with nature, and reconstruct their view of the *quality of life* to reflect "being" rather than "having." Rather than becoming slaves to things, people should seek self-realization in intellectual and spiritual fulfillment. Finally, such a person will be able to "*value and respect future consequences* of the actions that person takes . . . " (PKE 1989b, 13–14, emphases in the original). The Polish Ecological Club, then, saw itself as striving for nothing less than a radical change in the nature of society.

Many of the same goals and elements of self-understanding were picked up by *Wolę Być*, a decentralized youth movement concentrating on ecology, peace and personal growth. The translation of this movement's name is "I prefer to be." It was initiated in response to a July 1984 issue of the youth weekly *Na Przełaj* dedicated to the environment and containing an appeal for change.

Participants in *Wolę Być* saw themselves as involved in a youth movement that promulgated a new cultural perspective.

> We can counter the egocentric principle of "to have" with a life ordered by the philosophy of "to be" . . .
>
> An alternative to the exploitation of our common good, that is nature, is . . . to return it to a balanced state and struggle against committing new harm . . .

> An alternative to a life ordered solely by the accumulation of things is to learn how to experience satisfaction arising not only from material incentives but also from spiritual ones. . . . Also, intellectual endeavors . . . may result in just as much satisfaction . . .
>
> An alternative to treating people instrumentally and through the prism of one's own egocentrism is mutual goodwill . . . ("Odezwa programowa" 1984, 47–48)

These original ideals were developed further by some groups within the movement to reflect the philosophy of "deep ecology."

> Deep ecology, as distinct from narrowly understood protection of the natural environment, concerns not only countering the negative *effects* of the development of civilization to this point, but also and above all concerns the *causes*, deeply understood, bringing about those effects: convictions stemming from world views, values by which people direct their actions, attitudes, habits—generally contemporary lifestyles. Deep ecology postulates change in practices and attitudes destructive of human life and nature in favor of attitudes affirming all life.[1]

In interactions within the movement and in their daily lives members strove to act and think positively with tolerance, openness, respect, honesty and whole-heartedness; they eschewed the use of force or coercion.

Also blending environmental and peace activism during the 1980s was the "Freedom and Peace" (*Wolność i Pokój*) movement. It was established in Kraków and Warsaw in April 1985 as an anti-militarist peace movement, whose main trait was conscientious objection to military service and to the military oath which swore fraternal alliance to the Soviet army.[2] The group was firmly in political opposition (though *not* a part of the Solidarity underground), due largely to its tactics, prime among them being refusal to serve in the military. In addition to activism in the peace movement, Freedom and Peace carried out a number of strong protests against environmental destruction and was particularly active on issues surrounding nuclear energy and waste. Although the group was small, it was visible because of its stridency and the repression its members experienced for their activities.

Two of Freedom and Peace's main goals—a change in the military oath and legalization of alternative service—were achieved to a large extent before the end of communism. The group's influence on the new law on conscientious objection can be seen in the fact that one of the alternatives to military service is service in environmental protection. After the passage of this law, there was some redefinition of identity. A central group of members who were part of the Independent Students' Association in

1980–81 and Freedom and Peace in 1985–88 broadened the thrust of their activism into a "movement for civil society" by the name of "Future Times." In addition to the prior efforts to reform and reduce the military, promote environmental protection, abolish the death penalty and bring the problems of national minorities to light, the new group intended to support and help create local self-administration and social, economic, and political pluralism ("Program Theses" 1989, 24). They foresaw the gradual melding of the two blocs into one Europe and believed that society must accomplish this as well. Despite this group's claim that the Freedom and Peace movement ended in 1988, that movement continued to exist and be active in environmental protests well into 1989.[3]

Another group that contributed to the development of the environmental movement's new identity was the Ecological Movement of St. Francis of Assisi (*Ruch Ekologiczny Świętego Franciszka z Asyżu* or REFA), a movement of Franciscan clergy based in Kraków. The REFA movement concentrated on moral responsibility toward and love of nature as well as on the education necessary to enhance one's actions on behalf of these goals.

> The purpose of the movement is active participation in building a civilization of love based on the primacy:
> • of person before thing,
> • of ethics before technique,
> • of cherishing "being more" before achieving "having more,"
> • of compassion before justice through brotherly treatment of man and nature (REFA 1988b, art. 1).

Again, we see the struggle against material values, the emphasis on change in one's perspective on self and one's place, and the attempt to reshape patterns of interaction both among people and with the environment.

Fellow-Traveler Identity

Many of the groups active in the Polish ecological movement viewed themselves as participants in this movement defined by others, i.e. by the movements and organizations discussed above. Often those with this "fellow-traveler" identity were socio-occupational or territorially based groups with a policy orientation. They pursued environmental protection with little thought to the change in norms that was central to the identity of the movement's primary actors. Actors with a sense of being a secondary participant, of building on and acting among already existing groups, included participants in ongoing seminars and a few of the territorial groups. These actors shared the view that change in norms was the central task of the environmental movement, but saw coordination or territorial focus as their contribution to promoting such change. Thus, "fellow-traveler" or participant identity was not "old" or "new," "strategic" or "normative." Rather, it demonstrated an appreciation that certain actors were more holistic in their approaches or more active, therefore more central to the movement. In so defining themselves, participants with a "fellow-traveler" identity reaffirmed the existence of an overall movement.

Political Identity

A very important aspect of identity in Poland during the 1980s was one's place in the political spectrum. The predominant divisions were among actors that consider themselves part of the opposition, politically independent, or incorporated into the official system. The bulk of the environmental movement placed itself firmly in the independent public sphere. Notable examples were the Polish Ecological Club, *Wolę Być*, the Catholic Groups and the "Green Cross" seminar. Others were officially sanctioned organizations such as the League for the Protection of Nature, or parts of various official associations. Most of the occupationally based groups and the PRON Social Ecological Movement (discussed below) are good examples of environmental groups that were parts of broader official organizations. Finally, a few of the actors in the environmental movement identified themselves with political opposition—Freedom and Peace, the Great Poland Ecological Seminar, and the Silesian Ecological Movement being the most notable examples.

Levels of Identity

Three levels of identity emerge from this overview—identities of individual groups and actors, the ecological movement's identity, and society's understanding of itself. Examples of individual group identities have been discussed above. A few themes coalesced to form the identity of the movement. The most striking was that symbolized by the phrase " 'to be' over 'to have' " which appeared in the statements of principles of the Polish Ecological Club, *Wolę Być* and REFA, among those cited here. This phrase and the values associated with it also linked the Polish movement with environmental movements elsewhere in the world. Another point of coalescence was the conscious understanding that the movement was endeavoring to change social norms regarding the relation of the human race to nature. While the first point contradicted the materialism of modern life, the second contradicted the official development image of "man's conquering nature."[4] A third common theme was embodied in most groups' organizational principles, discussed in greater detail in the next chapter, but also essential to the identity of these groups: an egalitarian, associative structure and interaction patterns.

The third level of identity—society's understanding of itself—and the attempt to change it were a central concern of the environmental movement. This emphasis came through and was intertwined with the movement's own identity. Yet, the two should not be merged because the distinction clarifies the role of the social movement. Formation of and change within the movement are the start of the change in society. The movement becomes the bridge to new societal norms and, as Touraine pointed out, to new forms of political life. In not only adopting new values but also attempting to reshape social norms through both the content and form of their action, Polish environmental activists were paralleling the role of new social movements in the West.

All of these levels of identity taken together clearly placed the formation of the movement outside of the officially controlled public sphere. At the same time, the ecological movement was not explicitly anti-state. Although its values and activism meshed with or supported the strategy of the political opposition in fostering social and political pluralism, the movement's participants were drawn from the entire political spectrum, worked through whichever vehicles—including the state—might best achieve their goals, and remained focused on the goals of raising ecological consciousness and protecting the environment. In sum, the movement remained politically independent of the state and the opposition even as it was strategically dependent on their interaction for defining the means available to it to promote its cause.

A brief summary of movement development and networking will confirm the existence of an overall identity and lay the foundation for the more detailed discussion of organization and activism in the next chapter. Then we will turn to more extensive examination of the movement's relationship to the political opposition and its evolution through interaction with the regime.

The Development of the Ecological Movement

Poland's independent ecological movement emerged from the midst of major political and social changes in the first "Solidarity period" (1980–81). Until that break in censorship and blossoming of social initiatives, environmental problems were not discussed publicly by officials or critics. There were two reasons for this silence. First, the 1970s censorship laws prohibited the mention of serious environmental hazards and especially of the connections between the environment and human health (Curry 1984, 211–27). Second, environmental consciousness was still limited to the few experts and legal scholars active in relevant administrations and the drafting of regulations.

During the initial period of environmental activism, there was a tendency to gravitate toward Solidarity. Both weakness and this association with Solidarity forced the ecological groups to either disband or "lay low" during martial law. Once martial law was lifted activism started to mount, especially in Kraków with the reactivation of the Polish Ecological Club and the development of REFA. By 1985–86 several groups had formed—*Wolę Być* and Freedom and Peace as well as many smaller ones—and press coverage of the environment had expanded markedly. After that, environmental activism simply mushroomed. Movement-regime interaction during these stages of development will be examined in greater detail in chapter 7, but at this point a review of a couple of key periods is essential to understanding movement formation.

Milestones

Two clusters of turning points were crucial to the development of the Polish ecological movement. While the first cluster should be interpreted as part of the wave of social mobilization that gripped Poland in 1980–81, the second was comprised of more specific events and decisions that encouraged the development of collective identities at the level of specific groups, of the movement as a whole, and of ecological consciousness in the broader society.

The first cluster was part of the emergence of an independent civil society from the underground and its rapid development in 1980–81. Here we see the birth of environmentalism as a social movement. The starting points were regional marches against the ecological destruction of the Baltic and Kraków and the formation of the Polish Ecological Club during environmental activism to close down a smelter in the Skawina Aluminum Works (Hrynkiewicz 1988, 26). It is not altogether clear whether this activism or supporting strikes by Solidarity should be credited with shutting down the smelter, but the club did form and was registered in May 1981. That year also saw the seminars which were the roots of REFA. Moreover, many older organizations, such as the League for the Protection of Nature and the Polish Association for Tourism and Knowledge of the Country (*Polskie Towarzystwo Turystyczno-Krajoznawcze* or PTTK), became more critical and active.

Besides providing the opportunity and inspiration for social activism, the first Solidarity period caused a virtual explosion in information-gathering and exchange. With regard to the environment, there was the lifting of censorship and an increase in writing by specialists for the general public. Information previously withheld or published only in professional journals made its way into the opposition and official press. By the time of Solidarity's National Congress in Fall 1981, the political opposition had become conscious enough of the need for action on the environmental front that the Congress adopted a series of ten demands and three measures of its own regarding environmental protection ("Program NSZZ 'Solidarność'" 1981, teza 16).

The second cluster of milestones came in 1985–86. Contributing to the publicity of environmental concerns was the publication in 1985 of a report on the environment by an institute associated with the Central Committee (Wójcik ed. 1985). (An earlier scientific report on chemical pollution had already raised concern among the academic community.) The institute report, meant for limited circulation, was very critical, even alarming. More importantly, some of its findings were broadcast back into Poland by the foreign media. Government spokesman Jerzy Urban downplayed the seriousness of the problems when confronted with the findings at a press conference, which raised a controversy and brought the problem even more into focus.[5] Increasing awareness was reflected in the fact that citizens raised many questions about local and national environmental issues during campaign meetings with candidates for the parliament that fall.[6] Two of Poland's more visible environmental groups—Wolę Być and Freedom and Peace—were founded that same year.

A year after the publication of that report, the accident occurred at the Chernobyl nuclear power plant. Ecological fragility and the effects of the environment on human health impinged upon the consciousness of the entire society. This eventually made citizens more attentive to the state of Poland's environment, even though it did not lead to an immediate jump in environmental activism among the general population. The political opposition, which for a year had been stepping up its discussion of environmental problems in the underground press, mobilized quickly. Two new ecological groups were formed in Lublin and Wrocław in the first week after the accident and a number of bulletins were published with as much information as could be obtained to counteract the lack of official information. Against the background of the accident, environmental activism caught the public eye.

Perhaps one of the most important changes of this period was the government's move to normalization through inclusion (cf. Kolankiewicz 1988). For the environmental movement inclusion meant representatives on the Social Consultative Council, Jaruzelski's sanctioning of the environment as an issue of concern in his speech at the Tenth Party Congress (June 1986) and the creation of an ecological movement by PRON (*Patriotyczny Ruch Odrodzenia Narodowego*), the officially sponsored front of social organizations. Most ecologists met these efforts with a strategy of participating in whatever endeavors they thought might benefit environmental protection without compromising values or autonomy. Thus, the cooptive element of the inclusion strategy failed. Moreover, with official expressions of concern over the environment, press coverage of ecology increased from its already heightened level. The result was increased consciousness throughout society.

Networking

Beyond the coincidences and connections described in the historical summary above, a look at the more explicit interactions among actors in the environmental movement should show that there was such an overall entity and that individual groups and movements saw themselves as part of that entity. Three main types of connections among actors seem most prevalent in this movement: links through individuals who acted on several fronts, group cooperation and joint action, and similarities in the identities of individual groups which forged a common identity.

Individual Connections.

A number of people were integrally linked to the development of the environmental movement as a whole and its success in placing ecology on the national political agenda.

A major figure of the movement was Professor of Sociology Zbigniew Wierzbicki. His career in ecology began in the days of Stalinism. By 1952 he was president of the Poznań section of the League for the Protection of Nature and he remained a member of the scientific council to that organization's Executive Board throughout the communist period. For several years in the 1960s he was a member of the scientific council of Wielkopolski National Park. After unsuccessful attempts to create such a group in the late 1970s, he became co-founder of the Polish Ecological Club during the Solidarity period. Even though he resigned the vice presidency of the club in 1984, he continued to be an active member. It is also to Wierzbicki's Kraków seminar in 1981 that REFA traced its roots. In 1986, he started the Green Cross seminar in Warsaw which pulled together environmental activists from all over the country and from all the major groups and movements. Wierzbicki was also one of the co-organizers of the Polish Academy of Sciences' seminar on Nature, Man, and Values; and he was invited to teach at the 1987 *Wolę Być* jamboree.

Academically, Wierzbicki is credited with introducing environmental problems into sociology's study of the village in the 1970s and slowly creating a small field of study called "sozoecology," or the study of human society as it relates and adapts to the environment. He has published extensively in both areas. Politically, Professor Wierzbicki has also been active on many fronts. He was one of the initiators of the "green movement," which was dispersed almost at its inception by martial law, and a founder of the independent party "Green Movement" in December 1988. In more direct relation to the state, he was the episcopate's environmental expert on the Social Consultative Council to the President of the Council of State from its formation in 1986 until it was abolished with the political changes of 1989. At the Polish Round-Table talks (February–April 1989), he was an environmental expert for Solidarity. His seminars and his Warsaw apartment with its extensive library of official, independent, and opposition publications were meeting places for activists from the entire spectrum of ecological groups and movements.

A central figure in both the movement and the government advisory structure was Professor Andrzej Kassenberg. He is a former vice-president of the Polish Ecological Club, professor at Warsaw's Central School of Planning and Statistics (now the Central School of Trade), and a former member of Poland's Central Planning Commission. As a member of the planning commission, Kassenberg was able to take the movement's concerns to the highest decisionmaking level. His books on spatial planning and the environment are also central works in the environmental literature and used for self-education purposes by other ecologists.

Professor Stefan Kozłowski, a geologist, was a very important contributor to the ecological movement for his recognized expertise and heavy involvement in the policy advisory structure. He worked on a number of reports, including the 1985 report mentioned above. Kozłowski was a Senator in the first Parliament elected after the Round-Table, Chair of that body's commission on the environment, Chair of the State Council for Environmental Protection, a member of the Polish Ecological Club, and a participant in the Green Cross Seminar. In the summer of 1992, he became Minister of Environmental Protection, Natural Resources, and Forestry in one of Poland's post-communist governments. As one of the country's leading experts, he has participated in many seminars, conferences, and meetings of environmentalists, including accompanying members of *Wolę Być* to the Żarnowiec nuclear energy plant.

Zofia Odechowska, a member of the Polish Home Army during the war, was a very strong activist in the Polish Ecological Club and the regional group Mazovian Landscapes (*Krajobrazy Mazowieckie*). She was one of the principal activists in PRON's ecological movement and led the formation of the new Polish Ecological Association in Fall 1989. Along with Wierzbicki, Kozłowski, Roman Andrzejewski (the first post-communist Vice-Minister for Environmental Protection), and another well-known activist, Odechowska wrote and signed the "Ecological Manifesto" published widely in the Polish press in early 1989. The manifesto was a sharp statement of the reality of ecological degradation in Poland and of the need to reshape the vision and process of industrialization and empower the agencies and laws responsible for protection of the environment ("Manifesto Ekologiczne 1989).

Iwona Jacyna, an award-winning journalist writing in the daily *Życie Warszawy*, was one of the first to turn public attention to Poland's serious environmental problems. Her articles covered all dimensions of the environmental debate—physical destruction, administration, legal matters, activism, political stalemate. She was also a contributing author to 1985 report to the Central Committee which caused such a controversy once its findings were reported in the mass-circulation press. As members of the group *Ekos*, she and her assistant Krzysztof Walczak continued to keep these problems in the public eye. Another very active journalist was Ewa Charkiewicz of *Na Przełaj*, one of the originators of *Wolę Być*.

Several other prominent activists participated in more than one environmental group as well, including a growing core of younger activists who would step into leadership roles in the movement as the regime transition began. These few examples, however, suffice to show informal links among many of the key collective actors in the environmental movement. Another phenomenon illustrated by these examples is that an activist's participation in multiple initiatives often cut across the spheres of political identity—e.g. a state commission or newspaper, an independent group, and an opposition meeting, demonstration or publication.

Group Cooperation.

The second element helping to create an overall movement identity was direct cooperation between collective actors within the movement and participation in the same initiatives.

Many of these ecological groups, movements and organizations explicitly stated that one of their basic tenets was cooperation with other such groups: the Polish Ecological Club, *Wolę Być*, Freedom and Peace, REFA, and the Green Cross seminar, to name those whose statements to that effect have been cited above. Though cooperation in seminars, political lobbying, and education was fairly high, the groups tended to engage in other sorts of activism more unilaterally. There were, however, several instances of cooperative collective action. It seems that local level activism was more likely to bring a coordinated effort, though some initiatives on the national level did also bring groups together.

Perhaps the single issue that galvanized the ecological movement most was the campaign to prevent storage of radioactive waste in the World War II bunkers at Międzyrzecz (Messeritz). Between their central role in Europe's bat habitat and their proximity to the water table and the Warta and Odra river systems, the bunkers were judged by ecologists to be a particularly poor place to store radioactive wastes. The most visible and vociferous actor in the campaign to overturn the government's storage plans was Freedom and Peace. Local residents had not made any inroads into the decision to store radioactive waste in the bunkers by May 3, 1987 when 1,500 of them marched in silent protest after a mass in the local church and announced that there would be marches every month.[7] Throughout the summer Freedom and Peace activists led demonstrations and handed out leaflets explaining the issue. Though attendance ebbed during the summer, the citizens' September march drew between three and four thousand participants.[8] A hunger strike to protest arrests, fines, and police harassment after the march included some members of Freedom and Peace and was ended with an even larger gathering of supporters (Kossakowski 1988, 48). Meanwhile, numerous ecologists, including members of Wolę Być, the League for the Protection of Nature, the Polish Nature Society and the Polish Ecological Club had written letters of protest to various local and national authorities and conducted awareness campaigns throughout the country. The local PRON council and PRON's Social Ecological Movement actively intervened with local authorities, but to no avail. Although there were no immediate results, a prolonged campaign and controversy over the storage plans eventually reversed the decision.

The Międzyrzecz issue was part of the bigger problem of nuclear energy. This was the one issue on which the ecological subgroup of the Polish Round-Table talks in early 1989 could not come to agreement ("Protokoł Rozbieżnośći" 1989). Even some ecologists felt that Poland's excessive reliance on high-sulfur coal must be reduced at all costs, justifying the risks of nuclear energy. Nevertheless, the major environmental groups protested the construction of nuclear power plants in Żarnowiec and Klempicz with demonstrations, petitions, letters and reports of the possible ecological dangers.

Wolę Być and the Polish Ecological Club worked together on a few demonstrations. One was a campaign to shut down a chemical textile plant in Jelenia Góra (Wyka 1988, 70), a cause later taken up by the ecological round-table as one of the test cases of government goodwill (*Protokoł Podzespołu* 1989, 21). *Wolę Być* also worked with the Polish Ecological Club to organize the bicycle rides that publicized PKE's "Day without a Car" as part of its celebration of International Day of the Environment in 1987 and 1988.[9] In addition, *Wolę Być* demonstrated together with the new Polish Ecological Party (Kraków) in protest against the building of the Czechoslovak coking plant in Stronava, which borders Poland.

A major regional effort to protect ancient forests and delicate ecosystems also drew together a number of actors in the environmental movement. The "Green Lungs of Poland" project was signed in May 1988. Its purpose is to coordinate the protection of the environment by abiding by the principles of eco-development in five Eastern, relatively undeveloped voivodships. Active in developing and supporting that project were the PTTK, the League for the Protection of Nature, PRON's Social Ecological Movement, and the journalists' group *Ekos* (Walczak 1988). Other territorially based efforts, e.g. in the Karkanose and Bieszczady mountain regions, also elicited direct cooperation among environmental groups.

These few examples of cooperative and parallel efforts on the part of ecological groups indicate not only their consciousness of one another but also their willingness to work together toward shared goals. At the same time, however, there seems to have been a preponderance of parallel efforts over cooperative efforts when it came to demonstrations and petitions, as well as more unconventional activity. This tendency on the part of groups not only to maintain autonomy but, most of all, to be in control of the political connotations of their actions was especially evident during communist rule.

Although there were no institutionalized connections among movement groups, two somewhat overlapping centers of information and communication emerge from these individual connections and instances of group cooperation and from other available evidence. In the official sphere, the League for the Protection of Nature was often an initiator or coordinator of activism. It was also a center of information for many sorts of actors inside and outside of the movement. The Polish Ecological Club served a similar, though smaller-scale, function as an information base in the unofficial sphere. This role was largely a result of the emphasis placed by the PKE on expertise and the group's more visible profile and established organizational structure (when compared to other nonofficial actors). Augmenting the density of communication between PKE and other unofficial groups was the PKE membership of some of these other groups' activists.[10]

These two "hubs" of communication and information did *not*, however, remain contained to their respective spheres. First of all, their memberships overlapped slightly. In their professional lives, many PKE members also participated in official research institutes and commissions. By 1987, even reporters in the official media would consult the PKE as an independent expert. The League, on the other hand, provided information to and supported some initiatives of unofficial groups, if the intiatives themselves were legal.

Common Identity.

Finally, as discussed above, key parts of the self-definitions of various ecological groups were identical to each other. The strongest similarities were the recurrence of the theme (and the phrases) "to be" over "to have" and recognition of the need for all of society to reexamine and change its values. Value change was connected with plans and expectations for economic development. All of the movement's more central groups, Catholic groups, territorial groups, seminars, and ecological parties embraced ecodevelopment, though understanding of what this process should look like was generally weak. Most groups also placed cooperation with other groups toward these goals at the hearts of their programs. This consciousness of other groups and of the need to cooperate with them in coordinating environmental activism demonstrates that individual and collective participants—even though they may have wished to retain organizational and strategic autonomy—did see themselves as part of a larger movement.

Conclusion

The existence of a Polish environmental movement was clearly expressed in a collective identity before the transformation of the political and economic systems began. However, the movement was fragmented, held together only by that identity, several activists and episodic cooperation among groups. This fragmentation affected directly the development of environmental politics in the official public arena. It frustrated government efforts at cooptation, sparked the growth of environmentalism in many sectors of society, and kept the environmental movement nonaligned with respect to the two main political camps in Poland.

A closer look at identity formation and the origins of the various collective actors in the movement shows that, although the self-definition and goals of these actors and of the movement as a whole were those emphasized in the Western discussion of "new social movements," the impetus for the formation of these groups can be found in the Polish political process. Even though the primary grounds for environmental activism—worsening ecological conditions and failure of the government to ameliorate them—had been developing for quite some time, the first major catalyst for political action came in the wave of social mobilization accompanying the birth and growth of Solidarity. The changes in political opportunities introduced during that period and carried through Solidarity's underground existence then allowed the development of independent groups, movements, and seminars in the course of or in reaction to the inclusion strategies of the Jaruzelski regime, specific decision-processes and the environmental consequences of those decisions.

The range of political identities extant in the environmental movement assured that the movement as a whole remained focused on its issue area as a source of its independent identity, rather than on "choosing sides" in the political contest between the party-state and the opposition. However, given the nature of social control in the post-Stalinist system and the strategy of the political opposition, the very existence of a politically independent movement meshed more favorably with the opposition's strategies than with those of the regime and contributed to the breakdown of the authoritarian regime.

Thus, the ecological movement both stemmed from changes in civil society and contributed to further change. As individuals changed their perspectives and formed collective identities which deliberately attempted to change both general societal norms and actual political and economic decisionmaking processes, they moved from the private sphere to the public, linking the two in the process. That this "new" identity-centered movement with a heterogeneous, decentralized structure developed under Soviet-type state socialism suggests that theorists should look beyond the social and political structure of advanced capitalism for explanations of new movements. More likely roots are societies' attempts to absorb the new technological forms that Touraine cites and changing values associated with generational experience. Whatever the roots of these new movements, the question remains as to whether they become marginalized searches for identity and cultural change or whether they become actors in the political arena. Although necessary, it is not sufficient for political change that collective identities merely form. They have to be expressed in organizational entities that undertake various forms of activism. And, it is to these aspects of Poland's ecological movement that we now turn.

5

The Independent Ecological Movement: Organization and Activism

The existence of an "ecological movement" was widely recognized at least three years before the end of communist rule. Those seeking to change attitudes toward the environment and development in the entire society defined themselves as part of an environmental movement. State and societal actors not involved in ecology referred to the movement in the press. Yet, the Polish environmental movement had no overarching organizational structure, nor did it have a division of functions or set patterns of interaction among its members. Rather, it was comprised of a variety of smaller movements, organizations, groups, and individuals with differing goals and strategies. A fluid network of interactions among its actors created the overall entity known as the environmental movement. This entity was then reaffirmed in the ongoing process of identity formation and in the broader society's interpretations of the actions taken by movement participants.

As parts of a social movement, these component actors addressed the issues of individual and collective consciousness and identity. They worked to change the ways in which individuals and households in their society thought about the environment and carried out their daily lives. At the same time, some were new actors in an emerging civil society, striving to develop their own identity and organization and to develop civil society itself. In these endeavors they addressed themselves to participating in and changing political processes, institutions, and specific policies. These groups, then, were actively transforming society, trying to be the instruments by which individuals became collective actors in civil society, and both influenced the state.

In their attempts to participate in and transform political life, the smaller actors of the environmental movement developed a heterogeneity of organizational forms. There were no direct correlations between organizational form and the types of activism in which particular groups engaged. Although, for example, decentralized movements *tended* to engage more in demonstrations and protests and occupational groups *tended* to work more through political institutions, groups combined identity, organization, goals, and means differently. For this reason, we will look at forms of organization and types of activism separately before pulling them back together at the end of the chapter. Ultimately it seems that a collective actor's types of activism were limited more by political identity than by the organizational form it developed. (See table 5.1 for an overview.)

Organization and Participation in the Movement

Since the movement had no overall organizational expression, this section will focus on organizations of the actors within the movement and their social bases. This focus is appropriate because the groups that comprised the movement were actually the arenas in which individual participation became collective action. Concerns about organization—i.e. about whether it is open or closed, hierarchical or associative, democratic or authoritarian, effective or not—are really concerns about the structures and processes that enhance, submerge, or alter individual goals and actions in the pursuit of collective goals through collective action. In a movement without some degree of unitary structure these processes necessarily take place at the level of that movement's component groups.

Movements

The Polish Ecological Club was identified by the press, as well as most environmentalists and outside observers, as the core of the ecological movement. Politicians also recognized PKE's centrality in the environmental movement and its expertise. Club members comprised 40 percent of all the experts at the Government–Solidarity Round-Table talks on ecology.[1] In the broader public the PKE's name gained ever wider recognition, mostly due to references to its opinions in press coverage of environmental problems. For this reason the Polish Ecological Club will be examined here in some detail.

TABLE 5.1 *Political Identity, Organization, and Activism of Selected Movement Actors*

Actor	Political Identity	Organizational Form[1]	Most Important Forms of Activism
League for the Protection of Nature (LOP)	official	*scope*: national *form*: complex organization *membership*: large, entire range of ages, regions, and social groups	education, direct action on the env't, policy advice/intervention
Polish Association for Tourism and Knowledge of the Country (PTTK)[2]	official	*scope*: national *form*: complex organization *membership*: large, employed in tourism or hikers/tourists, mixed ages and social groups	direct action in recreational areas, policy intervention, raising awareness about responsible tourism and use of nature
Social Ecological Movement (ERS) - in PRON	official	*scope*: national *form*: association within a complex organization *membership*: small core with many formally enrolled collective members; mixed	coordination of initiatives, policy intervention
Union of Village Youth (ZMW)[2]	official	*scope*: national *form*: complex organization *membership*: large, rural youth and young adults	education, in formation-sharing, raising awareness (especially regarding agriculture)
Ekos (within LOP)	official	*scope*: national *form*: informal circle *membership*: small, professional journalists centered in Warsaw	self-education of journalists, publication
Polish Chemical Society[2]	official	*scope*: national *form*: complex organization *membership*: large (though only a portion was involved in ecology), professional chemists	expert studies, policy intervention, seminars
Society for the Protection of the Tatras (TOT)	official	*scope*: regional *form*: formally structured association *membership*: small, activists from mixed backgrounds	shaping development in and protecting Tatra National Park
Polish Fishermen's Union[2]	official	*scope*: national *form*: complex organization *membership*: large (though only a portion was involved in ecology), largely male working class	monitoring, policy intervention to assure water quality

Actor	Political Identity	Organizational Form[1]	Most Important Forms of Activism
Polish Hunters' Union[2]	official	*scope*: national *form*: complex organization *membership*: large (though only a portion was involved in ecology), male, mixed social background	policy intervention to assure forest/habitat protection
Nature — Man — Values (under the auspices of the Polish Academy of Sciences)	official	*scope*: national/Warsaw *form*: bi-weekly seminar *membership*: small, core activists from other groups and scholars	self-education, exchange of views among various movement actors
Wigry	official	*scope*: national *form*: bi-annual seminar *membership*: small, creative artists	aesthetic change, consciousness-raising among artists
Polish Ecological Club (PKE)	independent	*scope*: national *form*: formally structured association *membership*: mid-sized, highly educated professionals, social activists	expert studies, policy intervention, education, consciousness-raising
Wolę Być	independent	*scope*: national *form*: informal regional circles *membership*: mid-sized, youth, generally urban	self-education, consciousness-raising through happenings
Ecological Movement of St.Francis of Assisi (REFA)	independent	*scope*: national *form*: informal regional circles (in Church seminaries) *membership*: small, clergy, concentrated in a few centers	value change, consciousness-raising, education
Priesthood of Ecologists	independent	*scope*: local/Kraków *form*: informal circle *membership*: small, lay and clerical activists in Kraków	promoting alternative values
Green Cross	independent	*scope*: national *form*: periodic seminar *membership*: small, core activists of other groups, scholars	self-education, in formation-sharing, coordination
Clubs of Catholic Intelligentsia (KIK)[2]	independent (though officially approved)	*membership*: small, *scope*: national *form*: informal circles highly educated professionals, Catholic	self-education, seminars among influential elite
Freedom and Peace (WiP)	opposition	*scope*: national *form*: networked informal regional circles *membership*: small, young adults, concentrated in a few	consciousness-raising, protest intervention in policy (especially anti-nuclear)

Actor	Political Identity	Organizational Form[1]	Most Important Forms of Activism
		urban centers	
Silesian Ecological Movement	opposition	*scope*: regional *form*: networked informal circles *membership*: small, varied, urban	gathering and disseminating information, consciousness-raising, policy intervention, protest
Great Poland Ecological Seminar (WSE)	opposition	*scope*: regional *form*: networked informal circles *membership*: small, varied including farmers	self-education, mobilization for policy intervention, development of organic farming
Ecology and Peace	opposition	*scope*: national *form*: networked informal circles *membership*: small, young adults - activists	consciousness-raising, protest

Notes

Selection of groups for this table was made by two criteria. The most important actors in each political sphere are listed first in their category, then some other examples are listed to illustrate the variety of actors and activities present in the movement. The nascent political parties formed in the last few months of 1988 have been left out of the table, not only because they were formed after the government and opposition agreed to negotiate (thus beginning the transition) but also because they were too small and new to have influenced the general structure of the movement before the transition.

[1] "*Scope*" refers to the level of policy or debate to which the group aspired. Most of the membership in independent and opposition groups remained concentrated in several regional circles and did not cover the entire country.

"*Form*" is divided into four categories for the purpose of comparison. From the most institutionalized and formal to the most fluid and informal, the categories are:

- complex organization—actor is a bureaucratized institution or organization, or a formal part of one; this type of organization has different departments, a staff, and multiple offices

- formally structured association—has a formal ongoing organizational structure but is not as densely institutionalized as the organizations mentioned above; it may not have separate departments or more than one permanent office; membership is formalized by registration and/or dues

- networked informal circles—ongoing regional circles linked together by communication among key members, but no ongoing structure over them; membership in circles tends to be fairly fluid

- periodic seminar—no ongoing organizational structure between meetings aside from one or a few seminar leaders

"*Membership*" gives the predominant social bases of the group and a rough estimate of size. This estimate is rough as membership figures are not available for independent and opposition groups. Environmentally active members within official organizations are also hard to estimate. "Large" refers to organizations over 10,000 strong. "Mid-sized" groups generally have from 1000–7000 members. "Small" refers to groups likely to have had fewer than 500 members.

[2] Environmental protection is NOT the main focus of these organizations. In some cases, the organization has formed a separate section to deal with environmental problems, but these sections are generally subject to the priorities of the parent organization and receive resources from that organization.

The Polish Ecological Club saw itself as a movement with a loose formal organization, i.e. a movement undergoing a process of limited institutionalization. It was organized in a three-tiered territorially based hierarchy that extended throughout the country, but its activity was more intensive in certain regions, namely Kraków, Poznań, Wrocław, Katowice, and Warsaw. PKE's national-level headquarters were located in the city of the club's origin, Kraków. Although the structure of the club was somewhat hierarchical, activities of various levels were not tightly controlled by the center. An important exception to this rule was the instance where the proposed activity was not along the lines and in the subject areas laid out by the program established at the General Congress. Then the matter was referred to the Executive Board at the national level.[2]

The Executive Board, chosen by the democratically elected General Congress of Delegates, was responsible for all activism on the national level and for authorizing regional-level bodies. Most of the decisions regarding activism on a given territory were taken at the regional (*okręg*) level, which corresponded to the old, larger, geographically defined voivodships. Regions had to report their activities to the national level periodically and needed to receive permission for actions that crossed the boundaries of their territories. Within their territories, these groups were free to decide on their style and points of activism, as long as they fell within the guidelines set by the Congress in the program. Often it was the regional groups that cooperated with other environmental groups. Since the regional groups functioned independently, it was common to see only one of them listed as a sponsor of an activity. Some even referred to the PKE in the plural as the Polish Ecological Clubs. Finally, the basic unit of organization was the *koło* or circle. These were small local groups approved by the regional executive council.

The first section of the Polish Ecological Club's programmatic statement envisioned the creation of a number of commissions to the Executive Council to deal with law, health, ecology-safe agriculture, international cooperation, economics, and publishing. With the exception of the legal commission most of these bodies had already been created by the end of 1987. Other commissions already active by then were those concerned with ecological education, national parks, and spatial planning (Hrynkiewicz 1988, 42). Still other committees dealing with specific subjects of the eco-development program were created under the regional councils. The PKE also reactivated its scientific council at the national level. Reaffirming this commitment to knowledge and competence, the program recognized the impracticality of pursuing this line and mass membership at the same time (PKE 1989b, 38).

The Polish Ecological Club had both individual and institutional members. Although it did not actively recruit a large following, the club doubled in size between 1987 and 1989 to a total of between 5,000 and 6,000 members.[3] Hrynkiewicz divides the PKE membership into three categories: leaders, who represented the club to outsiders, were extremely well-informed and made the central decisions; activists responsible for most of the organizational work and "event" organizing; and rank and file members, whose support varied from mere dues-paying to attending all meetings and events (1988, 44–45).[4]

A clear majority of the membership at the time of the Second Congress in 1987 had university degrees and there were numerous advanced degree holders, more from the sciences and technical fields, but also some from the humanities and social sciences (Hrynkiewicz 1988, 47). Several of the activist members were involved in environmental protection professionally and saw the club as a means to pursue environmental goals more effectively, often circumventing bureaucratic channels.[5] This strong "expert" base was not surprising given the club's dedication to advancing the most authoritative studies and arguments on behalf of ecology. Both the concentration of professionals and the direction of club activism can be traced to the decisions of the First General Congress. They also caused some internal rifts when non-expert activists felt that experts were at times too cautious to allow for timely action in concrete matters. That this tension was fairly constant is partially explained by the roots of the club in the Solidarity period and the influx of former Solidarity activists seeking a channel for their social energies immediately following martial law.[6]

One of the major problems facing the club was a constant lack of resources. Strict internal rules as to legitimate sources of income were designed to maintain the club's political and scientific independence. All resources came from membership fees, donations, and sales of some of its publications. Members asked to do independent studies of specific ecological problems or other reports were not allowed to receive commissions, nor was the club as a whole, regardless of the organization requesting the report. The fear was that sponsorship might be seen as coloring findings, thus compromising the integrity of the club.

Although the Polish Ecological Club started as a movement of local and regional activists and it maintained that character in several regions, there was an evolution toward a more formal organization, especially at the national level, in the mid to late 1980s. Yet, internal resistance and regional autonomy within the club checked the development of a hierarchy. On the other end of the spectrum, though, more radical members began to take up activism in other groups and movements. In one case, a group of them—"Ecology and Peace" (*Ekologia i Pokój*)—was even excluded from the club (Gliński 1989, 50–51). This countervailing of extremes left the club between a grassroots, informal movement and a more formal institution.

In addition to the Polish Ecological Club, the ecological movement included a few smaller movements with no formal organization.

The youth movement *Wolę Być* grew out of an appeal by the editors of the youth magazine *Na Przełaj*. Anna Wyka, a sociologist at the Polish Academy of Sciences who has observed the movement closely since its origins, emphasizes the fact that the appeal never mentioned a movement (1988, 59). The text of the appeal bears this point out; the invitation was to change one's own perspective and share this experience through letters with others who had done the same. *Na Przełaj* editors promised to write about people and events promoting the ideas of ecology and deep ecology—environmental protection, humane values, healthy lifestyle and harmonious, noncoercive interactions among people ("Odezwa programowa" 1984, 45–53). The *Wolę Być* movement organized itself after this call and quickly numbered over a thousand members.[7] It remained politically independent in its organization, activities, and cultural perspective.

Despite its role as initiator, *Na Przełaj* was not directly responsible for the further development of the movement. After writing the appeal, the editors printed responses and invited those responding to meet one another at the editorial offices (Wyka 1988, 59). *Na Przełaj* also served as the group's central post office box for three years. In early 1987 at their winter festival members set up a system of "contact post boxes." These contacts were individuals who passed on information and thus became linchpins in organizing activities (Wyka 1988, 80). With this system intact the movement was able to reduce its dependence on the editorial offices of *Na Przełaj* for internal communication. Still there were some strong connections remaining between the two: *Wolę Być* had a regular column in the magazine, which was the base of its communication with other youth, the Warsaw group maintained the editorial office as its meeting site for a few years, and a couple of *Na Przełaj* editors—who were also movement members—were involved in finding financial support for the national meetings and ecology camps, getting permission for demonstrations, and finding lecturers (Wyka 1988, 88).

Wolę Być was loosely organized into regional groups which met with differing degrees of regularity, depending on logistics and the level of activism. The oldest and most active groups were in the most ecologically degraded areas (Wyka 1988, 80). There was no hierarchy and, in fact, no constant organization aside from the contacts. Moreover, the groups deliberately did not intend to institutionalize their activism (p.60). National meetings once and often twice a year drew movement participants from the entire country. They took the form of ecological camps or jamborees. At the winter jamboree in 1987 members began to create groups based on interests (issue groups), one of the most active of which was a group involved in biodynamic agriculture. Another group was interested in "green schools," also called "green anti-schools," which, in addition to focusing on ecology and other problems of life in the twentieth century, maintained an atmosphere free of competition, stress, and coercion.[8] These issue groups drew together movement participants from different geographical areas, thus cross-cutting the regional groups.

Since the movement was informal it did not have the legal right to carry on its own financial activity. Financial resources were therefore minimal, raised mostly from group activities and donations. Some of these resources were given, in turn, to other causes.[9] With no constant organization to support and a forum in *Na Przełaj* for reporting its activities and spreading its ideas, the movement had few steady expenses. Individuals absorbed their own transportation and mailing costs. For national meetings members sought support from a number of institutions, including the Minister for Youth Affairs[10], and relied on the goodwill of expert speakers who donated their time, energy and own transportation costs.

Although *Na Przełaj*'s main target was Poland's large population of scouts, it was read by young people from all social groups, whether they were scouts or not. The vast majority of *Wolę Być* members, therefore, were between the ages of 15 and 24. The movement favored event-oriented mobilization over membership drives, yet well over a thousand members attended national jamborees. They came from large cities, small towns, and rural villages all over Poland. Their socioeconomic backgrounds also ran the full gamut of Polish society—intellectual, working class, peasant.[11]

Freedom and Peace was also an informal, nonhierarchical movement. It was comprised of regional groups in association with one another and a spokesperson that represented the movement at the national level. These groups tended to be tightly knit because of the dangers members invited by joining. So, although membership extended throughout the country, it was small and activism was strongest in a few pockets: Warsaw, Kraków, Wrocław, and Gdańsk.[12] As an opposition group, the movement obviously received no financing from any official source. All resources were donated by supporters or members themselves. Though Freedom and Peace had no real organization to support, resources were needed for lawyers, fines and, most of all, for printing bulletins, appeals, and leaflets in the underground press. Some of the financial pressures of publication were eased by cooperation among opposition groups in obtaining materials and access to equipment, printing, and distributing underground press. Members of Freedom and Peace were young adults from the age of eighteen to their early thirties. As a result of the emphasis on draft resistance, there was a preponderance of males in the group.

Institutionalized Organizations

The only fully institutionalized organization centered in the Polish environmental movement was the League for the Protection of Nature. Since the formation and activism of this organization was discussed at some length in Chapter 3, here it will suffice to summarize the characteristics most relevant to the current discussion.

The League for the Protection of Nature had 1.7 million members in 1988, which accounted for about 4 percent of the Polish population. This membership was organized into both occupational and territorial structures: the League had more than 13,000 units in schools, youth organizations, industry, universities, villages, cities, and voivodships ("Z działalności LOP" 1988, 25). Thus, it was not only officially recognized by the Polish government, but also well integrated into the educational, economic, and political systems. Because of its size and its incorporation into the officially controlled social sector, the League for Nature protection became quite bureaucratic. Its summit and official voice was the *Zarząd Główny*, or Executive Board.

The League was well-funded compared to other environmental organizations. Its main sources of revenue were its Divisions of Tree-Plantation, Greenery, and Cultivation, which operated like firms (Komitet Obchodów 1988, 4–5). Some revenue came from membership fees and donations. As an officially endorsed social organization, the League had access to locations for its offices and to potential groups of members it might not otherwise reach. It received other indirect subsidies as well; e.g. its publication, *Przyroda Polska*, was underwritten by the central publisher of mass press in Poland.[13] The ministry responsible for environment at a given time (see the discussion of changing environmental administration in chapter 3) and the education ministry also provided financing for various projects at different points in the League's history.[14]

A secure position, relative wealth, and size enabled the League to sponsor other smaller groups and many local environmental initiatives. It established and funded the the Nature Protection Guards, most of whose 40,000 members were recruited from the League's membership. One example of a smaller group formed under the wing of the Executive Council was *Ekos*, a group of ecologically minded journalists, some of whom were instrumental in raising public awareness of environmental problems. Several activists in other environmental groups also belonged to the League. Because of its units throughout the occupational structure, the League for the Protection of Nature pulled together people from all walks of life and all political leanings. In this case, the most important question was: how active was this huge membership? The answer is that activism varied greatly. In the general membership there were large sections of passive, dues-paying card holders. The school circles provide a clear picture of these differences. In schools or classes the teacher and students often decided which social endeavor to support at the beginning of the year. If a class signed up with the League for the Protection of Nature, members paid their dues and then decided what to do. Depending on the teacher or circle leader, the group could be very active in terms of both education and direct environmental projects; it could also do nothing.

Catholic Groups

Special attention should be given Church and lay Catholic ecological groups. Their existence implied approval by the Church hierarchy—confirmed in Cardinal Glemp's 1987 "Pastoral Letter of the Polish Episcopate on Environmental Protection"—and implicated this central symbol of Polish society in the critique of Poland's ecological situation and the policies that led to it. In terms of organization these groups provided an interesting case; they were nonhierarchical, associative groups and movements embedded in the hierarchy of the Catholic Church. Although the intra-group relations strove to break the patterns established by the Church context, the organization of the Church and various orders defined to a large extent the realms in which these groups operated, their audiences, and their participants.

The clerical movement REFA began with a seminar led by Professor Zbigniew Wierzbicki in late spring 1981, which made it the oldest ecological group connected with Poland's Franciscan Orders (Jaromi 1988, 15). "REFA renounce[d] the legal form of association and all attributes of formal organizations, with the exception of using a sign (symbol) of the movement."[15] Comprised of circles attached to Franciscan seminaries, REFA was active in Kraków, Łódź, Legnica, Wrocław, and Gdańsk. The circles were founded spontaneously by three or more interested initiators. They organized meetings, trips, and schooling in ecology (REFA 1988a, 4). The movement had potential for growth and greater influence than its small size implied given the popularity of the Church in general and the Franciscan order in particular in Poland. This potential could be seen in the case of Legnica, the center of Poland's copper mining and processing industry. The priest who was vice rector of the Franciscan high school and lower seminary there and co-founder of REFA's Legnica circle had been a long time member of REFA in Kraków.[16]

The Clubs of Catholic Intelligentsia (*Kluby Intelegencji Katolickiej* or KIK) were intellectual discussion groups allowed to continue after the Polish October of 1956 as part of a reconciliation between the Polish state and the Roman Catholic Church. Though permitted various degrees of political freedom over the years, members were influential opinion-makers, seen by much of society as maintaining their intellectual integrity, and therefore able to play an important advisory role to Solidarity in the 1980–81.[17] In 1987 KIK formed an ecological section which concentrated its efforts on self-education, seminars and discussions.

There were a number of other Catholic groups, reflecting a growing interest among both clergy and lay Catholics in ecology. The "Priesthood of Ecologists" (*Duszpasterstwo Ekologów*), created in 1984, was associated with a reformist Franciscan order in Kraków. Unlike the clerical movement REFA, this group combined lay and clerical activists. Also formed in 1984, the Franciscan Ecological Movement (*Franciszkański Ruch Ekologiczny*) was a lay Catholic group located in Gdańsk. The Association PAX, seen as the government's Catholic group, also had some ecological sections. In 1988, the "Free Ecological Movement" associated with St. Brigid's Church in Gdańsk took up resistance to Żarnowiec, Poland's first nuclear energy plant, and the cause of cleaning up the Baltic Gulf. Yet, another group, the Franciscan Ecological Unity, formed in Kraków in the late 1980s.

Occupational Groups

Occupational groups participating in the environmental movement were almost always parts of other associations and organizations. These parent associations were generally well institutionalized. Many had direct economic interests in some aspect of environmental protection; others had no direct interests beyond those of every citizen.

Concerned with tourism, parks, trails, and recreation areas, the Polish Society for Tourism and Knowledge of the Country (PTTK) had an intimate interest in protecting the environment. This association was both the professional organization of those working in tourism and recreation and a popular organization for those who spend their leisure time traveling, hiking, fishing, skiing, etc. PTTK had environmental commissions under its Executive Board and the boards of its regional and city branches (Hrynkiewicz 1988, 31). Along with the League for the Protection of Nature, PTTK coordinated the activities of the volunteer Nature Protection Guards (discussed in chapter 3). Like that of other official organizations, however, PTTK activism was formalistic and piecemeal until 1980 (ibid., 30). Despite attempts to step up activism after that, the organization met a number of obstacles to timely activism and to growth. A major obstacle was PTTK's enrollment in the government ecological movement created in PRON. A number of activists on the environmental commissions resigned in protest that membership in the PRON movement placed another system of bureaucratic control on them, making effective and timely action impossible.

The Polish Chemical Society (*Polskie Towarzystwo Chemiczne*) had a section on environmental protection, as well as a very active section on chemistry and environmental engineering. Chemists were also quite active in the Polish Ecological Club and on environmental advisory committees. One indication of chemists' involvement was the joint Seminar on Environmental Protection of the Polish Ecological Club and the Polish Chemical Society, which was in turn a source of information for the "Green Cross" seminars discussed below. A landmark report commissioned by the Polish Academy of Sciences' Committee on Chemical Sciences on the "Chemical Pollutions of the Environment in Poland," appeared in the profession's leading journal in 1984 and widely increased concern for the environment in both academic circles and the press. The authors' technical analysis yielded the conclusion that

> . . . the degree of environmental degradation in Poland has reached a level threatening the biological survival of the nation and is much larger than could be assumed given the level of production and consumption. Such a state of affairs indicates unequivocally causes beyond technology, i.e. lying in the organizational-legal, systemic-economic and psychological spheres (Pawłowski and Kozak 1984, 495).

One of the co-authors of this article, Professor Lucjan Pawłowski, was also a central organizer of a series of international conferences on chemistry and environmental protection that dated back to 1976.[18]

Ekos was a circle of ecologically minded journalists meeting under the sponsorship of the Executive Board of the League for the Protection of Nature. Members' most significant activities centered around the articles and features they wrote for the mass-circulation press. This activism and the opportunity to reinforce it by raising the level of knowledge among colleagues through *Ekos* seminars, field trips, and other activities should not be underestimated. Members included noted journalists, such as Iwona Jacyna of *Życie Warszawy*, one of the first to write extensively and critically about Poland's environmental problems. As a group, *Ekos* also signed open appeals to the authorities of both a general and specific nature. A related group deserves mention as well: the Environmental Protection Club of the Association of Journalists of the PRL. The Chair of this club was Sylwester Bajor, whose articles appeared in newspapers all over the country. By sponsoring sessions on specific aspects of environmental protection, the club drew together officials responsible for the environment, academic experts, activists and newspaper, radio and television journalists for discussion and debate.

The Union of Village Youth (*Związek Młodzieży Wiejskiej*) also took up the issue of ecology. In 1982 a National Ecological Council formed in the union's Executive Board and the network of ecological groups inside the union grew to include 30 of Poland's 49 voivodships (Gliński 1989, 43). The Ecological Council set about popularizing environmental protection through a series of "ecological olympiads" in agricultural schools. To aid in the collection and spread of knowledge, the union's National Council created a "Social Information Center on Environmental Protection" which announced an ambitious program at the beginning of 1986 but was restrained in its activities by the financial difficulties of the cooperative sponsoring it (Hrynkiewicz 1988, 33). Still the union managed to organize a series of national courses on biodynamic agriculture during the second half of the 1980s (Gliński 1989, 44).

The Polish Fishermen's Union (*Polski Związek Wędkarski*) had both a large membership and a direct concern for water quality. From this interest it developed an ecological section with a broader orientation. Still, the union's most important contributions were its reports of sudden changes in water contamination to inspection authorities and repeated warnings of the general deterioration in Poland's water quality. Fishermen were also instrumental in initiating a local movement to protect the Hel peninsula in 1988 (Gliński 1989, 65).

The Polish Hunters' Union (*Polski Związek Łowiecki*), like the fisherman's union, had a large and diverse membership. Since it was most concerned with species preservation, the hunters' union took an active part in protecting endangered species. A parallel concern was habitat, mostly forest, protection.

Scores of other occupational groups declared a primary or additional interest in environmental protection as the 1980s wore on: the Polish Nature Association "Copernicus," the Polish Scouts' Union, the Association of Urbanists of Poland, a number of whose architects and urban planners were Polish Ecological Club members, the trade unions, the official political parties, the Central Technical Organization, etc. Some were more active than others and all served to sensitize their memberships more toward ecological concerns, but none of them gained much public attention for its activism.

Territorially Defined Groups and Associations

Local and regional issues brought together residents from different walks of life into territorially defined ecological groups. Of hundreds of initiatives from the neighborhood to the national level, several lasting groups were formed. Only a few will be mentioned as illustrative examples.

The Society for the Protection of the Tatras (*Towarzystwo Ochrony Tatr* or TOT) was a social organization created by local authorities in Zakopane in response to and absorbing an independent, local ecological movement to protect the Tatra Mountains and the Tatra National Park from further degradation (Hrynkiewicz 1988, 56). Local residents living in and around the park were greatly concerned that heavy tourism was ruining some parts of the park and that the park's administration was interested more in the income obtained by control of the park than in its preservation. These interests were blamed for the failure of the Polish Tatra Association to gain approval for reactivation.[19] They were also protected by overlapping the personnel of the park administration with that of TOT.

The Great Poland Ecological Seminar (*Wielkopolskie Seminarium Ekologiczne*) considered itself a co-creator of an ecological movement and acted in a more radically political fashion than other seminars. Its activities included creating ecological groups and establishing contacts with other such groups in the region and throughout the country.[20] The group was created in September 1986 and its bulletin (*Wielkopolski Informator Ekologiczny*), published in the underground press and designed to reach village, working-class, and academic audiences, began in March 1987. It took the form of small circles that met for a seminar once a month in a room provided by the Dominican Order of the Catholic Church in Poznań. Costs were limited to speakers' travel, photocopying, and postage and were covered by members' voluntary donations (Gliński 1988, 73–74). The Seminar focused on issues central to the *Wielkopolska* or "Great Poland" region of the country: the Międzyrzecz controversy, the government decision to build Poland's second nuclear energy plant in Klempicz, and plans for exploitation of an extensive and deep brown coal vein. This group was also one of the more interesting for its combination of influences: the All-Poland Committee for Peasant Resistance "Rural Solidarity" (a political opposition group) and Freedom and Peace cooperated in publishing its information bulletin; there was also a strong religious dimension to the group's identity, reflected in citations from and reliance on Church documents regarding environmental protection.[21] The seminar's emphases in both its activism and self-education on biodynamic agriculture and alternative energy reflected the closeness of the group to village constituencies (hence also the strong religious tone) and local opposition to national plans for the development of nuclear energy.

The Social Committee for the Protection of the Great Mazurian Lakes in Orzysz (*Społeczny Komitet Ochrony Wielkich Jezior Mazurskich w Orzyszu*) started as a local initiative and spread to the rest of the Western region of Suwałki voivodship, which is a major tourist region. Started by sailing and nature enthusiasts, the committee worked to limit and undo the damage done by local industries and communities, stock farms, agriculture, and tourist and sanitorium facilities. In addition to intervening when environmental laws were broken and raising ecological consciousness, the group attempted to expand the area under special legal protection. It invited and cooperated with anyone of similar intention, which provided PRON with a chance to enter and take control of the group (Hrynkiewicz 1988, 34–35).

As was the case with the occupationally based groups, there were so many different territorially based groups functioning at various levels and from various political perspectives that it is impossible to discuss even a representative sample. Other notable examples of this type of group would be: Mazovian Landscapes, which focused on the preservation of the landscape in the central region of the country, the Silesian Ecological Movement (*Śląski Ruch Ekologiczny*), the Gdańsk Ecological Program (*Gdański Program Ekologiczny*), the Citizen's Committee for the Environmental Protection of Jelenia Góra Valley (*Komitet Obywatelski na rzecz Ochrony Środowiska w Kotlinie Jeleniej-Górskiej*), and the entire "Green Lungs of Poland" project.

Periodic Seminars and Conferences

A number of seminars and conferences focusing on various aspects of Poland's environmental problems sprang up after 1984. They were a self-conscious part of the networking between actors that integrated them into a movement. What follows is a description of a few of the expressly environmental seminars. Many other bodies devoted from one to several meetings to ecology, but it was not their central concern.

The "Green Cross" (*Zielony Krzyż*) was a regular, critical and heavily attended seminar in Warsaw. The seminar leader was long-time environmental activist Zbigniew Wierzbicki. Organized in the end of 1986, the seminar was held under the auspices of the Society for a Free Polish University (TWWP) of whose Warsaw branch Wierzbicki was president.[22] According to its invitation to participate, the seminar was never intended to be "yet another form of activism in competition with other already existing ones." Its only purpose was to "examine the greatest actual ecological dangers and formulate 'up to the minute' information and postulates addressed to the authorities and public opinion (Wierzbicki 1987)." In order to produce the most well-informed propositions, the seminar worked with a number of academic institutions and the scientific councils of environmental organizations.

Nature, Man and Values (*Przyroda–Człowiek–Wartości*) was a biweekly interdisciplinary colloquium held at the Warsaw seat of the Polish Academy of Sciences. It was organized by the Research Team on Lifestyles of the Institute of Philosophy and Sociology. These colloquia drew together members of all the major ecological groups, clergy, scholars, and local activists with a wide variety of interests. The topics ranged from the philosophy of "deep ecology" to administrative and legal issues. Discussions were wide-ranging and at times heated as it was not unusual for government representatives to be sitting next to members of the opposition and clergy next to atheists.[23] The transcripts of the colloquia were to be published as a source of wide-ranging information on ecology.

Named for a lake in Northeastern Poland, the site of its meetings, *Wigry* was a symposium linking culture and environmental protection. The symposia occurred once every year or two, depending on logistics, and brought professors and practitioners of the fine arts together with naturalists and ecologists. Their purpose was to develop consciousness of the importance of environmental protection for culture, broadly understood. Supported by the Ministry of Culture and Art, the symposia attracted important opinion-makers in the arts from Poland and from abroad.

Political Parties

The formation of political parties and participation in electoral politics was the last new direction in environmental organization and activism under communist rule.

Starting in the mid-1980s the communist party's two coalition parties—the Democratic Party and the United Peasants' Party—both claimed "green" sympathies. Articles appeared in their press and environmental problems were discussed at their congresses. The best of the articles was Inez Wiatr's series "Encyklopedia Ekologiczna" in *Tygodnik Demokratyczny*; the most visibly concerned congress was the 1988 peasant party congress.[24] Still, neither of these parties was primarily ecological and in policymaking neither opted for ecology when it clashed with its more traditional interests.

True ecological parties were born only after the 1988 strikes. The Polish Ecological Party (*Polska Partia Ekologiczna*), founded in Kraków at the end of summer 1988, developed some branches in other cities. It quickly gained a local Kraków rival in the Polish Green Party (*Polska Partia Zielonych*). Many of the founding members of these parties were also members of the Polish Ecological Club. Among the Polish Ecological Party's most visible actions were protests against an enormous coking plant which the Czechoslovak government was building in Stronava on the Polish border. The Independent Party "Green Movement" (*Niezależne Stronnictwo "Ruch Zielonych"*) was formed in Warsaw in December 1988.[25] This party consisted of only a Warsaw nucleus, but it established an office and oriented itself primarily to the protection of environment in the countryside. This more specific orientation came with a political move toward alliance with Solidarity of Individual Farmers. The "Federation of Greens" (*Federacja Zielonych*) considered itself an alternative political party. The federation had member groups in various parts of the country. Members were proponents of "deep ecology" and eschewed participation in elections to national governing bodies for the development of local self-government and direct democracy. Grassroots groups sent representatives to a coordinating group whose functions were limited to exchange of information and coordinating action taken on matters that cross-cut or combine the localities (Gliński 1988, 53–54).

These new parties added yet another dimension to both the environmental movement and the rapidly growing pluralism of Polish political society in the late 1980s. However, they never became a significant force in Polish politics. As political parties they did not fall under the new law on associations and therefore did not register either as associations or parties (there was no new law on political parties) before the historic June

1989 elections. Their political goals were representation in the Sejm (parliament) and participation in elections. As of the end of communist rule they intended to boycott elections where no candidates campaign for ecology.[26] Since that first parliamentary election, however, these parties have been absent from the national political scene. While some of their activists have entered more mainstream parties, others have focused on local politics.

An Attempt to Impose Organization

The government-supported social front PRON created the "Social Ecological Movement" (*Społeczny Ruch Ekologiczny* or ERS) in September 1986 to give the numerous environmental groups and movements springing up around the country "a head." The intention was to bring these movements under one umbrella and the control of PRON.[27] This "Social Ecological Movement" was visible on the national level due to its official sponsorship and subsequent press coverage. It was clearly a group created "from above" and not a grassroots movement.

The creation of this movement was publicized widely. Yet, except for general statements about enhancing the effectiveness of environmental actions, the initial articles neglected to describe the "movement" and its goals and modes of action. Instead, they contained only a list of unsuccessful environmental initiatives and generally worded descriptions of some of Poland's environmental problems.[28] The PRON movement aimed to integrate and coordinate the hundreds of environmental groups and initiatives developing throughout the country. Seeing this as an attempt to control and limit the movement, most activists criticized and few joined ERS. Those groups who joined were generally parts of larger organizations who were already PRON members.

Although action taken by activists inside ERS was easily bogged down in the bureaucracy of PRON, there were a few dedicated individuals working in this group. Official declarations of support for the environment gave them a chance to pursue some environmental initiatives more critically. Thus, ERS served as a partial inroad into the official bureaucracy for certain ecologists. Some local councils of PRON supported efforts to achieve change in official policy. The most vigorous case was the attempt of the PRON's city council in Międzyrzecz to intervene in the decision regarding radioactive waste storage in old bunkers. Its efforts were rendered ineffective by PRON's own bureaucracy as well as other official organs.[29] What remained were weak initiatives and sharp articles about ecological problems in the PRON bulletin. After the establishment of a Solidarity-led government, the core activists of this movement broke away from PRON and its stigma to create their own Polish Ecological Association.

Overview of Organization

From this review of key actors in Poland's ecological movement, a few generalizations can be made about the movement's organization when the transition from communism started. The ecological movement was clearly heterogeneous with interest groups, informal movements, bureaucratic organizations, nascent political parties, and seminars. Moreover, these actors made no attempt to bring a degree of organizational uniformity to the movement. The one attempt to do so by an external actor, the government via PRON, was rebuffed. Ecological groups were also heterogeneous regarding the level on which they acted (national, voivodship, local), strategies (from serving on official advisory councils to demonstrating), political views (from members of the communist party to members of the opposition), and their own level of politicization (from apolitical to overtly political).

This heterogeneity applied to the social base of the movement as well as its organizational forms. Intellectual groups were clearly the most influential in terms of policy change. Youth groups, however, played just as important a role in consciousness-raising. The youth groups and the occupational groups brought in participants from the village and the industrial working class. General initiatives based on a defined territory pulled together residents of all ages and social backgrounds. Thus, the movement did cut across the country's social structure, and its identity was not class-based. Having established this much, however, it is also true that most of the core environmental activists were well-educated and urban, as has been the case in the West.

Although many of the actors in the environmental movement had traditional organizational forms, some were clearly different. *Wolę Być*, Freedom and Peace, REFA and the "Federation of Greens" all had informal, associative structures. Interactions within the circles and regional groups of these movements were based on equality and noncoercion; each regional group enjoyed autonomy *within* these environmental actors. There were no hierarchies and decisions regarding activism were taken in a directly democratic manner. Since the ecological movement as a whole had no structure and no group had financial or political control over others, interaction and collaboration *among* actors also took place on the basis of full autonomy. In sum, the Polish movement exhibited the same organizational traits that new social movement theorists emphasize in Western environmental movements and in "new" movements in general.

Goals and Activism in the Polish Ecological Movement

The two most fundamental goals of individual groups in the environmental movement have already been discussed: identity-formation and change in social norms regarding the environment. This section will concentrate on the more programmatic goals of the environmental movement and the types of activism in which its participants engaged. Of all the actors in the environmental movement, the Polish Ecological Club had the most developed program or action plan.[30] Since it encompassed most of the goals, though not all of the methods, supported by other groups, the PKE program will be discussed more extensively. A review of the main categories of activism will follow, each containing specific examples of groups that engaged in such activism and of actions that were undertaken. Some actions bridged types of activism; for example, they were simultaneously consciousness-raising and targeted at changing specific policies. The relevant points of these actions will be discussed in each category in which they fit.

Program of the Polish Ecological Club

There was always a lively internal debate over the proper nature of the Polish Ecological Club's activities, a debate that at times bordered on outright factionalism. As a result of the dangers of both factionalism and martial law (December 1981–July 1983), there was a noticeable change in emphasis in the club's activism. This change was consolidated at the First General Congress in October 1983. There the club adopted longer term goals of change in the environment over immediate political goals. An emphasis on apolitical "expert" activism was the result.[31] Along with the PKE's increasing institutionalization over time, this "expert" emphasis served to move the club along the road from an independent grassroots movement toward a mixture of movement and independent pressure group.

The club's programmatic statement proclaimed "eco-development" as the basic goal and prescription of the club, dividing the tasks of this development into eleven categories:

- ecological education
- science
- demographic problems

- air protection
- water protection
- protection of ecosystems, including flora and fauna
- soil protection, agriculture and food
- protection of human health
- protection of cultural landmarks
- socioeconomic development, including economic planning, spatial planning, energy, industry, transportation, human settlements, and the use of waste
- protection and use of mineral resources (PKE 1989b, 14–37)

Studies, proposals, petitions, education, and policy intervention were organized according to these categories. Club activism was divided into three broad areas: organizational matters within the club, information and education activities, and intervention and advisory activities. Activism in the first area focused on strengthening the value placed by the PKE's own members on environmental protection, cooperation among different branches of the club, and "cooperation with other organizations, movements, and associations involved in environmental protection, as well as the Church, effectively maintaining the club's principle of apoliticism and independence" (PKE 1989b, 37). It also dealt with organizational issues of jurisdiction, authority, and finance.

On the informational-educational front the Second General Congress of the PKE decided to initiate an Information Bulletin or an Ecological Quarterly and publish a series of "Green Notebooks" with the positions of the Executive Board and Regional Boards on various ecological issues.[32] Attempts were also made to publish more of the materials coming out of seminars, symposia, and discussion circles. For the more general public, the club decided to put out an elementary school primer and a university textbook, as well as a calendar containing its ecological principles and program goals. For generalists and specialists, the PKE hoped to start a data bank and archive and get its own chronicles in order. The club also prepared a national symposium on ecological threats to human health and a seminar on eco-development.

In addition, the Congress produced an agenda of the PKE's more immediate activities in environmental politics. On a general level the club used the following mechanisms to pursue its goals:

> . . . its legal rights to be consulted with and give its opinion on land use plans and plans for socioeconomic development, . . . to the maximum degree possible the forum of People's Councils [elected local government organs] on all levels for communicating information about the environment, bringing pressure on offices and institutions through the People's

Councils, influencing the development of the ecological consciousness of
representative and administrative organs,

    . . . [promotion of a] resolution that works on ecological topics be pub-
lished in large quantities . . . ,

    . . . work intended to expand, complete and update the Law on the
Protection and Shaping of the Environment and the Law on the Protection
of Nature,

    . . . demand[s] that an inspector for environmental affairs have access to
each village and neighborhood,

    . . . demand [for] changes in the methods used by the Environmental
Protection administrations to make them more effective,

    . . . interven[tion] with various authorities and institutions in pressing mat-
ters. Thus, it will prepare a series of written petitions:

    1) to the Minister of Environmental Protection and Natural Resources . . .

    2) to the Council of Ministers (via the Premier) . . .

    3) to the Government Presidium of the PRL . . .

    4) to the Sejm [Parliament] . . . (PKE 1989b, 39–41)

Then the program specifies a number of issues to be addressed to each of
the institutions listed above.

With the exception of some committees that remained in the planning
stage and some delays in publishing, the Polish Ecological Club pursued
the tasks laid down in its program while continuing other activities that
became traditions. Prominent among its regular activities were public
meetings with ecologists, exhibits, book sales, educational demonstrations, reports, letters to city and national leaders, and petitions.

Consciousness-Raising

Prime in the movement's activism were efforts to raise social awareness of
environmental problems, their causes, and their results. The most popular tactics were demonstrations, publication, and public meetings. There
were also unusual events such as religious masses for the environment.
Consciousness-raising activities and education overlapped to a great
extent. Here we will focus on activities aimed at general awareness.
Efforts to achieve more in-depth knowledge will be covered in the next
section.

Those groups that staged demonstrations most frequently were *Wolę
Być*, Freedom and Peace, and the Polish Ecological Club. *Wolę Być* members' street demonstrations or "happenings" were usually colorful and
had an "alternative" atmosphere. Unlike Freedom and Peace demonstrations, which were not legally sanctioned, *Wolę Być* demonstrations were

always legal, meaning that permits were obtained beforehand. Examples of this type of activism included a bicycle ride through Warsaw to publicize the need for bicycle paths and alternatives to pollution-causing transportation, sales of potted Christmas trees to reduce the number of trees destroyed and encourage tree-planting, a demonstration against water pollution in Łódź, and a march in gas masks through Wałbrzych, an industrial city in one of Poland's 27 officially declared areas of ecological danger, to raise ecological consciousness.

Publication was another major form of consciousness-raising in the ecological movement. Several ecological groups published everything from leaflets and bulletins to magazines and reports. Freedom and Peace and the Great Poland Ecological Seminar published regular newsletters and bulletins in the underground press. Open letters and appeals published in the *Wolę Być* section of *Na Przełaj* could aim at mobilizing members for action on a specific issue or at a reconsideration of general values on the part of the magazine's wider readership. The Catholic group REFA also published a regular bulletin. In addition to its more ambitious reports, the Polish Ecological Club published short bulletins when pressing issues were under consideration by the authorities or quick action was necessary to respond to a problem.

Another medium for activism was the Church. Since the vast majority of Poles identify themselves as Catholic[33], the influence of Catholic ecological groups was potentially enormous. As Poland was preparing for Pope John Paul II's second visit and emerging from martial law, the clergy of REFA put together an impressive ecological exhibit titled "The Blue Patron of Ecologists" which later toured other Polish cities (Jaromi 1988, 14). Another Catholic group, the Priesthood of Ecologists, co-sponsored two conferences, the first titled "Christians in the Face of Ecological Danger" and a 1987 symposium on "A Christian and the World of Creation." The latter produced a number of propositions and calls to action for those of goodwill who were ready to act. Perhaps the most unconventional means of consciousness raising were "masses for the environment" organized by the Priesthood of Ecologists (Gliński 1989, 40). Some parishes also distributed environmental literature by REFA and other ecology groups.

Education

Education and self-education were central to the activities of almost every environmental group. The emphasis in education, however, differed somewhat from group to group. Some concentrated on scientific knowledge about processes occurring in nature. Others took a more anthropogenic approach that focused on the extent of human destruction of nature and the effects of ecological degradation on human health and human society.

The League for the Protection of Nature published Poland's most widely circulated monthly about nature, *Przyroda Polska*, and an internal newsletter. Most of its educational activities took place in its circles, or basic membership units. In addition, the League sponsored competitions of environmental knowledge and exhibitions. Courses in biodynamic agriculture and "ecological olympiads" were also run and promoted by the Union of Village Youth. Self-education and education of colleagues were the main activities of the *Ekos* group of journalists and the Clubs of Catholic Intelligentsia. *Wolę Być* had a self-education movement in the form of "green schools." One of REFA's most successful initiatives was a series of ecological schools for Franciscan clergy and seminary students of all branches of the Franciscan order. Other REFA educational initiatives included a series on healthy food and publishing articles about ecology in the religious press (Jaromi 1988, 17). The Polish Ecological Club published books and "notebooks" on ecology for use in these types of activities. Lecturers and guest speakers were a major part of ecological groups' meetings and several seminars facilitated the exchange of information.

The Polish Ecological Club also combined its consciousness-raising activities with education. The Kraków branch's Thursday meetings with ecologists became an important forum for public discussions of environmental problems. These discussions were generally well-attended, drawing from thirty to a few hundred people, depending on the topic. As can be surmised from its agenda, the Polish Ecological Club did not shy away from addressing issues that were controversial or fundamental to current policy. This was also true of the club's public meetings which addressed the entire range of ecological topics, among them the effects of economic reform on environmental protection, nuclear energy, and the environment and health.[34]

Policy Intervention

Another main direction in environmental activism was to effect change in policy decisions and, less frequently, policy implementation. Intervention in policy took both conventional and unconventional forms.

Almost all of Poland's ecological groups exercised conventional means of influencing policy, such as letters and petitions to relevant authorities. *Wolę Być* activism included meetings with factory managers as well. The tourism association also used official channels, for example, to press for the creation of a landscape park near the city of Wrocław. Others, especially members of the Polish Ecological Club, the Polish Chemical Society, and the League for the Protection of Nature, participated in the advisory bodies whose studies and opinions were to inform policymakers. There was also intervention to assure implementation, one example of which might be the reporting of sudden water quality changes to inspection agencies by the fishermen's union.

The main unconventional means for influencing policy decisions were demonstrations and protests linked to specific decisions. The *Wolę Być* march through Wałbrzych, besides raising consciousness, had the specific goal of inspiring residents to demand that changes ordered in air pollution control be implemented (Stępniak 1988, 11–13). Among other such actions *Wolę Być* undertook were a 1987 campaign to remove hazardous building materials from an elementary school in Gdańsk and a campaign to change the course of a car race that was planned through a closed reserve for birds.

Freedom and Peace initiated particularly visible anti-nuclear protests in Międzyrzecz, Wrocław, and Kraków. In Międzyrzecz the movement waged the campaign to overturn the government's decision to store radioactive waste in old German bunkers near the town. Freedom and Peace members repeatedly demonstrated, mobilized the local population, and were arrested in Międzyrzecz in 1987 and 1988. The group's first protests in response to the Chernobyl accident (April 26, 1986) and the Polish government's handling of the disaster took place on May 2 and May 9 in Wrocław and drew crowds of a few hundred. On June 1 in Kraków 2,000 people marched in protest against nuclear energy and the construction of the Żarnowiec power plant.[35] The march was covered in both the unofficial and Western press.

Direct Action on the Environment

Compared to its political and social activism, the environmental movement undertook little direct action on the environment. Many circles of the League for the Protection of Nature engaged in action that was generally of a conservationist nature—tree-planting and clean-up campaigns. The Polish Scout's Union and the tourism association also took part in these types of activities. The Nature Protection Guards, in addition to leading some of these campaigns, also served as society's environmental inspectorate, reporting violations it uncovered. *Wolę Być* undertook tree-plantings and clean-up actions, as well as some social labor such as work on a water treatment plant in Jelenia Góra Valley (Wyka 1988, 70). Freedom and Peace increased the potential growth of such action by campaigning to have service in environmental protection accepted as an alternative to the draft.

Activism, Organization and Identity

Although environmental groups held many of the same goals, there was a great variety of activism in the ecological movement. Organizational form was not directly linked to differences in types of activism undertaken, as the bureaucratic League for the Protection of Nature and the informal movement *Wolę Być* clearly demonstrated. The one exception was that sustained educational efforts, which were carried out primarily by official organizations, seminars and the Polish Ecological Club, required some structure.

In general, types of activism seem to have been guided more by place on the political spectrum than by the organizational nature of the group. The officially sanctioned groups engaged in consciousness-raising only to a limited degree, stopping before fundamental critique of development policies. Although quite active in policy intervention, these groups did not resort to unconventional means. On the other hand, official organizations were much more likely to be involved in direct action on the environment than either independent or opposition groups. The nonofficial groups tended to focus their energies more on broader problems that required changes in policy, plans, or structure. Differences according to political identity were also visible in the places where groups decided to publish and in the policies they critiqued. Thus, the collective actors in the movement often acted along the lines of the split between officialdom and opposition, even though individual participation in the movement and the identity of the movement as a whole superseded the split. As would be expected, this was particularly true of the movement's official organizations and opposition groups.

Conclusion

The Polish environmental movement definitely exhibited the traits Cohen indicates as defining "new" movements. It was heterogeneous. Not only were there ecological groups with bases of support in different sectors of society, but also several combined members from a variety of social backgrounds within the same group. Particularly good examples were the Great Poland Ecological Seminar and the League for the Protection of Nature. None of the groups discussed above viewed itself primarily in terms of socioeconomic class, even though occupational identities were the basis of some collective actors (notably the village-based groups and the ecological sections of professional associations). The movement had no overall structure; it was comprised of various types of collective actors: informal movements, institutionalized movements, large bureaucracies, interest groups, periodic seminars, and nascent political parties. Moreover, some of these groups—*Wolę Być*, Freedom and Peace, REFA and the Federation of Greens—had the directly democratic structures with only loose national federation which Cohen sees as characteristic of new movements.

The ecologists of the Polish Ecological Club, *Wolę Być*, the Franciscan movements, Freedom and Peace, *Wigry*, the Federation of Greens, Green Cross, and the Great Poland Ecological Seminar sought to change society's view of itself and development. The new visions and action in accordance with them were essential to the identities of these groups. Finally, in regard to Cohen's "self-limiting radicalism," these groups encouraged pluralism; they also recognized the autonomous functioning of the state and economy, though they sought to influence the norms that guided that functioning.

Although strategy plays only a secondary role in new social movement theory, it is an essential aspect of any political action. Actors in the Polish environmental movement used a multitude of tactics in their overall campaign to change the norms by which society and the economy related to the environment. These tactics were employed in strategies aimed at state policy (lobbying, petitioning, consulting, advising, demonstrations, implicit or explicit threat of political opposition), at change in civil society through the medium of the state (education, media attention to the environment), and directly at civil society (education, self-education, demonstrations, exhibits, direct action on the environment). Taking advantage of political changes at the end of the decade, environmentalists became active in the local government movement and ran for positions in the new, post-communist People's Councils.[36] A new direction of environmental activism has thus become electoral and lobbying politics. Another major direction has been to step up activities that raise awareness and knowledge of the environment. With more political and economic control in the hands of civil society, educating and reshaping values become all the more critical.

Since the environmental movement was in dialogue with a centralized state and economy during the communist period, its success and development were partially shaped by government policy toward its actors. Regime policy toward the environmental movement was made with the intention of keeping ecology from becoming an opposition issue. Hence the inclusion strategy, visible foremost in PRON's attempt to create an integrative structure for the various ecological initiatives. However, diversity in the movement's organization and activism, as well as actors' dedication to the development of ecological values in society, rendered cooptation through inclusion impossible.

Regime strategy will be discussed in further detail in chapter 7. Government treatment of the ecological movement depended to some extent on the credibility of the threat that the political opposition would take up ecology as a weapon in the political battle. Before examining state policy toward the movement, then, it is necessary to look at the opposition's interest in ecology.

6

The Opposition and Ecology

Although it was also "independent" from official control, the political opposition in Poland in the 1980s must be considered separately from issue-oriented independent social movements of the period. Whereas participants in independent movements, especially the environmental movement, defined their identities primarily with respect to their causes, opposition movements defined their identities with respect to the existing political system. The primary goal of opposition participants was to modify and eventually bring down communist party rule of the country. However salient, issues were ultimately weapons with which to discredit communist rule further and mobilize social opposition to the existing regime.

Ecology was potentially a strong weapon. The state of Poland's natural environment and lack of significant government action to halt its deterioration blatantly contradicted official claims of the constitutional right of all citizens to enjoy the natural environment.[1] Along with this right came every citizen's obligation to protect the environment,[2] an obligation clearly not being met by the citizens in the strongest positions to do so. With growing social concerns about the level of pollution and its effects on human health, the potency of the issue as a critique of the existing system increased. Ideological claims of a state of and for the working class were openly contradicted not only by the workers' opposition embodied in Solidarity but also by the clear priority of industrial output over the health of workers and, indeed, all citizens. The ecological critique reached to the very foundations of the economy, political sys-

ginning to recognize ecology as an issue to be covered, had
eness of what it entailed.

ment was originally the purview of the eighth problem
of the Congress, labeled "Man and Environment—Social
ajowy Zjazd Delegatów" 1981, 5). After presentation and
working groups' materials, the work of the thirteen prob-
s combined into a program document of eight sections,
he environment being included in the fifth section on
idarity—Social Policies." The environmental provisions
entioned during debate at the Congress.[9] This oversight
ted to the enormity of the tasks facing that Congress and
f the debate, which grouped the material into three sec-
he environment in with the main economic discussions.[10]
he dearth of discussion reflects the fact that the environ-
a high priority in the political opposition at the time. Even
o discuss the environment went unheeded.[11] A National
n Environmental Protection (*Krajowa Komisja Ochrony*
SZZ "S") had been set up within Solidarity at the end of
onth before the Congress, but it seems not to have accom-
efore the imposition of martial law cut off almost all social

ground Opposition and Its Press

ortly after martial law, ecology was not at all a priority of
pposition. Concerned with immediate repression, those
vists who had escaped internment established an under-
rk and press to inform society of repressive moves by the
d keep social resistance to the communist regime mobi-
erground press was filled with news of arrests and protests.
repression eased off, articles about union issues and oppo-
increased. Environmental degradation was not discussed,
t came into discussions of working conditions.[12] The role
round and its press had become maintaining Solidarity's
ong industrial workers, especially in large factories central
economy, and supporting cultural freedom and an alter-
of information and views among the broader society.
were useful and pursued toward these ends, but the oppo-
et out to affect the official policymaking process in partic-
s.

tem, and society itself. Yet, for the most part, the political opposition did
not choose to pick up this weapon.

Even though the political opposition supported the environmental
movement from the latter's inception, passive support rarely became
active engagement. The issue of ecology remained close to, but not at the
heart of, the opposition throughout the 1980s. Still, even marginal opposition interest in ecological issues served a politically useful role for the
environmental movement. When the Chernobyl accident brought the
environment into the core of opposition concerns—at least temporarily—
in the spring of 1986, the Jaruzelski-Messner government reacted swiftly
by making the environmental movement an early and clear target for
inclusion policies. The threat that the environment would become
another potent "opposition issue" was the final push that placed the issue
firmly on the government's own political agenda.

Environment Under the Solidarity Umbrella

From August 1980 on, the political opposition in Poland could be identified as Solidarity, more specifically its core network of leaders, advisers,
and activists. Solidarity's support for the environmental movement came
in part from conviction and in part from Solidarity's role as an umbrella
for almost all social movements during the 1980–81 period. It was under
this umbrella and backed by Solidarity strike support that the ecological
movement first formed.

The environmental movement began as a series of sporadic protests
and independent actions targeting local and regional problems. Hrynkiewicz identifies the beginning of the movement with June 1981 marches
against pollution of the Baltic Sea. These marches were organized by the
Union of Deep Water Fishermen, the League of the Sea, the Kashubian-
Pomorskian Association and other social organizations. Yet, these were
by no means the first public actions on behalf of the environment. Similar
marches and demonstrations had already protested the destruction of
Kraków's environment and monuments by neighboring industry
(Hrynkiewicz 1988, 26). The significance of the Baltic Sea protests lay in
the fact that they signaled the spread of ecological concerns and mani-
fested broader organizational efforts.

In addition to the sporadic actions and protests that began to draw
attention to environmental problems, the Solidarity period saw the organizational beginnings of the environmental movement. The first successful collective action by environmentalists was the protest in Kraków that

closed an aluminum smelter at the Skawina works. Although the Skawina controversy had begun before the formation of Solidarity,[3] public action to close the plant began only after the Polish Ecological Club was founded in September 1980. The formation of such a club, in turn, was possible only after Solidarity's founding strike and the government's acquiescence to the formation of independent groups and organizations. Contamination from Skawina became the issue on which the new ecological club started its public activism and through which it first became visible to the public. A memorandum to the Mayor of Kraków a few weeks after PKE's founding listed closing and completely renovating Skawina as the first requirement for controlling ecological damage to the city. Among the tactics employed were a law suit against the plant's management and local administrators on behalf of local residents and meetings with local authorities and the Minister of the Iron and Steel Industry.[4] In its efforts the PKE enjoyed the support of labor activists concerned with employee health and able to deliver a credible threat of strike action at major plants in the area.[5]

The formation of the Polish Ecological Club and its extension throughout the country constituted the first organizational expression of an independent environmental movement. Starting in Kraków and Warsaw, the club first organized as a circle of regionally based clubs. The number of these regional clubs increased and they eventually grew into the loose three-tiered national organization discussed in chapter 5. This network gave the movement a self-conscious identity as a social movement on the national level at an early point in its development. The club's first national congress, however, was not held until October 1983, after martial law restrictions had been lifted. The combination of popular pressure (marches), working-class action (demonstrations), and a mobilizing core of experts and activists, formalized as the Polish Ecological Club, signaled the potential for broad-based support and networking of a social movement. The marches in the Baltic area were a sign that environmentalism was not contained to the particular context of Kraków, that indeed there was a growing environmental movement.

Although the movement was just beginning to develop, an awareness of the concerns raised by ecologists penetrated to the leadership of a political opposition embroiled in debates over the nature of fundamental economic and political change. Solidarity's First National Congress, meeting in two sessions from September 5–10 and September 26–October 7, 1981, adopted a number of programmatic theses concerning the environment:

1. Assurance of a proper place for en and realization of economic ref

2. Establishment of an appropriately-s mental protection, the upkeep and its relegation to disposition b

3. Updating of legislation and impler ronmental protection so that, *in* able to execute them.

4. Assuring participation in the repre sentatives from social organizati mental protection.

5. Halting of production by firms w Particularly necessary are immec of projects for cleaning up water ment facilities for communal and

6. Introduction of mandatory publicat threats to the environment and s school programs on the topic of

In order to realize these tasks we propc

1. Initiating activism at the level of inter control of the functioning and ful of the observance of technologi enterprises.

2. Inspection of the state of the environn development of different types of e on environmental protection as we ing enterprises.

3. Formation of Union opinions and pos bills.[6]

As well-intentioned and inclusive a concerns never entered Solidarity's pr kiewicz 1988, 25–26). Even the mo drawn up for debate at the Congres 1981 documents, had failed to consic reform process.[7] The first point of th environmental protection in the disc from ecologists in the subgroup of th responsible for social policies.[8] Indec discussions throughout the Congress

Solidarity as Arena for Civil Society: Opposition Press Survey

Solidarity's role as the network that allowed civil society to flourish by maintaining a public sphere outside of official control centered around its perpetuation and distribution of an opposition press.[13] The Solidarity network was also linked to the Catholic church, especially to certain parishes, which provided space for independent interaction in civil society. In this role, the political opposition facilitated activity and discourse far beyond its own activism to escape government control. Although ecology remained outside the core interests of the political opposition at least until the Chernobyl accident, the environmental movement was a beneficiary of the more general role of the opposition press.

By the mid-1980s the underground press was facilitating communication among environmental activists and, especially, between activists and the rest of society in several ways. First, it reported unofficial demonstrations, petitions, and other actions, as well as any official repression of groups and individuals. Second, the regular serial section of the opposition press (weekly and biweekly newspapers) provided an alternative source of information about both policy issues and actual conditions in the country. Meanwhile the more irregular publication of longer works, in particular the series of "notebooks" for alternative education, provided a third avenue through which activists in various sectors of society, including ecologists, could take up more complicated problems and present lengthier studies. Fourth, the underground press reached a large proportion of the society through informal circulation among readers, and it surely reached those more inclined toward activism.[14] Thus, environmentalists were able to reach a potential source of increased support for and participation in the movement. Finally, the press facilities of the underground were used by some environmental groups to print their own bulletins, leaflets, newsletters, and founding documents.

Having noted the number of ways in which the opposition press supported the environmental movement, it is instructive to return to a review of that press for what it reveals about the political opposition's own activism on behalf of the environment. Neither the underground press nor other underground activity showed much involvement in environmentalism from the beginning of martial law to the end of 1983. The few short articles or news briefs that did mention environmental concerns during this period focused on the "union issues" of working conditions or mismanagement of firms, especially of the heavy industry firms where Solidarity membership was the strongest.[15] At the end of the year the opposition Committee for Social Resistance (KOS) put out a two-page special on environmental contamination in its regular newsletter.[16] This special was written by and announced a Social Committee for Environmental Protection which had been set up under Solidarity's Temporary Coordinating Commission ten months earlier. The article was largely a copy of the committee's founding declaration, dated June 1983. It is likely that the publication of a two-part series on the environment in *Życie Gospodarcze*, an official weekly written primarily for managers and bureaucrats, prompted the announcement of this committee. This series was the first general, critical discussion of the environment in the official press after the imposition of martial law.[17] Most of the committee's efforts from that time on went into gathering and selecting information for publication in the opposition press.

During 1984, occasional articles on the environment began appearing in the underground press. These articles, moreover, started to go beyond working conditions and other "union issues" to discuss general ecological and health concerns.[18] Besides more general articles, the underground also stepped up its publication of short notices and bulletins. Many of these notices focused on specific factories or episodes based on information garnered by workers, while some also reported new data on ecological destruction at the regional or national level.[19] Although the opposition press coverage of the environment remained sparse, ecology seems to have become a topic in its own right in the eyes of opposition intellectuals by the end of 1984.

Throughout 1985, coverage of the environment was picking up in the underground press, as it was in the official press. A public controversy over the degree of degradation facing Poland's natural environment erupted in August of that year.[20] This controversy spurred both government and opposition media to devote more attention to ecology. Another main contributing factor to increased underground press coverage of environmental issues was the formation of the radical anti-militarist group Freedom and Peace and the rather rapid extension of its activism into the area of ecology. This ecological emphasis developed primarily through the conduit of anti-nuclear activism but quickly became a part of the overall philosophy and identity of the Freedom and Peace movement. What first attracted the opposition press was the group's radical tactics— e.g. draft resistance and hunger strikes—and the subsequent repression meted out by the authorities. Still, until the Chernobyl accident, the environment was not a central opposition issue. The opposition press tended to parallel official press coverage of environmental topics, relaying more critical information and interpretations but not taking the initiative in pressing ecological concerns. One example of this type of coverage was an article in *Tygodnik Mazowsze* at the beginning of 1985. The article merely cited official but unpublished statistics on environmental destruction.[21]

Information about environmental hazards, once in the public domain, spurred both demand for more coverage of these issues and the willingness of the underground press to pursue them. This dynamic was particularly visible with the publication of an internal communist party report as a "*zeszyt*," or notebook, in the underground press in March 1986. This report on ecological threats, discussed at greater length in the next chapter, was originally commissioned and written in an institute associated with the party Central Committee's Academy of Social Sciences. Published in a very small edition, it reappeared in the underground press as part of the Notebooks on Independent Medical Thought series.[22] Strong popular interest in this report was followed by increased coverage of environmental issues in the opposition press. The specialized underground press had, in effect, spurred greater coverage of the issue in the general underground press.

That the core of the opposition was sympathetic to the concerns of the environmental movement yet unwilling to engage in it actively is visible in the fate of a call to form opposition environmental bodies advanced by opposition leaders Tadeusz Jedynak, Adam Michnik and Jacek Kuroń. Appearing first in February 1985, this proposal called for the formation of "Independent Committees to Protect the Environment."[23] Their original appeal focused on Silesia, the most heavily degraded region in Poland, and called on workers, scholars and anyone else in a position to monitor and reduce ecological degradation to do so wherever possible. These groups were never formed, however, and the issue was dropped, to be remembered only once the Chernobyl accident had riveted public attention on the environment.

Chernobyl: The Opposition Engages

The explosion and fire at the Chernobyl nuclear energy plant on April 26, 1986 spurred the political opposition, at least temporarily, into environmental activism.

Poland had a small nuclear energy program of its own which, until Chernobyl, had never become a national political issue. Action against the development of nuclear energy and storage of radioactive waste remained the province of environmental groups—official, independent, and opposition. Even some environmentalists favored the development of nuclear energy, seeing it as the only way to reduce the country's extraordinary dependence on high-sulfur coal for most of its energy needs.[24] The core of the political opposition remained in the background of this debate. Chernobyl, however, brought the nuclear issue home to all Poles. Immediate opposition activism involved bulletins in the underground press, protest actions, and the creation of two new opposition environmental groups: an Independent Ecological Commission in Lublin (May 2) and a Working Group for Protection of the Environment in Wrocław (May 9), the latter born in the organization of a major demonstration against nuclear energy and the government's information policy regarding the Chernobyl accident.[25] The Międzyrzecz protests raised the nuclear issue in Poland soon after Chernobyl.

The underground press rose to the occasion when the Chernobyl reactor caught fire, the editors taking upon themselves the tasks of collecting information from scientists, from abroad, and from officials to warn and advise the population. Both underground publications and Solidarity leaders at the national and regional levels issued immediate bulletins.[26] Several publications put out lengthy special editions, explaining radiation and the effects of certain exposures on human health, as well as the course of the accident itself.[27] Activist networks' contacts with groups and individuals in other countries, especially in Lithuania, Belarus, and Ukraine, became the main conduit for information about conditions closer to the accident. The Western press was quoted extensively. (Unfortunately, this meant that some of the exaggerations and wild speculation going on in the West were also transmitted to an already panicked population.) True to its role as maintaining an arena for independent thought and action in Polish society, the opposition mobilized its resources to meet the crisis by filling in as best it could the information gaps left by the Polish and Soviet governments. Besides publishing warnings and organizing protests, there was little else the opposition, or for that matter the government, could do to protect society from the clouds that had already passed over. After the fire had been put out, the only thing left for the opposition to do was to monitor foodstuffs and try to assess the consequences of the accident.

Even its activism surrounding the Chernobyl crisis, however, belied the opposition's primary concerns. Shortly after the accident, the Temporary Coordinating Commission, the executive council of underground Solidarity, issued the following communique:

> . . . for production indicators all residents of Poland pay with their health.
> People are systematically poisoned at work, on the street, in their place of
> residence, and on vacation. The [nuclear] power plant currently being built

in Żarnowiec is based on Soviet technology. We do not know what security measures have been adopted and whether or not we are threatened by a catastrophe of inestimable consequences.

The tragic ecological situation in Poland is the consequence of the doctrinaire forced development of heavy and raw material industries. Also from doctrine come the authorities' attempts to liquidate all independent social organizations and to assure themselves a monopoly over information. Improvement can result only from fundamental changes in the political and economic system. Only organized pressure and social activism, expressed in the creation of independent institutions, will be able to force the authorities to call off the current politics.[28]

From this section of the communique it is apparent that opposition leaders had ruled out any hope of improving environmental protection within the existing system. Ecology, just two weeks after a major disaster, had become another reason to overthrow the communist system, but not a specific sphere of activism to achieve immediate change in existing policies that threatened the health of the population.

Opposition Ecological Groups

The Solidarity political opposition became engaged in direct environmental activism only after Chernobyl and then primarily around that issue and government handling of it. Yet, the opposition continued to support the activities of ecologists. The primary avenue of its support was access to underground printing and distribution facilities, as well as the reporting in the opposition press of unofficial activities and repression of environmental activists. A few new ecological groups took advantage of this role of the opposition press as civil society's communication network. In the political terms of the day, these groups must be considered oppositional, primarily because their actions were considered illegal by the regime.

The most visible of the opposition ecological groups was Freedom and Peace. Its ecological activism, focusing above all on opposition to nuclear energy, really began with protests against the government's inadequate response to Chernobyl and the regime's determination to continue developing Poland's own nuclear program. The first target of persistent activism against this program was the plan to bury radioactive waste in the Międzyrzecz bunkers. Residents of that area first took to the streets in the spring of 1986, shortly after the Chernobyl explosion. Freedom and Peace joined the protests and led a continuing campaign from the summer of 1987 until the decision was rescinded in 1988. By that time the group's environmental activism had expanded into other geographic and issue areas.

Most other opposition ecological groups were territorially defined. This basis for self-definition was logical, considering the type of mobilization necessary for opposition activity in a centralized authoritarian political system. Mobilization and activism took place largely through face-to-face communication and centered on the most acute ecological problems in the immediate area. The regional scope of these ecological groups corresponded not only to geographically delineated environments and economic activity, but also to Solidarity's regional underground networks, which were especially important in the writing, printing and distribution of the opposition press.

Among the small groups co-sponsored by various opposition networks or enjoying a close relationship with the opposition were the Great Poland Ecological Seminar, Ecology and Peace, the Gdańsk Ecological Program, the Silesian Ecological Movement and the Citizen's Committee for the Environmental Protection of Jelenia Góra Valley. Most of these groups were established between late 1986 and the Round-Table talks. The Great Poland Ecological Seminar was one of the first of these territorially based opposition groups. It tapped opposition networks associated with "Rural Solidarity" and with more oppositional parishes in that region. Its bulletin was published with the help of these networks and Freedom and Peace.[29]

Another opposition group, the Silesian Ecological Movement, was very closely linked to both Freedom and Peace and the Silesian region of the Solidarity underground. Founded in February 1988 at the First Independent Ecological Seminar bearing the title "How to Save Silesia," this movement declared its intent to engage in direct action, such as occupations and blockades, as well as protests, demonstrations, leafleting and petitioning (Gliński 1989, 46). The group Ecology and Peace was formed when more radical activists split from the Polish Ecological Club. Like the other opposition ecological groups, Ecology and Peace maintained close relations with Freedom and Peace and the Solidarity underground. After the fall of the Messner government in September 1988, this group transformed itself into an alternative political party called the "Federation of Greens." Other groups in such cities as Gdańsk and Jelenia Góra also enjoyed close relationships with their region's Solidarity activists and the activist parishes in their cities (e.g. the Free Ecological Movement's connection with St. Brigid's in Głogów).

Before the 1988 strikes began, the environment had become a widely discussed issue in both the official and underground press. The official press, in fact, had become so critical of environmental destruction that the main differences in coverage were only a matter of degree. Both sets of articles were bleak. Many of the articles in the official press, however, looked for more solutions within the framework of the socialist system, whereas articles in the opposition press stated or implied that nothing short of overhauling the socialist system would resolve the problem at hand. This difference in tone was also reflected to some extent in a difference in data used, though neither of these differences should be overstated. Although opposition data was generally more critical, both venues of publication showed wide internal variations in data used. In part, this was unavoidable given the sparse and unreliable nature of environmental data collected in the country.[30]

To the Round-Table

After the post-Chernobyl spate of action, the political opposition settled into a posture more supportive of independent and especially opposition environmental groups. Environmental destruction became a frequent topic of even general underground publications. Yet, the core of opposition concerns remained control over economic and political life of the country. It was over economic issues that the 1988 strikes started. However, the strikes mobilized a much broader cross-section of society into political opposition. These other segments of society had maintained or gained an alternative consciousness to that proffered by the regime through the underground press and independent activism, as well as through the memory of the 1980–81 period.

Following the demise of the Messner government, the new government agreed to meet with Solidarity to negotiate a way out of the economic and political stagnation of the 1980s. Independent activism flourished. Many groups were formed; nascent political parties sprang up; old political parties, submissive until then, began to challenge the policies and dominance of the communist party; even the official trade unions began to stake out an independent political stance. Environmentalism received an added impetus when the new Prime Minister, Mieczysław Rakowski, made environmental protection one of his administrations three "economic priorities" (Panek 1988, 5). The five-month period between the fall of the Messner government and the beginning of the Round-Table talks saw the creation of three small "ecology parties," a new independent bulletin (*Serwis Ochrony Środowiska, or SOS*), and an increase in protests and demonstrations.[31]

By the time the Round-Table talks began, government recognition of environmental problems had reached the point that Solidarity and government negotiators came to an agreement rather quickly on all issues with the exception of a non-negotiable difference in their positions concerning nuclear energy. Facilitating negotiation was the fact that most experts for the two sides were drawn from the independent ecological movement, notably from the Polish Ecological Club. The influence of the movement was also visible in the fifth section of the agreement, which consisted of a list of problems for immediate intervention, most of which were key demands of various regional or local ecological groups *(Protokoł Podzespołu . . . * 1989, section 5). On the point of nuclear energy they simply wrote a statement of difference ("Protokoł Rozbieżności" 1989). With this statement the opposition and government representatives at the sub-table for ecology completed their deliberations almost a month before the Round-Table talks themselves came to an end.[32]

Conclusion

Aside from that part of the opposition directly involved (opposition ecological groups formed from 1985 on), the core of the political opposition supported but was not the driving force behind the development of the environmental movement. Moreover, the opposition tended to use environmental arguments for the political purpose of raising social support for its anti-regime stance and activism. Self-interested though this tendency was, the political opposition served as a crucial foil for the independent environmental movement. The mere existence of opposition interest in ecological issues drew official attention. More significant for the development of official policy toward the movement, the threat of opposition engagement in environmentalism prompted the government to compete for control over the issue. To do so meant becoming engaged itself. At the very least, official engagement entailed opening a public dialogue on the problems facing Poland's ecology. It also meant tolerating the independent movement while trying to woo it. Independent collective action on behalf of the environment had succeeded in placing ecological concerns on the public agenda and this recognition of their goals encouraged environmental groups further. The relatively low level of government repression of environmental activists and the government's public professions of support for environmentalism, in turn, allowed the independent movement to grow stronger as public awareness rose.

7

Official Environmentalism: The Failure of Normalization

The official environmentalism of the second half of the eighties was a new phenomenon in Poland, begun in response to growing unofficial environmentalism. What existed before the 1980–81 Solidarity period was the traditional administration of the economy, public lands, and public waterways to the ends of economic development alongside conservation of parks and other designated wild areas. In these tasks the government was supported by a handful of officially controlled social organizations, such as the League for the Protection of Nature, the Nature Protection Guards, and the tourism and recreation association (PTTK). However, the fragmented nature of environmental administration assured its subordination to economic and development interests in the Council of Ministers and the party's Political Bureau.[1] Recommendations on the protection of nature by advisory bodies within the government and party structures were generally nonbinding.[2] Moreover, press articles and books on the environment were censored. Thus, no fundamental questioning of Poland's development pattern and priorities as they related to ecology came to light in public discussion until the entire system of government and economy became the topic of a raging debate that caught up the whole country in 1980–81.

Several factors contributed to the lack of public discussion about environmental degradation. In the 1970s, censorship laws prohibited discussion of serious environmental hazards; particularly forbidden was the mention of the effects of environmental degradation on human health.

According to documents smuggled out of the country by a worker in the censor's office,

> Information on direct threats to life or health caused by industry or chemical agents used in agriculture, or threats to the natural environment in Poland should be eliminated from works on environmental protection. This prohibition applies to specific examples of air, water and soil pollution and impurities in food that are an endangerment to life or health (Curry 1984, 212).

These documents contain examples of specific events and problems not to be discussed as well as crucial parts of texts deleted from articles in the mass circulation press and from a book on the environment.[3] The second reason for silence was a low level of environmental consciousness in the society as a whole. This lack of awareness, of course, is tied to but cannot be blamed wholly on censorship. An ideology trumpeting the technical ability of human beings to conquer nature and society's preoccupation with consumption also come into play.

The communist development ideology with its emphasis on conquering nature and the lack of ecological awareness on the part of party and government officials was reflected in society's complacency as well. According to a July 1975 public opinion survey, at a time when environmental movements were springing up in the West, the Polish population was relatively satisfied with the state of the environment. Of a representative sample of the population, 77% positively evaluated the amount of greenery, 75% evaluated air quality positively, and 74% were of the opinion that the noise level was satisfactory. The only negative result came in evaluation of water quality in neighboring reservoirs or lakes: only one third of those respondents living in proximity to a reservoir or lake considered water quality satisfactory. A full 47% of those surveyed thought that Poland was doing much or very much to protect the environment at that time, while 36% thought little or very little was being done. Given the high and increasing levels of air and water pollution at the time (see the discussion in chapter 2) and the lack of any serious attempt to control them, the number of positive evaluations (47%) is surprising. Moreover, 57% of all respondents expressed the view that new technology would resolve the conflict between development and environment, while another 7% saw no conflict at all. Only 23% were skeptical about the fate of the environment. Authors of the study noticed that respondents critical of the state of Poland's environment lived in cities or industrial areas rather than in villages, tended to be better educated, and were more often women. Contrary to expectations, critical views did *not* correlate to age.[4] Still, the overall picture emerging from the study, three years after the Club of Rome published *The Limits to Growth* and during the rise of environmentalism in the West and in international organizations, is of a nation unaware of ecological hazards and placing faith in development and technology.

The debates and social protest of 1980–81 and the environmental movement arising out of this period challenged both Poland's development policies and its administrative structure. Official groups became more active, but the impetus of environmentalism remained outside the official sphere (see the discussion of the environmental movement in chapters 4 and 5). It was as a normalization policy after the imposition of martial law that the government became engaged on the issue of environmental protection.

Normalization: Conceptual Problems and a Model

The term "normalization" was coined by participants in the process itself: political authorities in the Soviet Union, Hungary, Czechoslovakia, and Poland. It is a specific type of a broader phenomenon: the reimposition of an authoritarian regime. Jiri Valenta traces this use of the term normalization to the Russian word *normalizatsiia* which he claims "describes the complex policies developed and fostered by the Soviets, under specific national conditions and over a long period spanning a decade or more, to partly or fully reverse revolutionary change in a given eastern European country" (Valenta 1984, 128). From these roots "normalization" has a teleological element that both introduces semantic contradictions over the meaning of "normal" and fails to clarify the limits of the process it labels. Moreover, the term itself becomes a linguistic tool for reimposing the Soviet-type system on a population that has rejected it. Normalization was to be a process that returned "the situation" to "normal" as defined by Soviet leaders. There are a number of problems with this usage. First, "normal" is not usually a quality attributed by those studying comparative politics to Soviet-type systems. Political processes in these systems are more likely to be considered unique. Use of the term "normalization" in the West, moreover, is likely to mean bringing unique systems more in line with others or the Western "norms"—in other words, something quite different from restoring and buttressing a Soviet-type system. Use of the term in the East implies that those living under Soviet-type systems should accept that condition as normal, a premise that has already been rejected in any "normalizing" country, as evidenced by the dissent that brought the regime to the point of imposing normalization policies.[5]

The second confusion wrought by this term is the implication that returning to "normal" is returning to the *status quo ante*. This implication is confirmed by normalizing authorities' use of terms like "deviation" and "abnormal" to describe behavior during the period of reform, change, or crisis preceding normalization policies. Yet, these "abnormalities" were usually explicable social responses provoked by features of the *status quo ante*. Return to the *status quo ante*, therefore, would not "normalize the situation" since the potential would remain for recurrence of disruption. On the other hand, if normalization changes those elements of the *status quo ante* which provoke dissent and disruption, then the use of that term tends to brush over the significance of these changes.

A third problem arises with periodization. When can a country be considered normalized? Most scholars studying these processes consider them to be fairly long-term, a decade or more (cf. Valenta 1984; Gitelman 1981; Brus, Kende and Mlynar 1982). At least one author sees normalization as the shorter process of restoration of order, principally the restoration of Soviet control over East European governments (Hutchings 1983, 47–52). The problem with this approach is that stable domestic polities are necessary for a full restoration of Soviet control over the bloc. The instability of these polities is reflected in the fact that conditions in these countries after the initial military interventions were not "normal" by the standards of post-Stalinist Soviet-type systems. Parties were weak and in turmoil; extraordinary controls remained on all public interactions; there were purges and verification campaigns in the workplace; and military might was more visible than during "normal times." It seems reasonable to mark the end of normalization at the point where politics and the economy are stable without extraordinary measures, the primary goal of the normalization process. If accurate studies of public opinion were available, achievement of the other main goal of normalization—the populace's abandonment of all hope that reform efforts from below can bring change—would also help to mark the end of the process. Here the best secondary indicator is the lack of widespread societal support for political opposition, though the dearth of opposition could signify strong repression rather than resignation.

Despite all of these problems with the term normalization, it is used in this study for the primary reason that it was used consciously by Polish authorities in designing and describing the policies they implemented from the beginning of martial law to the late 1980s.[6] The goals of normalization also affected the authorities' perceptions of what was permissible on the part of society. The three basic foundations of Soviet-type systems in satellite countries were: (1) guarantee of the leading role of the (Marxist-Leninist) communist party, (2) state ownership of the means of production and a functioning centrally planned economy, and (3) the acceptance of Soviet hegemony. In the literature on Eastern Europe and the Soviet Union, "normalization" therefore means the return to a functioning post-Stalinist system with a centrally administered economy and polity which guarantee the leading role of the communist party and Soviet hegemony. How much leeway there is for reform of the *status quo ante* within these guidelines is the essential question involved in the debates about the meaning of "normalization."

The most comprehensive model of post-crisis normalization in East European countries was developed by Włodzimerz Brus, Pierre Kende, and Zdenek Mlynar and summarized in chapter 1 of this study. According to this model, normalization has three phases, each with essential tasks to be performed despite variations among individual countries. The first stage is irrevocable crushing of what Soviet leaders deem to be the cause of the crisis. All social initiatives and reform activity are blocked and the country "is plunged . . . into conditions visibly worse than the those against which it has revolted." During the second phase the population is atomized and any remaining social institutions of suspect character are dismantled. This stage is not complete until people have given up hope of bringing about any changes, recognized defeat as irreversible, and accepted the official stance that change, if it is to come, will come through official channels. The third stage is the differentiated linking of economic rewards to political obedience based on acknowledgement that all change or "improvements come 'from above,' that none of the pillars of the Soviet-type system is jeopardized, and that Soviet hegemony is secured . . ." (Mlynar 1982, citations pp. 3 and 4 respectively). It is at the end of this third stage, i.e., once the regime's control of the polity, economy and society is firmly established, that the government can begin to offer general concessions in the form of consumer goods and reforms of certain practices or features of the economic or political systems. Small, partial reforms are to bring the country to the point of being fully "normalized" in that they remove the impetus for dissent, rather than simply imposing conditions where dissent is impossible.

The course of the ecological movement in martial law and post-martial law Poland demonstrates the failure of policies designed to bring about political normalization. The Polish case not only deviated from the pattern set by previous East European normalization processes; in some ways it actually violated the very logic of the normalization process. Even allowing for a fair amount of reform within the rubric of normalization, the Polish party-state never "normalized" the polity since the measures required to reform the economy threatened the leading role of the party and eventually toppled it from power. In this failure of normalization are the beginnings of the current systemic changes.

Normalization in Polish Environmental Politics

The general tasks associated with the three stages of normalization were complicated by specific features of the Polish case. Foremost among them were the immediate development of a strong underground opposition, the need to diffuse a high level of mobilization in a variety of directions and most sectors of society, a delegitimizing legacy of failed reforms, and severe economic crisis.

The Tasks of Normalization in Poland

The Jaruzelski government could not demobilize and atomize society by repression alone, since high levels of general repression strengthened solidarity in the underground and social support for it. Beyond the immediate crackdown, the government's normalization policies had to target three separate spheres of social life not directly under the control of state institutions, breaking the links among them: (1) the private domain, individuals not engaged in nonofficial public activities; (2) those engaged in political opposition; and (3) those publicly active in independent groups, movements, or organizations, including the Roman Catholic Church, which were neither officially controlled nor part of the opposition. One can visualize these policies as the government trying to keep three spheres of society separated (diagram 7.1). Thus, normalization, through control over the media, state institutions, the economy, and the part of society supportive of the government, had to prevent those not publicly active from becoming so outside of official channels. Another task was to keep those who were independently active from becoming part of the political opposition. The primary means by which the government sought to isolate independent groups and movements from the opposition were cooptation and incorporation. Meanwhile, change from above, atomization of society, propaganda, and repression targeted at specific points of opposition were to reduce both the independent and opposition public spheres.

These sociopolitical tasks were complicated by the dire need to rejuvenate and reform the economy. In the economic sphere alone, the government faced contradictory demands. While systematic reforms, designed to overcome economic crisis in the long run, could be instituted, they would be disruptive to recovery in the short run. Moreover, the hardships

Diagram 7.1 *Spheres of Societal Mobilization*

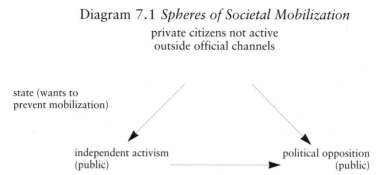

imposed by systemic reform would fuel opposition to the regime and further corrode the ability of the authorities to use economic rewards in order to buy political cooperation. The need to boost economic performance also served as an official justification for postponing both comprehensive and specific measures to reduce ecological degradation. These economic limitations on policies to achieve political normalization forced the government to focus on legal, institutional, and propagandistic measures to reduce nonofficial public activism.[7]

Part of the normalization process was to prevent the development of political issues that could mobilize the inactive parts of society into opposition. The environment was one such issue. It was made a political issue by independently active ecologists and by the increasingly obvious problems affecting the quality of life. In order to keep it from becoming an opposition issue, the government had to become engaged itself or repress the issue completely. Environmental politics went through the government's three main phases of normalization policies from the imposition of martial law to the 1989 elections: repression and restoration of socialist order, preemption, and inclusion. (See diagram 7.2 at the end of this section for a summary of these phases.) These policies were conducted in the press, legislation and administration. Ultimately, they failed. The environmental movement became one of the independent social forces sustaining the pressure for political change.

Phase I: Repression and the Restoration of Order

With the introduction of martial law on December 13, 1981 all unofficial groups and activity were suspended. Most of these groups were then disbanded through a combination of delegalization, repression, and tight administrative control over the venues and materials needed for their activity. Fledgling environmental initiatives, for example the 1981 "Green

Movement" in Warsaw were also disbanded or not allowed to re-register after martial law. The Polish Ecological Club was suspended, but it was one of the few independent social organizations not completely disbanded or outlawed.

Poland's first point of deviation from the established pattern of normalization was the survival of hope and social initiative after the original crackdown. Solidarity members set up a large, well-organized underground with strong social support. In the case of environmental politics, the main sign was the survival of the Polish Ecological Club, especially in its Kraków home base. When asked how the PKE survived martial law, its president Stanisław Juchnowicz replied that it remained quiet and local.[8] The club had supporters both in the Kraków municipal government and in local Church circles. Long-term environmentalists remained engaged and formed a strong core of the association. As far as political will was concerned, the club enjoyed the enthusiasm of many former Solidarity activists who saw in environmentalism a relatively secure channel for the social energy awakened during the Solidarity period.[9]

Even before the end of martial law in July 1983, environmental activism began to stir in Kraków. The clerical movement REFA—at that time little more than a single group of seminary students and priests—prepared a major ecological exhibit for Pope John Paul II's second visit to Poland. (The Pope's visit signaled the coming end to martial law and symbolized the regime's readiness to make peace with society, albeit on the government's terms.) The ecological exhibit went on to other churches in Poland. Meanwhile, the Polish Ecological Club began preparations for its first General Congress to take place in October of the same year. The purpose of the Congress was to take stock of the PKE's new situation and decide on its goals and course of action in post-martial law Poland. The major political outcome of the Congress was the club's distancing itself from the opposition in favor of a clearly "independent" status. Since this decision was made early, before many of the groups in the movement had formed, it had the effect of placing the movement as a whole firmly in the independent sphere, despite the variance in political leanings of groups which developed later.

Phase II: Preemptive Strategy

Having failed to accomplish full demobilization of social resistance during martial law, the Polish government approached the deactivation of remaining social initiative with a preemptive strategy. On the general level this strategy was exemplified by the creation of a number of institutions for channeling social initiative and gauging discontent. The main channel for public action became PRON, The Patriotic Movement for National Rebirth, which was a front of social organizations supportive of government policy. These were the organizations funded and supported in other ways by the government and, in turn, they often served as transmission belts of official policy. Among the new organizations were new trade unions designed to replace the ones Solidarity had rejected and to pull in rank and file workers, many of whom had joined Solidarity in 1980–81. Preemption, therefore, sought to dissolve the independent sphere of social activity, thereby isolating the opposition. At the same time channeling and controlling social initiative would atomize the general society by breaking up autonomous links among its members.

Once martial law was lifted environmental activism mounted. When environmentalism began to increase again in 1983 and 1984, the preemptive strategy appeared as attempts to "clean up" citizen action in various regions by channeling it through official organizations. A few examples of such channeling are: the creation of the Society for the Protection of the Tatras (TOT) by local authorities in Zakopane to supersede a suspended citizen action group; the adoption of the "Green Lungs of Poland" project; and PRON's takeover of a local initiative in the Mazurian lake district.[10] That leading government officials were conscious of the potential power of this issue was further confirmed at a 1983 meeting with social scientists, where Rakowski, then deputy prime minister, mentioned the political danger for the government should the opposition take up this issue.[11]

Two new institutions for gauging social discontent were the Institute for the Study of the Working Class under the Central Committee's Academy of Social Sciences and the Center for the Study of Societal Opinion (CBOS). Created after the imposition of martial law, these institutions were to identify potential problem areas where policy change might prevent social upheaval.[12] The Center for the Study of Societal Opinion carried out several interesting studies. Some were unpublished and used by the government to gain information about potential political problems. Others (or parts of them) were used to show society that there was support for government policies. However, little heed was paid in the broader public to claims based on these reports due to widespread distrust of government sampling techniques, wording, and interpretation of results.

The Institute for the Study of the Working Class produced a series of seven in-depth studies on problems facing workers. Environmental degradation was the topic of one of these studies. This Central Committee report requires more thorough consideration both because it was a key

part of the 1985–86 turning point in the development of the environmental movement and because it demonstrates how the normalization
process tended to backfire. The report was published by the Central
Committee in April 1985. Meant for limited circulation, it was very critical, even alarming. One of its introductory paragraphs summarizes the
overall findings this way:

> . . . industrial activity in our country brings about highly dangerous con-
> sequences in the form of poisoning the environment. Workers are poisoned
> in their place of residence along with all other citizens. One could say that
> this is the single area in which the process of class levelling has been most
> advanced (Wójcik, ed. 1985, 3)

Far from providing information for preemptive policy, this report caused
a furor that raised social awareness of environmental problems even
higher and pushed the authorities into the position of having to recognize
the problems publicly. The Western media published articles on the
report, and Radio Free Europe broadcast the introduction and a five-part
summary of the entire text.[13] If Polish citizens did not listen to the broadcasts or have access to the foreign press, either directly or through
Poland's underground press, they noticed government spokesperson Jerzy
Urban deny the seriousness of Poland's ecological situation when he was
confronted with the report's results by foreign correspondents.[14] Then
they saw a series of articles and interviews in the press confirming the
report's findings. Roundly criticized by the Minister for Environmental
Protection (Jarzębski 1986), the report's evidence and conclusions were
shocking to a public that had not heard much about environmental
degradation. Increasing awareness was reflected in the fact that citizens
raised many questions about local and national environmental issues during campaign meetings with candidates for the parliament that fall, which
started within a month of this controversy.[15]

This report not only spurred public concern and the growth of
the environmental movement; it also helped to place the environment on
the agenda of the political elite, most notably that of General Jaruzelski
himself. Four of the institute's reports, including the environmental report,
were finally discussed at a Political Bureau meeting in Spring 1987, two
years after the report on ecology had been published. The institite directors were invited to the Political Bureau to answer questions. During the
meeting, party officials tore into the reports and attacked the institite. The
debate became very heated and the directors were not being allowed to
answer fully. Finally, Jaruzelski had to remind his colleagues that "gentle-
men do not debate facts," that the professors were professionals and
should be listened to, and that it was better for "a few of us to have heart

attacks than for Poland to have one." Any objections to the contents of the reports should be submitted in writing to the authors.[16] After that meeting, Jaruzelski ordered that a summary of each of the reports in this series be written and circulated to all party first secretaries at the *województwo* level and to members of the Presidium of the Council of Ministers.[17]

This episode shows that those authorizing the report and choosing the authors were trying to do at least three things at once. First, as commissioned, they were trying to collect true information for policies that would preempt social protest by addressing key issues, even if these problems could not be fully resolved. The second intention from above was to coopt these experts into the advisory process. The third goal came from below: on this count, the report was a classic case of those inside the party structure trying to influence the priorities and policies of the top. In this case, choice of topics and authors gave the institute directors power to influence policy.

The report and its reception also show the pivotal role of the intelligentsia which, as a community, pulls together people staffing the government, universities and advisory commissions of the opposition to exchange ideas. Of the seven contributors, Stefan Kozłowski, who had been active in high level advisory commissions for over a decade, became a senator during the political transition and headed the new parliament's commission on the environment, before moving over to the post of Minister for Environmental Protection, Natural Resources, and Forestry. Another author, Iwona Jacyna, was one of the first journalists to start writing critical articles on this topic in the official press. One contributor, Roman Andrzejewski, became Vice-Minister for the Protection of the Environment and Natural Resources under the first Solidarity-led government. Another, Andrzej Walewski, was appointed Chief Environmental Inspector in the first Solidarity government. Two of these people were members of the Polish Ecological Club, and at least two other ecological groups could claim one of the contributors as a member. Thus, a report commissioned by an official party institute was written by a team of scholar-activists whose political identities spanned the entire spectrum from opposition to official. The text of the report reveals the influence of perspectives very critical of the regime and the use to which the report was put suggests that the exchange of views among intellectuals from various milieux was an avenue by which alternative views reached the political center.

The preemptive phase of normalization also saw changes in environmental administration and legislation. In the administrative reorganization that followed martial law, responsibility for the environment was separated from its subordinate position under the ministry for territorial administration and given its own central office.[18] The Sejm raised the

Office of Environmental Protection and Water Economy to the Ministry of Environmental Protection and Natural Resources in November 1985 (effective January 1986).[19] This change was largely symbolic as the new ministry did not gain more power over industrial and mining ministries. Still, the upgrading of the office symbolized a willingness on the part of the government to hear environmental concerns voiced and a recognition that environmental problems should be tackled.

Politically, the preemptive policy was not effective either on the general level or with regard to the environmental movement. This is visible in the rapid growth of social initiatives, including the environmental movement, and in the move to a more permissive normalization policy of inclusion. Beyond politics, there was no noticeable improvement in the state of the environment. Fines for exceeding emissions norms were raised repeatedly during the 1980s, but the high costs of compliance and spotty enforce-. ment of such legislation negated any positive effect higher fines might have had.

Phase III: Inclusion

The year 1986 saw the government's move to normalization through inclusion.[20] Inclusion policies embraced the independent sphere and tried to pull some more moderate parts of the opposition into official public life. The only part of society excluded would be the most radical elements of the political opposition. Presumably, exclusion would isolate these elements from having relevance for public life and eventually reduce them to an insignificant fringe. For the environmental movement inclusion meant General Jaruzelski's sanctioning of the environment as an issue of concern in his speech at the Tenth Congress of the communist party (June 1986), the creation of an official ecological movement (September 1986), and the appointment of an ecologist to the Social Consultative Council (December 1986).

The real landmark of the general inclusion effort was the creation of the Social Consultative Council to the President of the Council of State in 1986 (Kolankiewicz 1988, 152). This council was a policy advisory committee meeting directly with General Jaruzelski, then head of state and communist party First Secretary. In an approach that could be considered corporatist, the government formed the Social Consultative Council by soliciting representatives from the Roman Catholic Church and the Solidarity opposition to join representatives of the party in discussing major policy decisions. Since the overwhelming majority of the Polish population identifies itself as Catholic, the Church was seen as a voice for both the private and independent public spheres. One intention behind the council was to get alternative perspectives on key issues. The main purpose of the council, however, was to obtain the adherence to major policy initiatives of those sectors of society that considered the Episcopate and some Solidarity leaders to be legitimate representatives of their interests. The Episcopate sent representatives, including an ecologist, but the opposition split over whether to participate. Although most leading opposition figures declined to participate, others did represent the opposition sphere on the council. Seen as merely the sounding board it was, the council never lent policy the legitimacy and social cooperation the government sought. It did, however, increase the variety of voices heard in the upper echelons of government and in the official press, since transcripts of the meetings were published.

This new approach to building a rapprochement with society strong enough to withstand the trials of economic reform came out of the Tenth Party Congress of Polish United Workers' Party in June 1986. Not only were the speeches of key leaders conciliatory, but the government also announced an amnesty of political prisoners and the creation of the Consultative Council shortly after the congress. The rapprochement included environmental concerns. During his address to the congress on behalf of the Central Committee, General Jaruzelski stressed the need for environmental protection as one of the six most pressing problems affecting the quality of life in Poland.[21] Since parts of the press had covered environmental problems off and on and from differing angles for almost a year, Jaruzelski's sanctioning of the issue was not a sudden policy change. Rather, it enunciated the government's position, clearing the way for less adventurous newspaper editors, television directors, and public officials to deal with environmental topics. The previous year had been confusing with growing popular concern, Chernobyl, and no clear official line on either the issues or press coverage of them.

Three months after the party congress, PRON, the official social front, created its own "Social Ecological Movement" (ERS) in an attempt to put "a head" on the many and varied initiatives springing up all over the country.[22] In the language of its founding declaration, the PRON ecological movement was to be the instrument for creating the "organizational system allowing the integration of all sorts of movements" (as quoted in Hrynkiewicz 1988, 37). By controlling the process of integration and the organization of initiatives, PRON would establish effective control over the ecological groups and their activities. The establishment of this official "movement" was the crowning effort of the government's inclusion policy toward the ecology movement.

Environmentalists, if they participated in the official endeavors at all, saw the new institutions as merely an additional forum for pressing their demands and not as central to their activism.[23] Participation would not come at the cost of compromising values or autonomy.[24] That inclusion meant more for the regime's attempt to validate its rule[25] than it did for its targets is evident in the failure to coopt those targets. Even had the regime succeeded in coopting members of the Polish Ecological Club or other groups, this would have made little difference to the movement as a whole since it was comprised of a plethora of different groups with no formal connection to one another. With no one group in a position of authority over any other, the government would have had to coopt each group individually.

The government's inclusion strategy not only failed to achieve its desired aim of coopting the environmental movement, it also violated a main tenet of normalization. By placing ecology on the official policy agenda, the government in effect *conceded the success of the environmental movement's independent, collective initiative* in making ecology a political issue. Official expressions of concern over the environment, designed to garner support or at least neutralize the issue, encouraged increased press coverage of ecology. The result was increased consciousness throughout society and more support for the independent environmental movement. In view of the skepticism with which many in Polish society regarded official declarations of intent to change living conditions and the dire condition of the environment, the government simply could not coopt the environmental issue without enacting effective policies. Viewed as the culprit in the first place, the communist system could not stop at mere propaganda. The Jaruzelski regime, however, lacked the resources and monitoring systems required even to begin effective policies and, at any rate, was preoccupied with economic crisis and the perceived need to increase production.

Inclusion took on a more genuine and less cooptive character after the May and August strikes of 1988 and the subsequent fall of the Messner government. In August, the environmental ministry unveiled the first draft of its long-awaited comprehensive program to the year 2010.[26] The new premier, Mieczysław Rakowski, placed the environment among the three most pressing socioeconomic tasks facing Poland.[27] His appointment of an economist as Minister of Environmental Protection and Natural Resources showed intent to tackle the real problems holding back environmental protection. Rakowski's tenure in office, however, was preoccupied with preparing for, holding, and carrying out the decisions of the Round-Table talks between the government and Solidarity.[28]

Discussions at the "sub-table" for ecology went smoothly and the parties reached an agreement on all issues except nuclear energy before the end of March. The Round-Table talks ended in the beginning of April 1989 and the elections that brought Solidarity into government were held in mid-June. The communist party's inability to form a government brought Solidarity into power two months later.

By the time the Round-Table convened, the inclusion policy had succumbed to real change in the relationship between the government and various social forces. By June, the very nature of state-society relations had changed. By August, communist rule had been overturned.

Environment, Normalization and the Press

The press played a central role in conveying normalization policies.[29] Although press coverage of environmental problems and politics fell largely within the same pattern as the general normalization effort, some early critical voices raised the level and openness of discussion of the environment more quickly than the government seems to have expected. The press was also the primary arena in which political "issues" were made. Against the argument that the official press was controlled and therefore served only to make the political "issues" deemed appropriate by the government, one can advance a few observations: (1) the Polish press was quite lively by the mid-1980s, this liveliness itself being an element of the normalization strategy; (2) issues brought up outside the Polish official press, especially in the other main vehicle for the creation of political issues—the opposition press, often infiltrated the official press as the government reacted to those issues in an attempt to control them; (3) experience had taught citizens how to read the press for what was missing; and (4) the official press reached the vast majority of the population, so it was still the main arena in which political issues were made or at least consummated. Thus, the effect of the critical voices in the official press was to push environmental politics through successive (but not successful) normalization policies and into the open quite rapidly.

During the martial law phase of normalization, the government controlled the press very tightly, stressing order, stability, and the totality of its control. This emphasis on stability was an attempt to capitalize on society's fatigue with constant change, uncertainty, and economic crisis, thereby justifying the imposition of martial law. Portraying its control as total, the Jaruzelski regime hoped to effect society's resignation to that control and its abandonment of political activism. There was no room for the press to discuss issues that would either question the communist gov-

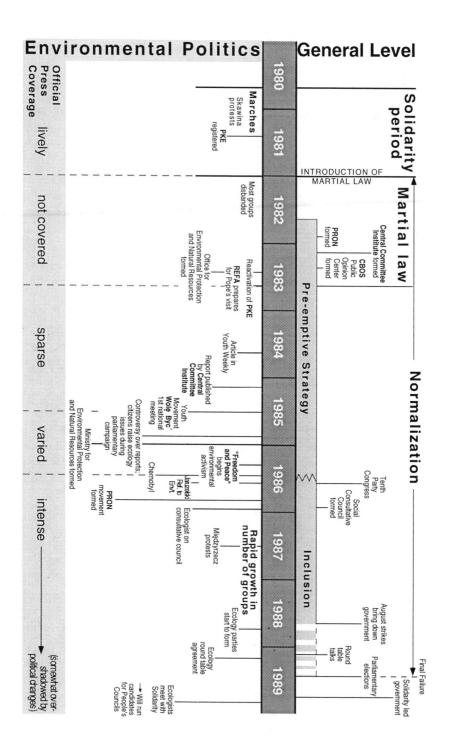

ernment's policies or raise social concern. Not surprisingly, the environment was not a topic of press coverage. A break in this imposed silence
came three months before the formal end of martial law, when a weekly
for enterprise managers, economists, and other professionals featured a
two-part series on the environment summarizing a report by the State
Inspectorate for Environmental Protection.[30] A few months earlier the
same newspaper had carried an article on water resources and pollution.
Still, this serial had a small circulation among a specific group of people.
Such specialist publications had always been more thorough and critical
than the mass circulation press.

The most interesting, indeed strangest, period of press coverage of environmental problems came between martial law and the Tenth Congress of
the communist party, or during normalization's "preemptive" phase.
During this period (mid-1983 to mid-1986) there was a great deal of variance in how the environment was discussed in the mass circulation press.
In the study of communist systems, differences in the press have generally
been taken as signs of struggle over policy or political position. In this
case, variance reflects more a lack of a clear official "line" on the environment. Traditionally given a low priority, the potency of the issue
caught the government by surprise.

After martial law, two of the 1970s most vigilant and censored journalists covering the environment, Iwona Jacyna and Krzysztof Walczak,
brought out a series of blistering articles in *Życie Warszawy*.[31] Other
newspapers also began discussing environmental problems before the
1985 controversy at Minister Urban's press conferences and that fall's
election campaign for the Sejm. At least four weeklies covered the environment regularly in the mid-1980s. *Przegląd Tygodniowy* and *Polityka*
carried longer, more in-depth features than the daily press. Both of them,
especially *Polityka*, targeted well-educated, thinking audiences, who
tended to be involved in politics, economic management, social organizations, or academia. *Tygodnik Demokratyczny* was the organ of one of
the communist party's obedient ally parties and carried a series entitled
"Ecological Encyclopedia," which covered a variety of topics from both
policy and scientific standpoints. The youth weekly *Na Przełaj* with its
close ties to the *Wolę Być* movement covered and promoted environmental activism.

Since part of the normalization strategy was to convince society that
the regime appreciated and was grappling with the complexity of the
problems facing the country, discussions of environmental problems,
their solutions, and the limitations the government faced in dealing with
those problems may have been acceptable to censors when they appeared

in press targeted at the intelligentsia. This strategy dovetailed with a very careful attempt to avoid raising expectations through a typical communist "propaganda of success" like the one Polish authorities had used during the 1970s.[32] At times during normalization, deflation of expectations even bordered on a propaganda of hopelessness. Coverage of the environment often crossed that border. In the last analysis both the government and the press often came down to the observation that environmental protection costs money and may cut production, neither of which Poland could afford in this time of economic crisis.[33] The implicit argument was that environmental protection was a luxury that only wealthy countries could afford: when Poland reforms its economy and catches up to the West, it will be able to concentrate on protecting the environment. Since everyone knew that point was far away, Poland would have to settle for partial measures to ease the worst of the ecological degradation.

While official statements and more conservative journalists alternated between cautiously encouraging discussions of new policy measures and the lowering of expectations, i.e. within the range of the normalization strategy, scholars and more daring journalists challenged not only the poor record of environmental protection, but also new policies, the statistics, and defeatism designed to paralyze activism and bury the issue. Economists began to estimate the obvious and hidden costs of pollution to the economy, often arriving at sums over 10% of Poland's national income.[34] A few of these studies were then reported in the press, which challenged the economic arguments against environmental protection. The one area in which the government prided itself on improvement was the reduction of dust emissions into the air. A *Życie Warszawy* article questioned the reductions claimed, pointing out that production had fallen temporarily and that the Supreme Control Chamber had found the data published by the Central Statistical Administration to be unreliable, especially as 40% of the enterprises had reported their emissions on the basis of their own estimates, not on the basis of actual measurement (Walczak 1984e). The press, especially periodicals targeting youth, also covered examples of environmental activism. Measures not requiring heavy financial investment were discussed as well. Among others, these included stricter controls and prosecution, administrative reforms, basic repairs of existing equipment, alternative uses for industrial waste, and the establishment of protective zones around steel mills, factories, and power plants. Thus, while the bulk of the government-controlled press tried to maintain a delicate balance between a sincere-sounding pessimism that would lower expectations and will to engage in independent activism and an emphasis on partial improvements that would build the government's credibility as effective policymaker, a handful of dedicated journalists consistently pointed out inaccuracies, dangers, and ways around the limitations claimed by officials.

Late summer and fall 1985 pushed the issue of the environment to the forefront of the media. This process began with the controversy at the government spokesperson's press conferences and accelerated with the pre-election public meetings with candidates for the Sejm. The controversy started over an article in *Życie Warszawy*, summarizing recent ecological reports by Polish specialists and the European Commission on the Environment, all of which showed Poland severely contaminated and leading Europe in environmental degradation (Kastrofy 1985). When foreign journalists questioned the government spokesperson, Jerzy Urban, about the findings at his weekly press conference a few days later, he replied that the government attached a great deal of importance to environmental protection despite a lack of economic resources. At the same time he pointed out that the press had exhibited a tendency toward alarmism. When questioned further about the claim that Poland was Europe's most ecologically degraded country, he declined a formal answer on the basis of his own lack of expertise and because the Polish government did not carry out such studies. Still he surmised that the statement was not true.[35] The next week, after a spate of articles on the environment and criticism from several quarters, Minister Urban made a prepared statement on the topic in which he emphasized the measures already being taken in Poland to protect the environment, claimed that Poland was not the most destroyed country in Europe based on statistics of sulfur dioxide emissions, and pointed out that no studies had proved a growth in disease related to environmental contamination in Poland.[36] Criticism increased to the point where two weeks later another journalist asked him directly about society's reaction to his comments. After admitting that there had been a number of polemical texts in the press, Minister Urban stated that in part he had been misunderstood as he had not belittled the importance of threats to the environment in Poland. Rather, he had only opposed the exaggeration and hysteria couched in the statements that Poland was Europe's worst case of degradation and that there were ecological disaster areas in Poland. (These arguments were then and have been continually advanced in ecological studies both in Poland and abroad.) Still he recognized that social concern in several specific localities was justified.[37] This month-long debate, running as it did through press conferences watched by a large part of the public[38], raised both consciousness and discussion of the environment in the press and in the public at large.

One manifestation of how the government press dealt with coverage of the environment during the uncertain year between the press conferences and the Tenth Congress of the Polish United Workers' Party (the communist party) was the campaign against *brud*, or dirt, starting at the end of winter in 1986. Spring cleaning campaigns occur every year in the Polish press, but the 1986 campaign was quite intense. Articles often linked the poor state of sanitation and the bad habits of individuals with environmental problems, implying that the environment would improve significantly if people would be responsible. Thus, attention was channeled away from Poland's main problems of industrial pollution and inadequate treatment facilities for municipal waste. Singling out individuals rather than policies or systemic flaws had always been a mechanism used in communist press coverage of negative phenomena; the channeling role of the *brud* campaign exhibited a slight refinement of this mechanism.

Chernobyl, however, focused attention back on larger ecological issues. The nuclear accident at the end of April 1986 was covered belatedly and cautiously in the Polish press. A full 37.6% of the population living in the 14 most-affected counties of northeastern Poland first heard about the accident from a source other than the Polish official press.[39] Well over half of those responding felt that the Polish press did not devote enough attention to the disaster (57.2% no, 28.7% yes, 14.1% could not tell or did not answer—CBOS 1986c, question 5). When asked if they felt that the information presented by the Polish press was true, the respondents answered: 8.0%, yes; 33.4%, rather so; 25.6%, rather not; 11.3%, no; 21.2%, hard to tell; 0.5%, no answer (CBOS 1986a, question 6).

Of the bloc countries, Poland was the only one to attempt a prophylactic measure—mass distribution of iodine. The goal of this action was to decrease iodine deficiencies that would prompt the body to absorb the radioactive iodine comprising the largest share of the Chernobyl fallout. The medical effectiveness of this measure was questionable, particularly as it was carried out five to seven days after the initial fallout. Yet, there is no evidence to question the sincerity of intent behind this decision. If, however, the government hoped to reassure the population and gain public recognition for undertaking this action to protect the Polish population at the risk of antagonizing the Soviet leadership (whose people across the border received nothing), the plan backfired. The measure induced a certain amount of panic as people waited hours in the (radioactive) rain to get the iodine. When word got around that high government officials (*nomenklatura*) and their families had received the iodine at least two days earlier than the general population, resentment, suspicion and fear increased.[40]

During and for a short period after the Chernobyl fire, the Polish press carried selective warnings about contaminated food, stories about dumping milk and other products suspected to be contaminated in the northeast region of the country, suggestions for cleaning and preparing food, and advice about working and playing outdoors.[41] Still, full accounts of the accident and its consequences were not published. The government consistently denied dangers beyond those already disclosed and did not allow the press to publish independent or even full official data on contamination. Above all, the government attempted to ease anxiety about the effects of the accident on the health of the Polish population. These efforts were little heeded as 61% of opinion poll respondents felt that the threats to health would be great, very great, or immense. Another 18.1% felt that they would be moderate or small ("not great" in Polish); only 1.1% felt that there would be no or close to no threats to human health (CBOS 1986c, question 12).

Despite the government's reassurances and efforts to tread the fine line between Soviet hegemony and defense of the national population, the Chernobyl accident raised ecology to the level of a national concern. It touched everyone. Journalists wrote a spate of articles on nuclear energy, one of the most sensitive ecological issues from the government's point of view. Coverage of the health effects of other types of environmental contamination—another highly sensitive issue—also increased.

The third phase of press coverage can be marked from the announcement of the new, official "Social Ecological Movement" in September 1986. In this phase the press became more uniformly open in its discussion of the environment and of environmental politics. Increased coverage followed logically from the inclusion policy, as the government had to embrace environmentalism to pull activists into the official public sphere. Articles announcing the official movement reported various facts attesting to the dismal state of the environment and the need for concerted action, but revealed nothing that had not already been reported.[42] In the widespread press coverage of environmental problems that followed, the role of official groups was accented, even enlarged. Nevertheless, all areas of the country and all topics became fair game to the press. Not immune to this new openness was the official movement itself. At least one lengthy article examined quite frankly its creation, organization, claims, and potential. The author pointed out that a social movement had already existed before the official one was created, that the official list of ecological groups, sections, etc. was inflated to include a number of official organizations that were not really active, and that after seven months the new movement had achieved nothing. Moreover, it would achieve nothing until it became less "polite," gained some courage, and utilized social pressure (Walczak 1987, 3). Again, critical journalists were exposing not only environmental problems and policy flaws, but also the political battle over control of the issue, i.e. the inclusion policy itself. The focus on the politics of environment and the actors involved was new, at least on the general scale.

The extent to which the press covered Poland's environmental problems during the inclusion period testifies to ecology's salience as a political issue, the growth of social activism, and the gravity of the ecological problems that prompted both the activism and the politics. An indication of the magnitude of this coverage can be gained from an intensive review of the central and regional printed press during what was an average period in terms of issue saliency. During the three-month period from May to July 1988, 116 serials of the Polish press printed at least 1,774 articles on the environment or articles with meaningful discussion of the environment.[43] The review period included the end of the campaign for election to the People's Councils and ended just prior to the August 1988 strikes that drove the government to the Round-Table talks with Solidarity. So, the review occurred at a time when the environment was not a particularly urgent issue in the mass press, but when some discussion of environmental issues might be expected in connection with local elections.

Although regional differences in coverage were not exceptional, there was heavier coverage in the most ecologically degraded areas of the country.[44] The regional newspapers of Katowice and Kraków, Poland's two most ecologically degraded counties, published more articles than the less destroyed regions.[45] When one considers the number of articles in the central press, though, regional differences in press coverage pale. Of the articles and references found, a little over half (906) were printed in the regional press while the rest (868) were printed in central publications for distribution throughout the country. Thus, the range of articles to which any one citizen had access was fairly small (from 887 to 1,000). Obviously no one read every publication available, but the extent of this coverage ensured that everyone in the country had ample opportunity to read about the environment.

Another angle from which to evaluate press coverage is by the socioeconomic groups targeted in various periodicals. Again, the dominant factor of press coverage was that it was aimed at the general population (1,372 articles, or 77.3%). Looking at the newspapers and magazines targeting specific sectors of the population, farmers, youth, humanist and technical intelligentsia, and activists in various parties and councils were those most targeted. There were also articles addressed to Catholics, women, whole families, the military, workers, and even Polonia, the Polish diaspora. Of all the groups, the working class appears to have been undertargeted the most, especially considering its size and role in politics (only 11 articles). In part, this can be explained by the low number of periodicals written especially for the working class. Often newspapers bearing titles that imply an emphasis on the working class were in fact the general population's daily newspapers for a given region. Also, in discussions involving industrial workers many environmental issues were raised under the rubric of "working conditions," which appears in this review as an issue but was not a defining condition of article selection. Political considerations also enter the explanation, as the working class was the base of both Solidarity's support and the regime's ideological claims to political legitimacy. In communist countries, control of the working class has always been a high priority, reflected in the propaganda, censorship, and often disproportionately high penalties meted out to workers for crossing official policy.

Finally, a review of the issues covered shows no real gaps. Given the timing of the review, there were many articles on the records of the People's Councils in environmental protection and new proposals for activism. There were general articles about water, air, and soil pollution and specific articles about individual cases and towns. Administration, fines, and court cases were discussed. Technical articles concentrated on new production processes, alternative uses for industrial waste, air filters, and water treatment plants. Political articles discussed both official and independent activists. Agriculture, industry, working conditions, and human health were popular topics. Several articles covered conflicts and cooperation with neighbors, especially Czechoslovakia and the German Democratic Republic. Environmental education became a common topic. Other articles discussed urban problems of noise, vibration, and lack of greenery. One of the most important themes—investment, economic management, and the relationship between environmental protection and economic reform—ran through many of the pieces, even though it was the central topic of only a handful of articles.

Despite such extensive coverage, the press was still not *totally* open. Censorship and, perhaps more importantly, self-censorship continued. In fact, a few astute observers made the nature of press coverage itself the subject of their articles. Even as late as July 1988, one commentator in the Polish official press noted:

> In the Kraków press, there exists an unfailing rule of thumb, whose sense can be summed up in one sentence: true, things are not so good, not as we

would like, but we are doing everything to make them better. In the meantime [the press] disinforms readers with half-truths, avoidance of uncomfortable and irritating problems, and superficial openness.

This remains the case despite the fact that " . . . one can write about the full extent of ecological threats in the county of Kraków, the perpetrators and the reasons for the continuing danger of ecological catastrophe" (Sabatowski 1988).

A similar theme was picked up the same day by the author of a column that focused on the press and its anomalies. The column starts with the author's terrifying realization that the new, open, exact tone of the press leaves no room for satirists to pick up on what is not said or only half said. Precise analysis of an article about an ammonia leak from a factory, however, reassures the satirist that his job is secure and points out a number of common elements in coverage of environmental problems. True, the title of the article on the ammonia leak is alarming, but the subtitle "Luck in Bad Luck" puts the reader at ease. Use of diminutive forms of words (fairly common in Polish) and choice of words (e.g. "mix up" rather than "emergency") also dispelled the sense of alarm and suggested exaggerated reaction to the threat on the part of workers. Another cause for relief is that had a different, larger pipe burst there would really have been cause for alarm; the danger of this leak paled in comparison. Moreover, all were fortunate that the enterprise's chemical emergency team, which had drilled such exercises before, took immediate action . . . even though eight firefighting units were also necessary to contain the problem and the action required shutting down production and evacuating the work team. "In this situation it is not fitting even to bother about the few hundred kilograms of ammonia that did get into the atmosphere, all the more since the rapid rescue action averted the evacuation of residents of a nearby apartment complex." Finally, the author points out that the accident was caused by the wearing out of faulty material, "which of course could not be foreseen" (Szmak 1988).

A number of tendencies emerge from both of these commentaries and from many of the rest of the articles in the press review. After 1986, there was indeed openness, but often not clarity. The fact that this could be said in the press itself and that some articles were more straightforward implies that much of the problem was to be found in journalists' and editors' own ingrained habits, particularly the habit of finding the positive in the negative. Some of the lingering tendency not to push half-truths into the open could also be attributed to differences in censors, but there does not appear to be a systematic distinction in type of coverage by region, a result one would expect from significant differences among regional censorship offices. Other elements of articles, like comparisons to "what if" scenarios or, more frequently, to past conditions reduced the significance of what happened and pushed it out of the center of attention.

Another common element in the coverage of "accidents" was the tendency to cite causes as though they were a given or fate. Unless blame could be ascribed to larger, overall development or investment policy or to human error (on the part of operator, inspector, or manager), news articles tended not to question smaller routine procedures and decisions whose correction could be possible but would require concerted implementation. When a reporter describing a disaster stressed some successful reaction or policy "given the circumstances," attention was again drawn away from the question of what caused those circumstances in the first place.

Coverage of the health effects of pollution was also complicated. In many cases it was simply hard to know what small effects a given event or condition might have, so this angle was not covered. Since pollution's effects on health are generally cumulative, the inability to pinpoint small increments of contamination left open the question of the extent of responsibility or liability. More importantly, confronted only with the large picture, the projected total effect of pollution on the health of residents in a given area, citizens were left impotent to protect themselves or demand protection against individual avenues of contamination. The result was a numbing effect and reduced hope that activism could accomplish change.

Although a lot of the press coverage of environmental issues fell into these patterns, i.e the normalization range between a propaganda of gloom that would reduce expectations and "it is bad, but we are doing what we can," the press was indeed the forum for developing the political issue of the environment. Some journalists dropped half-truths and broke the numbing effect of a gloomy future. Perhaps most importantly, the sheer extent of coverage reached everyone. This review has concentrated on the printed press, but the environment was also discussed in radio and television, on talk shows and in special programs. Widespread coverage of the environment becomes all the more noteworthy when one considers that this issue competed for the attention and energy of society with other very pressing crises, including the breakdown and reform of the economy, severe housing shortages, and the lack of basic medicines, materials, and services in the health care system. Beyond these economically based problems were the political issues of repression, control, and the reform of higher education. Holding its own with these topics, the environment had indeed become a major political issue.

Conclusion: Normalization's Failure

Normalization originally sought to deactivate society by discouraging attempts at change "from below" and especially the use of collective action to achieve such change. Yet, the switch to inclusion actually encouraged environmentalism. The process by which the government became engaged in the political issue of environmentalism raised the level of social awareness and pointed out the failure of official policy. The PRON ecological movement, Jaruzelski's reference to the environment at the party congress, increased press coverage, and inclusion of an ecologist on the Consultative Council could all be seen as acknowledging ecologists' success in focusing official and public attention on the issue. At the same time, inclusion attempts, though they brought new influences into the policy agenda and policy discussion, failed to extend the regime's control over social initiative.

Since the main ecological groups were not created by the government, they had a measure of legitimacy in the eyes of society and thus an independent base of support. They did not need government patronage to function. The Polish government's inclusion policy, therefore, came from a position of weakness, not strength. Because the regime had never achieved the first phases of normalization, it had never established the control and social submission to it that were necessary in order to make concessions to the population and still maintain authority. The failure of the inclusion policy to coopt ecologists and its inadvertent strengthening of the environmental movement sealed normalization's end with respect to the environmental movement. By the end of 1986 several groups had formed and press coverage of the environment had expanded markedly. After that, environmental activism simply mushroomed. A count published by Solidarity's Commission on the Protection of the Environment and Natural Resources at the time when regime change began listed 60 groups or organizations whose main purpose was environmentalism and another 80 which counted environmentalism among their fields of activism (Gliński 1989, 33).

Spanning all of the stages of normalization was the Polish government's failure to quiet social demands with effective reform policy. All of the attention given the environment during the "inclusion" phase only underlined the government's failure to achieve substantive change in that policy area. Most of all, the actual state of the environment continued to deteriorate. The predominant reason given by the government for slowness in combating ecological destruction was a lack of resources. Yet there were many areas where sorely needed change would not have taxed economic resources.

The rapid growth of the environmental movement also shows the regime's failure in the basic task of keeping the non-publicly active sections of society from becoming independently active. Inclusion embraced the independently active sector at least to keep it out of the opposition and at best to extend control over it. When the inclusion policy backfired by encouraging independent activism, more and more supporters came from the hitherto inactive sectors of society. Given the ineffectiveness of both preemptive and inclusion policies, the weapon of environmentalism as a fundamental critique of the communist system was still available, should the political opposition have chosen to pick it up. Chernobyl prompted the opposition to do so to some extent, although on the general level the opposition had more powerful weapons in the economic crisis and the authoritarian political system. While increasing environmental activism in both the opposition and official sectors of society, the movement remained independent.

At the same time, this growth in independent public activism was, in effect, part of the development of a civil society that could then support the dynamic changes put into motion by the opposition-led strikes of summer 1988. New environmental parties and groups sprang up immediately and ecology became the topic of one of the Round-Table's "subtables." The failure to normalize the environmental movement was one component of the general failure of normalization in Poland. While social refusal to be coopted undermined normalization, normalization policies actually contributed to the development of the movement and social support for it. What emerged were mutually reinforcing processes of the development of civil society and the failure of normalization. The relationship between these processes was heightened by the fact that the developing civil society was not simply anti-state, but took up issues and positions that went beyond the deep-seated split between officialdom and the opposition. This pluralistic, decentralized, and forward-looking civil society could not be reined in or "normalized" by the centralized state.

8

The Environmental Movement in Transition

With systemic change underway, the Polish environmental movement now faces a double transition. The first is its own transformation from a mobilizing movement into a regular political actor or set of actors. Thus, Polish environmentalists

> . . . face the classic dilemma of issue-oriented, expressive groups. That is, how to retain the support of the intense programmatic activists, who strongly value the group's protest tradition, and of those in the organization who view the group's long-term political effectiveness as tied to participation in mainstream legislative and electoral politics (Cigler 1986, 46).

The second transition confronting the movement comes in adjusting to the transformation of its political environment. The magnitude of the regime change alone compounds the usual identity crisis faced by an institutionalizing movement. At stake here are the political identities of several of the movement's individual and collective actors—in terms of their relation not only to the state but also to political ideologies and the major actors in the system. Moreover, the institutional and procedural changes in the political system have forced movement participants to learn new skills and develop new strategies and organizations for expanding their influence in political decisionmaking. These systemic changes have also made identifying points of influence more difficult. Finally, the political changes have been accompanied by a fundamental transformation of the economy. The latter is a complicated and largely decentralized process that directly affects the environment, yet is difficult for many movement participants to understand and influence.

This double transformation of the Polish ecological movement is still very much underway, but a few patterns are emerging. We can see some changes in internal structure, identity, and types of activism in the movement. Spurring on these internal transformations have been changes in the relationships between movement groups and external actors both within the country and abroad. Taken together, the changes in the movement and its context have extended the range of activities in which environmentalists engage, but also seem to have limited the movement's effectiveness at the level of national politics.

From the Round-Table: Democratic Transition in Poland

Although Poland was the first East European country to establish a government not led by the communist party, its political transition is by no means "accomplished." This transition is discussed in more detail elsewhere.[1] For our purposes, review of a few of its main features suffices to provide the context for the environmental movement's evolution since 1989.

Political party formation and consolidation in Poland's new democracy has been a protracted process. Five national elections in five and a half years (three parliamentary and two presidential elections) have produced a wide variety of party and coalition configurations.[2] The political transition started with the regime-founding election of June 1989 where Solidarity as a broad social movement won as much of the vote as the Round-Table agreements allowed it to contest (excluding one Senate seat which went to an independent businessman). This united approach to competing with the old regime allowed the Poles to become the first Soviet bloc country to break the barrier of installing a government not led by the communist party. Yet, this "umbrella movement" phase delayed until subsequent elections the formation of real political parties geared toward electoral competition (Jasiewicz 1993, 133). Although significant differences had emerged in visions of democracy, the presidential elections of late 1990 became largely a contest of personalities backed by two parts of the former Solidarity movement, the remnants of the communist era "parties," and a couple of new organizations. By the parliamentary elections of 1991, more than 150 parties were registered and 31 of them gained at least one parliamentary seat. This highly fragmented parliament and party spectrum produced a series of coalition governments during which the parties elected in 1991 continued to splinter. Lech Wałęsa, the President, finally disbanded parliament and called for new elections.[3] The September 1993 parliamentary elections resulted in the electoral failure of many parties on the right and a majority coalition government of the much reformed communist party and the reformed Polish Peasant Party of the communist era; five other parties entered the Sejm. The results of actual voting were intensified by a five percent threshold for parties, an eight percent threshold for coalitions, and a seat distribution scheme that almost doubled the proportion of seats gained by the victors. Only in 1994, therefore, did we begin to see the consolidation of a moderate number of consistent parties identifiable by the electorate. The November 1995 presidential elections resulted in the victory of the post-communist party candidate, Aleksander Kwaśniewski. Both the campaign and the election revealed continued fragmentation of the right end of the political spectrum and potential fissures in the more consolidated parties. Even though the hyperfragmentation of the early transition period has passed, the party system is still unstable and most parties remain underinstitutionalized. Although now clearer, party programs during the transition period have tended toward statements of general ideals and vague outlines of priorities. In many cases, it is difficult to distinguish among them. Organizationally and programmatically underdeveloped parties, in turn, have not provided good targets for lobbying by interest groups and movement activists.

One result of party fragmentation has been a series of weak coalition governments, which in turn has caused a fair amount of institutional instability in the political system as each government seeks not only to replace personnel but to develop its own vision of the structure of the new political system. At the very top of the system a power struggle emerged among the presidency under Wałęsa, the government, and the legislature (consisting of a strong lower house, the Sejm, and a weaker upper house, the Senat or Senate). The constitutional amendments passed as the provisional "Little Constitution" in 1992 defined more of the formal powers, particularly of the President, but left room for differences in interpretation, thus not resolving many of the conflicts over power and procedure.[4] The conflicts should lessen in the aftermath of Kwaśniewski's election, which placed all major branches of the political system under the control of the same party, and when the new constitution is adopted (probably in fall 1996). For the time being, however, the effects of these conflicts are still visible in gaps in legislation and decisionmaking processes that are less regularized than desirable. A little further down the governing institutions, continual turnover in top-level ministerial personnel brought shifting policy lines and, at times, vacuums in authority. Meanwhile many of the old mid-level bureaucrats remained in place and standard operating procedures from the pre-transition period persisted. The ministry in charge of environmental protection was no exception to this rule, as five different ministers passed through its doors in less than six years.[5]

Another feature of this political transition central to the fate of the environmental movement has been its link to a fundamental economic transformation. Modelled on Western capitalism, the emerging economic system in Poland follows its models in treating the environment as an externality. Debates over the nature and mechanics of the economic transformation have not shown much consideration of environmental imperatives. Although environmentalists have developed a keen interest in market-based measures for controlling pollution, progress in establishing such systems has been quite slow.[6] For ecologists perhaps the most hopeful trend in the economic transformation is the fact that some of the enterprises hardest hit by the recession and least able to adapt to market conditions are the worst polluters (e.g. the Lenin Steelworks in Nowa Huta, one of the largest sources of pollution in the Kraków area). These big metallurgical and chemical plants are also likely to face more reductions as the transition continues. To the detriment of activism, however, market constraints have raised the sensitive issues of plant closings and unemployment, making workers and their dependents less inclined to support environmental measures that would either strain enterprise budgets further or close down certain operations. Meanwhile, economic conditions compel Poles to work second and third jobs to make ends meet, leaving little energy or even will for environmental activism.

The economy and other overarching issues, particularly those concerning the power and influence of the Roman Catholic Church and "decommunization," have also crowded the national political agenda, pushing ecology off the list of issues receiving political and media attention.[7] Whereas the communist regime's attempt to coopt the issue of ecology led it to tolerate wider discussion of environmental issues and several journalists became activists taking advantage of the centralized press in the pre-transition era, the post-transition period has seen a revolution in journalism that paradoxically has lessened the impact of environmental coverage. Not only is there a plethora of other issues and developments, but personalities and scandals receive a great deal more attention in publications that must survive in the new market economy. The fact that the press is now decentralized and pluralist also means a much greater variety in the stories covered and the way they are covered from area to area and publication to publication. As a result, any specific issue does not usually have the same impact on environmental consciousness or mobilization as it might have had under the centralized yet liberalized press of the mid to late 1980s.

Finally, the role of external advisers in the transition process has been very visible both on the general level of politics and economics and in the specific area of environmental politics. Economic policies have been shaped by the neoliberal and fiscally oriented policies of international financial institutions and advisers. Ecology has not found a place in this debate. Countering this trend somewhat has been the visible role of international environmental organizations. Besides assisting local environmentalists in their efforts to reorganize their activities, these organizations have also been active in helping Poland get resources for specific projects designed to improve environmental monitoring and protection. The balance sheet, however, has leaned strongly toward fiscal and restructuring policies that do not consider the environment.

Movement Transformation in the Political Transition

What is happening to the issue-oriented social movements of the communist period? Have they continued? Are they becoming the interest groups of the democratizing period? One would assume that their drive to place issues on the social and political agendas and to make "society's" voice heard in political decisionmaking under more repressive conditions would predispose such movements to institutionalizing these interests in the new political process. This seems especially likely with the movements that received the support of the former political opposition taking power in the first phase of the transition. Institutionalization might be expected to take one or more of several forms. The most probable route to political influence would be to develop associations and organizations that lobby the legislature and bureaucracy, while garnering public support and resources to make their lobbying efforts more successful. In cases where the state institutions for achieving a movements' goals do not exist or need restructuring, the movement might become a part of the new state. In any case, some of its members could be expected to move over into positions of authority in these state institutions. Finally, with repression lifted, at least parts of the movement are likely to intensify and regularize their attempts to change social values. In other words, to the extent that their goals have not been met, the social movements of the communist period should be becoming the interest groups of new systems or, at least, continuing as more visible and less restricted social movements. The environmental movement has undergone some of these changes, yet its effectiveness as a set of interest groups and a grassroots movement has not increased appreciably. Shaping both these changes and their outcomes have been a number of political factors at the national level and new opportunities for engaging international and transnational actors in environmental protection in Poland.

Internal Changes in the Movement Since 1989

The Polish environmental movement has continued to both grow and fragment since the dismantling of communist rule. Some parts of the movement have proven more adaptive to the new political environment than others. New groups and temporary groups have also sprung up throughout the country, many in response to local and regional issues. Yet, the overall nature of the movement shows more continuity than change. Expressive protest groups still exist alongside institutes of "experts" and the movement is as decentralized as ever.

The uncertain direction of the Polish Ecological Club epitomizes the dilemmas facing the ecological movement as a whole. Looking toward the future, many activists see the "nongovernmental organizations" (NGOs) of the environmental movement dividing into two groups, purely professional associations with a paid staff—e.g. foundations and institutes—and local issue groups and activism, largely if not wholly on a volunteer basis.[8] This pattern is typical of institutionalizing issue movements in the West. Both types of groups are needed and support each other, but internal group dynamics have led many of the collective actors in the movement to hesitate in this decision. The PKE, too, does not know which way to go. A June 1993 meeting of the leadership decided that the club would not change its membership base and build a mass movement; rather, it would keep its apolitical, expert focus.[9] Membership remains highly educated, around 4,000, and concentrated in major cities (PKE 1993b, 6–7). Although its membership profile and external image tend toward a professional association, many of the club's members are not ready to abandon their earlier identity as social movement activists engaged in protest politics.

As an institution, the PKE is staying out of party politics and even green party politics. (This is not, however, true of its individual members.) The club supports all candidates with ecologically sound goals. Although the club has not discussed lobbying parties directly in order to influence their programs, its leaders recognize that they will probably have to develop a position on such activity soon. For now, the July 1993 Congress of the PKE has decided to plan a series of lectures for members of parliament, including members of the Environmental Commission.[10] Further decisions taken at the Congress continue PKE's style of activism from the pre-transition period. Public activism emphasizes ecological education even more than it did before the transition. The PKE is trying to expand its education efforts, as well as the base of materials available for instruction, at all age levels and for all social groups.[11] Aiming to establish influence at each level of government, the PKE wants to be visible and is developing a new strategy for using the mass media to exert pressure on political decisionmakers. Yet, the club does not want to be "loud" in the sense of staging protests and demonstrations.[12] This caution in its public image has left it a little further apart from other groups than one might expect. Although it was probably an oversight, the PKE did not invite other groups to send observers to the 1993 congress. (There were, however, observers from groups abroad, as well as other guests from Poland.) Even if, in terms of expertise and experience, the PKE would be the natural leader and coordinator for the movement, it seems to eschew that role.

As politics becomes decentralized and environmental groups continue to form, some new attempts have been made at facilitating coordination of efforts. Perhaps the most aggressive move in this direction has been the creation of a Service Bureau for the Environmental Movement (BORE) in Warsaw. Its goal is to become a comprehensive information bank for the use of all groups. The Bureau collects and distributes information on a variety of topics: laws and standards in Poland and elsewhere, technical information, handbooks for organizing, educational materials, press coverage, information about the political system and current issues, and address lists of other groups and specialists. The Bureau and its parent organization, the Social Ecological Institute, also lobby the environmental bureaucracy and write opinions of draft regulations, legislation, and plans. Many of the more than 200 identified ecological groups have used the Bureau at least once, but the smaller groups tend to use it more than major groups like the Polish Ecological Club.[13]

Activists' memberships in multiple groups also assure some contact, as do occasional general meetings of ecological groups—both those independently organized and those promoted by the Ministry of Environmental Protection, Natural Resources, and Forestry's Office for Contacts with Society. Also facilitating communication are *Serwis Ochrony Środowiska* (SOS), a monthly information bulletin circulated largely within the movement, and a new bimonthly periodical dealing exclusively with environmental issues and movement news, *Zielone Brygady*, which has appeared steadily since May 1989 and can be bought at some newsstands, academic bookstores, and the ministry for the environment. Still, contacts among environmental organizations at the national level are not what they could be.[14] In response, a few of the activists involved in BORE and PKE are contemplating stronger efforts to facilitate cooperation. Coordination does, however, tend to be better at the regional level and/or when an immediate issue comes up that calls for cooperation.

One can find examples in the last few years of all of the types of activism visible during the communist period. Still, there has been a general trend toward strengthening the types of activities typical of movements in established democracies. The focus of activism has evolved from an emphasis on symbolic politics to a more instrumental approach to decisionmaking, including an emphasis on expertise and consulting and new work on economic mechanisms of environmental protection. The locus of activism is also devolving from the national level to the regional and local levels. The PKE's July 1993 General Congress, for example, decided to support development of specialized centers in regions especially affected by a given problem. Thus, the club has established two Baltic Sea Bureaus in Gdańsk and Szczecin and an air quality center in Katowice.[15] This structure should strengthen both regional activism and interregional cooperation dealing with specific problems.

Environmental activism has begun to head into electoral and lobbying politics. Since penetrating the national legislature as a green party is now nearly impossible given the five percent threshold and the limited resources of environmental candidates, most green candidates have chosen to run at lower levels of government. Those who do run for national office affiliate themselves with other political parties. Some ecologists have become quite active in the local government movement, working for greater political decentralization and running for positions in the new, post-communist People's Councils in June 1994. These new candidacies and the fact that most of the movement's new groups are arising around local issues have combined to shift the emphasis of activism to specific policy decisions and implementation at the levels at which they occur.[16] Small (often temporary) groups focused on local and regional issues draw on the technological and organizing information provided by the new service bureau and the policy information provided by the ministry's office for contact with the movement. To date, they have scored some success in reversing government decisions, revising planned projects and changing decisionmaking procedures for the future. These little groups are also spawning the new environmental candidates for local and regional offices. This shift in emphasis is not without problems, however. Activism at the local level still tends to be episodic. At times it can also be shortsighted or centered on "not in my back yard" issues.[17] Finally, since the Polish government and parliament have not made a definitive decision regarding the plan to reorganize the country's administrative system by reintroducing districts (*powiaty*) and consolidating voivodships, it is still not clear how entrenched environmental interests can become at the local level.

Many of the collective actors in the ecological movement are beginning to function more like the interest groups of Western pluralist societies. They call themselves NGOs and study the activity of NGOs in the West. Encouraged by international agencies and groups in the West to do so, these activists are reshaping both their activities and their identities. They have come together to set up "funds" or foundations to help support environmental protection. New institutes and centers provide the technological and organizing information necessary to participate more effectively in decisionmaking practices and a flow of documentation and expert opinions to influence decisions currently on the table. The few full-time activists expend a great deal of effort seeking funding and cultivating contacts in the government and among other NGOs.

Meanwhile, others have continued the more "social movement" mission of changing social values and raising consciousness through protest activities and alternative "happenings." Interestingly, the more radical of the communist era groups have either disappeared or remained on the social movement end of the spectrum, while the more politically neutral and officially connected groups and organizations have moved the furthest toward interest group behavior. Thus, in the ongoing process of resolving the classic conflict of movement institutionalization, the respective values placed on protest activity and effectiveness within the political process have outweighed the questions of political identity that shaped movement activity before the transition. The change to Solidarity and post-Solidarity governments has *not* brought a major reversal of group roles within the movement.

Changes in the Movement's External Relationships

With both systemic change and leadership change, environmental activists have developed some new relationships with external actors for advancing their cause. These new relationships can be seen on the international, regional, national, and subnational levels. However, despite these expanding contacts, the effectiveness of the environmental movement in advancing its interests has been, at best, limited.

One opportunity the political transition has afforded ecological interests has been greater attention and assistance from the West.[18] This attention was in part derived from contacts established during the 1980s by East European activists with international organizations and foreign governmental agencies, including the United States Environmental Protection Agency. Some Western governments have targeted resources directly to environmental clean-up and education programs. (The U.S. EPA, for example, is funding a major water treatment and management program for Kraków.) However, most external funding for new projects has come through multilateral financial institutions. The World Bank has sponsored several projects throughout Central and Eastern Europe and particularly in Poland. The European Community has also been active, dispersing aid and encouraging investment through its PHARE program. The United Nations Development Program runs a small grants program for a variety of specific projects ranging from education to the purchase of land. On the other hand, the European Bank for Reconstruction and Development, one of whose main priorities was supposed to be investment in environmental protection, has been slow to engage. Taken together, all sources of international funding still comprise only a small part of the insufficient expenditures on environmental protection in the region (Manser 1993, 75–77, 86–92).

More importantly for the development of environmental interest groups, the interest of external actors has maintained some visibility for Polish ecologists in their own national political sphere at a time when many other factors are working to push them off the agenda. Several transnational groups have intensified their links with counterparts in Central and Eastern Europe and have developed programs focusing on the area.[19] These programs bring in funds and some publicity. Western assistance has also been instrumental in increasing regional cooperation among environmental activists. This cooperation takes the form of numerous seminars, conferences, and information exchanges. The Regional Environmental Center in Budapest (set up with a combination of local activism and Western funds) now has affiliates in Warsaw, Prague, Bratislava, and a growing list of other capitals. This new network has improved communication between activists and facilitated a few efforts to coordinate pressure on their respective governments for various forms of ecological cooperation. The Marshall Fund's Environmental Partnership for Central Europe has also put more resources into the environmental movements of the area, among other things funding equipment for some branches of the Polish Ecological Club.

At the national level, the Polish ecological movement's experience with transition has been rather mixed. Now free to engage in all sorts of activities, some movement participants are finding their influence to be even more limited than under the communist regime after martial law. While the movement as a whole has better ties to the bureaucracy than it did during communist rule, its influence over the national political agenda has if anything weakened since the late 1980s. This weakening is due to other pressing issues of the transition, structural factors resulting from the political and economic transitions, and—to some extent—the loss of a centralized press seeking to coopt ecological issues before they become opposition issues. Popular mobilization aimed at general policies and values at the national level has ebbed in the face of this crowded agenda and institutional fludity (although local initiatives can still draw at least episodic social participation). Beyond the plethora of issues and uncertainty about political processes, we may also be seeing some effects noticed by those studying social movements in other contexts: a very "open" political process can demobilize social movements, as can certain characteristics of policy implementation (cf. Kitschelt 1986, 62–67). In our case, even though "opennness" may mean little in terms of influence on policy because new political institutions are weak, it still focuses participation on particular decisionmaking processes within the political system rather than on broader mobilization to affect norm formation and major policy directions. On the positive side of the ledger, environmental activists have been able to influence more directly the development of specific projects and the allocation of some funds from both foreign and domestic sources. The results of daily consultative, networking, and lobbying activities, these achievements are not directly tied to mobilizing high degrees of social support or high visibility in public discourse.

The first change the transition brought was some administrative rationalization. In conjunction with a long-standing movement demand, the forests were placed under the Ministry of Environmental Protection and Natural Resources. This move should facilitate the establishment and implementation of coherent environmental policies. The expected results are yet to appear, however, due to the continuing weakness of the ministry with respect to economic and industrial ministries and due to the governmental instability that has led to a revolving door of ministers. The new Ministry of Environmental Protection, Natural Resources and Forestry has also established an office for contacts with environmental movements and other social forces inside the press spokesperson's office. Maintained essentially by one person, this office is supposed to facilitate communication in both directions. Movement participants and other citizens send letters and petitions for forwarding to appropriate offices in that ministry and elsewhere in the government bureaucracy. They turn to that office for information on policies, standards, current decisions, and any other matters that interest them. Often, the specialist running the office is able to obtain this information, but sometimes she runs into silence herself. In many parts of the ministry, a lingering suspicion of environmental activists and fear of negative repercussions from above leave officials reluctant to share even unclassified information about controversial issues. This office also sends out draft laws and regulations, plans, programs, and other decisions to key movement groups for their input. The groups most often consulted are the Polish Ecological Club and the League for the Protection of Nature, both of whom are well-established, connected with other groups, and inclined toward "expert" participation in policymaking rather than protest activity.[20] The channel of influence provided by environmental activists inside relevant state institutions has expanded since the transition started. After heading the Sejm's environmental commission in the Mazowiecki government, movement activist Stefan Kozłowski served as Minister of the Environment before a cabinet change replaced him with a more controversial and less effective candidate. Many old officials have maintained their positions throughout the transition, but personnel changes have occurred in department heads and some lower positions in the ministry. Several movement activists, including Kozłowski as Chair entered the new Ecological Council to the President, created by Wałęsa in 1992. Although generally positive for setting up an administrative base for ecological interests, the migration of some movement leaders into the governmental bureaucracy has also weakened leadership of the movement, leaving a new (and less experienced) generation to guide it through confusing times. This exodus may make the movement more adaptable in the long run, but it caused some lack of direction in many groups during the first few years of the transition.

In its influence on key national policy debates and the legislative agenda, the environmental movement is more a study of the limits remaining on interest group and movement effectiveness. Politically, environmentalists are weak. This is especially the case in legislative politics.[21] With the fall 1993 elections they started to establish genuine connections with a few political parties. Until then, some environmentalists formed and others supported a fractious set of weak "green" parties, while all of the main parties simply voiced ecological values and goals but initiated no actions to back up these claims. (The latter is not surprising as it is a common phenomenon even in developed democracies with stronger environmental lobbies.) In the 1993 elections, however, a new "ecological fraction" of the Democratic Union (*Unia Demokratyczna*), headed by Rodosław Gawlik, Vice Chair of the Sejm's Environmental Commission, actually ran environmental candidates and began to influence the party platform. (This party later joined with the small Congress of Liberal Democrats to become the Freedom Union [*Unia Wolności*].) That this fraction was an internal party development, rather than the result of a party's efforts to "capture" a group and some votes, suggests some real support for environmental efforts among certain politicians.

Even if one of the main political parties does adopt a "greener" agenda, its own weakness assures that the pursuit of ecological interests remains weak. In order for interest groups to achieve their goals through influencing parties, those parties have to be strong enough to press new policies through the legislative process. This is still not the case in Poland, especially when the legislative agenda is packed with other central issues of the transition.[22] Environmentalists are not strong enough to change the perspectives of central players—and of society—to the point that their interests can be understood as part and parcel of economic transformation rather than luxuries to be afforded once the transition has been accomplished. As the party system consolidates and political parties develop stronger organizations, attempts to lobby parties may prove more fruitful. Stabilization of governing coalitions and the further development of the legislative system should also stabilize membership in and contacts with parliamentary committees responsible for many of the key policy decisions and much of the text of laws passed by the legislature. (As this book goes to press, it looks as though the governing post-communist party will have this strength, since it will be unchallenged by an opposition President, as it was during 1993–1995. Ecology, however, is not a primary concern of this party.)

Values, Votes and Volunteerism: Public Support

The ability to mobilize social participation and support gives the movement the visibility necessary to affect public discourse, the policy agenda, and individual values. Although it is not the only means of influence open to movement activists, successful mobilization can carry the potential power of sway over general levels of political support for the government and various parties, even over votes. Even for strategies not requiring popular mobilization, however, movements need to show enough support to convince other political actors that they represent the interests of certain segments of society.

Public support for environmental causes in the post-communist system shows mixed trends. When surveyed about the environment, respondents affirm their concern about ecology, express ecological values, and even proclaim their willingness to make certain sacrifices in order to improve the environment. At the same time, concrete knowledge about ecological processes and current environmental action is fairly low. When it comes to other types of political support, the public is largely absent from the debate. Participation rates in groups are low; green parties have not attracted votes; and activists have not been able to muster social support when confronting other organized political and economic forces. In 1992, fully 80 percent of the respondents in a nationally representative sample were worried or very worried by the state of the environment, and only 14 percent felt that environmental protection had improved any since the transition (CBOS 1992b, 4). A year later, 88 percent of respondents indicated the poisoning of the natural environment as one of the most serious threats facing the country (up from 76% the year before). In both 1992 and 1993 the environment tied crime for first place on this list of threats (CBOS 1993a, 1). Passive concern, however, is one thing; action is another. Asked whether they would be prepared to change their behavior for ecological reasons, respondents expressed a fairly high willingness to make some changes in their consumption patterns:

- 94% would take the time and effort to sort and recycle
- 84% would buy a product with less convenient but more ecological packaging
- 83% would buy a more expensive product if it were less ecologically harmful
- 67% would commit to a regular (but unspecified) payment to be used for environmental protection
- 64% claim that the fact that a product is not harmful to the environment has a determining (20%) or significant ("large" - 44%) effect on the decision to buy it (CBOS 1993c, 6–9).

These declarations show a general acceptance of environmental values. Still, the question remains open as to what proportions of Polish society would actually carry out these intentions given the chance. For now, the opportunities to recycle are very limited, information about the ecological effects of using certain products and packaging is lacking, and no environmental tax is on the horizon.

Participation in and awareness of environmental activism is quite limited relative to the high level of societal concern about the environment. Two 1993 surveys revealed that between 1.8% and 2% of Poland's adult population are members of or participate in an ecological group.[23] This result somewhat underrepresents total participation as youth groups form an important component of the movement. Even so, active participation is fairly low, especially in view of the levels of concern voiced by citizens. (About 7% of adults declare having belonged to a group in the past—CBOS 1993c, 4.) One factor contributing to low participation and support of groups is lack of knowledge about concrete groups and actions undertaken, even when people have heard of some sort of ecological activism. A survey taken in 1993 on public knowledge about the activism of ecological groups shows a drop from the year before in the number of respondents who have heard of these groups (which the investigators attribute to the proximity of the 1991 parliamentary elections to the 1992 survey). Of those who have heard of these groups and organizations, only a little over half heard of any concrete activity undertaken by these groups over the last year.[24] Another factor depressing participation in environmental activism is the widespread belief that it does not or can not bring change. In 1992, only 2 percent of respondents believed that local activism brought results; the figures for voivodship and national level activism were 3 and 6 percent respectively (CBOS 1992a, 4). Those who had heard of ecological groups and organizations were of the opinion that most of their activism went into educating and raising social awareness as opposed to actions actually affecting the environment.[25] Results a year later show some improvement, especially in the evaluation of local activism (CBOS 1993b, 10), but skepticism about the effectiveness of environmental groups and organizations was still high. Another study suggested that the bulk of society expects various levels of government to take the lead in improving the environment in their locale, while few thought that ecological parties and organizations should be the primary actors in these endeavors.[26]

Despite the clear concern about the environment on the part of Polish society, the support environmentalists receive in general or when they are clashing with well-institutionalized economic interests is minimal. Some of this lack of support can be attributed to the low expectations of efficacy discussed above or to the fact that people are too busy trying to survive in a rapidly transforming economy to engage in activism. Another factor, however, is that they increasingly see their economic and environmental interests as conflicting, especially as societal experience with unemployment has intensified. From early 1992 to early 1993—while unemployment rose—the percentage of those surveyed who felt that increased unemployment was a social cost worth bearing to stop especially harmful production processes or even shut down whole factories contaminating the environment dropped from 58 to 45 percent. Only 37 percent of society thought that Poland could restructure industry and invest in environmental protection at the same time (CBOS 1993c, 1,3). These views on the economic transition may very well be placing ecology further down the average citizen's agenda, even as concern and passive support for environmental values remain high.

Conclusion: The National Political Process Revisited

In large part, the national political process—determined by the institutions and procedures of communist rule, the existence of a strong political opposition, and government strategies for controlling society— shaped the original formation and evolution of the movement; in many ways the new political processes are shaping and suspending its transformation. This environmental movement is transforming into a movement and set of interest groups more characteristic of Western democracies. Both internal changes in the movement's component groups and intergroup networks, as well as change in its external contacts, point in this direction. Yet, ecologists' influence on the national political agenda is not necessarily stronger; indeed, it appears even weaker than it was before the transition. In order to increase their influence these groups may have to follow their Western counterparts in building coalitions and even undertaking direct negotiation with other interests, especially producer groups. However, the explanation for their weakness lies primarily in factors beyond their control: weak parties, unstable governments, and an overriding concern on the part of both politicians and the public with rapid economic transformation along fairly orthodox neo-liberal lines. Effective interest groups need effective targets to which they can present their views and from which they can demand action. The lack of such targets in Poland is still hindering the development of effective means to represent interests in society.

It is a bit early yet to tell whether antecedent movements—movements that developed before the end of communist rule—have an advantage or "head start" over movements that have risen since the transition. Right now, it rather looks as though their antecedent status will not result in stronger interest representation than that enjoyed by the groups that are forming as the political and economic systems of the region consolidate. Inasmuch as the old movements are slow to adapt to the new circumstances, their abilities to institutionalize their interests may be even weaker than those of totally new groups. The new political process will spawn new forces more adept at using the system, forces that form precisely to get something done in the new setting.

Finally, a few words about how well these observations might "travel" to other post-communist countries in the region and other issue areas. From at least a preliminary glance, the experiences of Polish environmentalists have been similar to those of their colleagues throughout the region.[27] This is not surprising given that these movements are faced with similar transitions and similar perspectives on economic transformation. What the similarity does suggest, however, is that differences in the historical evolution of the movements before the transitions, although still visible, are less salient than the current transitions in shaping environmental activism. Again, political processes and institutions are having strong shaping effects on movement development. How well do these findings travel to other issues? The jury is still out. In part, the rather unique nature of ecology has made it a visible and constant issue, whereas other single-issue—peace, minority rights—movements have been affected more fundamentally by the change of regime. Judging by the level of political apathy and dissatisfaction with the transition, other interests seem to be experiencing similar difficulties in developing their identities and affecting the political process, but this is a topic for further study.

9
Conclusions

This study has focused on a number of themes in an attempt to show the complexity of Polish politics in the crucial decade of the 1980s through the window of environmental politics. That window, in many ways typical of the politics surrounding independent social initiatives in that period, is also a crucial and, in some respects, unique issue area in and of itself. If this study is to contribute to existing theory and to the understanding of communist systems and their disintegration beyond the knowledge it imparts of this case, it is time to untangle some of the themes that have been woven together to create that picture.

The fundamental theme that structured this study was the nature of the sociopolitical tasks facing the Jaruzelski regime during normalization and the contradictions of the government's policies meant to achieve that normalization. Normalization's failure was due, in part, to the development of a civil society beyond the regime's control, but it also contributed to that very process. In the case examined here, a social movement was able to grow stronger, increasing participation, expanding public debate and knowledge about ecology, and influencing policies. This second theme—the formation of this "new" social movement in Poland—has interesting implications for social movement theory and for our understanding of society in communist systems and in the breakdown of authoritarian regimes. The third theme set forth in this case study concerns the complexity of political dynamics in Poland during the 1980s, a complexity that went beyond the "us-them" perception of many Poles and of many Western observers focused on the relationship between

Solidarity and the government. Finally, we return to the substance of the case itself—the fundamental nature of the environmental challenge to any current political regime and the fate of ecology in the political and economic transformation.

Normalization: The Failure of Both Strategy and Concept

Clearly, "normalization" failed. Moreover, normalization's failure was the failure of the communist party's last chance to maintain its leading role in Polish politics. Poland has already embarked on a fundamental transformation of its political and socioeconomic systems. What this study shows is that the very strategy adopted by the Jaruzelski regime actually contributed to the development of social activism outside of officially controlled channels. In an attempt to gain some legitimacy after martial law, the government found itself compelled to include in the political process—or *appear* to include in the political process—as many groups and individuals as it could wean away from political opposition. That meant not only tolerating their independent activities, but also opening discussion of more issues in the centralized mass press. More open independent activism garnered more social support for nonofficial activities and the government simply lost the social control upon which its rule depended.

The formation of independent collective actors was initiated both outside of and within the normalization process. Successful collective action to force the government to address new issues, to reverse policy decisions, and to tolerate greater freedom of expression and association signalled the development of civil society. In this context, a normalization strategy of inclusion could not have achieved the acquiescence to control from above that was characteristic of earlier normalization processes in Eastern Europe. Inclusion was an attempt to develop a new social contract to replace the standard normalizing strategy of selectively using material incentives to atomize society and achieve political obedience. The latter strategy was ruled out by economic crisis in both Poland and the Soviet Union and by the nature of Solidarity's 1980–81 challenge to the regime. Because those being included in Poland were already collective actors, the social atomization necessary for intimidation and acquiescence was never achieved. The regime's efforts to include in the policy process groups not intimidated by the threat of exclusion or by other sanctions served not only to empower these autonomously formed social actors, but even to encourage others to form groups and press their demands. In the end, this normalization strategy was undermined by the regime's weakness and social resistance to cooptation. Moreover, the strategy's weaknesses contributed to the development of new collective actors who remained independent of state control—that is, they contributed to the further development of civil society.

After the martial-law stage, the Polish government's normalization strategy was riskier than those previously tried. In stressing more open dialogue, inclusion, institutional change, and legality, the government left itself vulnerable—at least inasmuch as it wanted to convince citizens that politics had changed—to having these tools used against it. Yet, more far-reaching change was the regime's only hope for reasserting stable authority after 1981. After a series of crises and small normalizations from 1956 on and the unifying experience of even partial and temporary victory in the prolonged and profound political challenge of the Solidarity period, few would be deceived by superficial change. The other alternative of maintaining outward social peace and conformity by force, if possible, would have been extremely costly and, ultimately, unstable. The Jaruzelski government's goal was to open up the political process sufficiently to identify and deal with problems before they became controversial political issues. In so doing, the government hoped to engage more citizens in day-to-day issues and to marginalize the opposition.

Had it worked, this strategy would have left in power a leaner communist party but one exercising less intrusive control over daily social and economic decisions. Broader and more meaningful political participation would have opened the policy agenda to more influence from society, preempting potential political crises. Indeed, the changes implied by such a strategy were sufficiently far-reaching that they no longer fell within the bounds of "normalization" as understood by its practitioners or analysts; it was a *perestroika* without the starting base of thorough social and political control. Rather than gradually liberalizing a repressed society (a strategy which also failed in Czechoslovakia in 1968 and the Soviet Union in the second half of the 1980s), the Jaruzelski regime in the mid-1980s was effectively pleading with a defiant society to meet the regime's compromises halfway. Although temporarily collared by martial law and dispirited, societal forces and average citizens had been empowered by the Solidarity experience and by continued underground resistance. In the face of grave economic and social crises, piecemeal change and compromises could not bring political allegiance. Rather, they were evidence of weaknesses and openings for further demands and further pressure on a tottering system.

Finally, the Polish case exposes the contradictions inherent in the concept of normalization. Logically, unless it is to be maintained by force—a situation far from "normal"—post-crisis normalization must bring change. Otherwise the circumstances that caused the original crisis would only be reestablished, setting the scene for another round of unrest. The change foreseen by East European and Soviet leaders trying to achieve normalization and by those studying it was two-fold: a resignation and acquiescence to political control and a social contract offering improvements in material conditions in exchange for this acquiescence. At best, normalization is a temporally limited concept. Even the most successful case of normalization—after the Hungarian Revolution of 1956—set in motion a series of economic and political reforms that first reformed the system and then undermined it. The Czechoslovak case resulted in a sullen and resentful society that united to overthrow its communist government almost spontaneously when people finally perceived the chance to do so. This was a political dynamic in sharp contrast to the support that a reforming communism enjoyed in 1968 before normalization began. The Polish government achieved neither the political resignation nor the economic stability necessary to offer material incentives, but normalization policies contributed to the development of independent political actors and the reconstitution of civil society. In sum, normalization was a process of political change, different in each context. Using the term "normalization" masked that change by emphasizing the reimposition of the political, social, and economic control that communist party-states exercised over their citizens. Actual though this control was, its extent proved to be more limited than either the leaders or the analysts of these systems—even their subjects—supposed. Both as propaganda and policy in the East and as an analytical concept in the West, "normalization" contributed to the tendency to overlook change—destructive or constructive—in the political systems and especially in the societies of the Soviet bloc.

Lessons from the Social Movement

If this case demonstrates how normalization strategies contributed to the growth of at least part of the civil society that undermined communist control, it also returns to the question of where these societal initiatives came from in the first place. Applied to this study, the question is: what were the roots of the ecological movement? To answer this question we need a more dynamic understanding of society in communist countries than was generally proffered in the literature on communist political systems.

The environmental movement developed in response to (1) the actual physical conditions resulting from economic policies made according to certain political procedures and priorities and (2) the political opportunities that arose in the 1980s. Both of these factors were rooted in the national political process. A particular set of institutions and decision-making processes had produced Poland's industrialization pattern and debilitated attempts at environmental protection. The results sparked concern among certain members of society who formed collective identities around changing both values and these political processes. These collective actors, as well as politically active individuals, functioned at various levels of the political system from the local to the national, in various policy areas and institutions, and in the media and the social sphere. While some worked within the political system; others remained outside of it. As more collective actors formed and as their concerns became visible, activists developed networks among the groups and the consciousness of an overall movement, which in turn encouraged more groups to form.

That individuals and groups were able to expand the nature and scope of their activism into a social movement was in part the result of changes in Polish politics beginning with the formation of a social, cultural, and political opposition in the late 1970s. More support and channels for expressing alternative views combined with the serious economic challenges facing the regime to shape the conditions for Solidarity's formation in 1980. And, the Solidarity challenge changed the political dynamics of Poland, not only during the union's legal existence, but afterward as well. For the environmental movement, the most crucial changes were the expansion of public dialogue, both in the official and unofficial media, and the regime's greater tolerance for social activism it did not directly control. Although preemption, establishment of bureaucratic, financial and logistical barriers, and cooptation were strategies for minimizing and controlling that activism, these strategies' failure did not often bring severe repression of those who continued their activities. Indeed, as argued above, inclusion attempts even brought some opportunities for further development of the movement.

Thus, this study lends support to the argument that the roots of social movements are to be found in the national political process.[1] The environmental movement, even in its focus on changing societal norms and its attempts to serve as a bridge between these new norms and political life, actually derived its impulse from the political system, the way it functioned, and the results of the policies it produced. Ultimately, the same can be said for the political opposition that served the environment well as a foil. Social refusal to submit to communist party authority stemmed from the very attempt to atomize and control society that was inherent to the Soviet-type political system in general and to normalization in particular. True to Marx's observations about all of the modes of production he had studied, Soviet-style state socialism contained the seeds of its own destruction.

More specifically, this study supports Robert Rohrschneider's finding for Western Europe that environmentalism as a national political issue inspired participation in the movement at the local level.[2] The rapid growth in local initiatives came after 1985 and the public controversy that placed environmentalism in the media and on the national agenda. Furthermore, many of the small local groups referred to national issues and aligned with other actors on the national political scene, such as Solidarity or the Church.

The case of the Polish ecological movement also has something to say to those studying new social movements. The organizational, ideological, and political characteristics of this movement define it as a new social movement. This should not be surprising as environmental movements are among the prime examples of new social movements in the West. What is instructive is that this movement developed under Soviet-type state socialism. While perhaps confirming theories that find the roots of new social movements in the technological, psychological, and cultural challenges of modern industrialized society, the fact that the movement developed under state socialism refutes theories that derive new social movements specifically from the class structure of advanced *capitalism* or *market* penetration of everyday life and culture. At the same time it suggests that the environmental movement will persist, albeit in somewhat different forms and with different strategies, under the new political system in Poland.

Finally, the experience of the Polish ecological movement speaks to those living under authoritarian systems who would like to mobilize for change in the political system or in a specific policy issue area. The abject failure of the government's attempt to create an official environmental movement that would pull together existing groups and channel their demands in acceptable directions (PRON's "Social Ecological Movement") suggests that it is difficult for even a strongly centralized authoritarian state with well-institutionalized mechanisms of social control to contain and regulate a heterogeneous, decentralized social movement. A pluralistic movement with informal networks of cooperation and no center has to be controlled or repressed at the level of each individual group. Repressing or gaining control over even an important group in the movement does not give the regime control over the others. Although controlling each group is certainly possible, it becomes increasingly difficult as the number and variety of groups multiply, particularly if the regime is facing similar movements in other issue areas and/or serious economic or legitimacy crises at the same time.

Beyond "Us vs. Them": Civil Society in Poland's Transition

The spectacular image of Solidarity, an independent labor union of almost ten million, locked in open political battle with the party-state for a year and a half reinforced the perception in Polish society of a great divide between the "us" of society and the "them" of the state. Martial law and the establishment of an extensive underground strengthened this perception. In Western theory, Polish politics became a prime case of a contest between state and society.[3] Indeed, both the contest and the perception existed. At a general level, the "us-them" dichotomy, along with economic crisis, defined the context of politics in Poland at least from 1980, if not earlier.

However, "us vs. them" is not the full story. On the level of daily politics, there were many different versions of "us" and the "thems" of the party-state were defined with varying levels of specificity depending on the "us" doing the defining. Moreover, as this study has argued, some people and groups formed their identities on a basis different from this dichotomy. One result was the development of social movements, such as the environmental movement, and other initiatives that remained independent of both the government and the opposition. Thus, even at the level of composite political actors, such as movements, "the Church," and "the opposition," the Polish regime's political tasks were more complex than just fighting its contest with the opposition. Preemption, repression, various uses of the press, tolerance, and the inclusion strategy were indicative of a more differentiated approach to the variety of social forces. At the same time regime interactions with each movement, or in each issue area, were imbedded in the general "us-them" confrontation between Solidarity and the party-state. The ecological movement, like other independent movements and groups and even the Roman Catholic Church, was able to use the conflict between the government and the political opposition to gain concessions from the former and support from the latter.

Moving down a step to the level of individual collective actors, the political dynamics in society become even more complex. Each group was an "us" in its interaction with the state. This perception existed in official groups, as well as in independent and opposition groups. Thus, the League for the Protection of Nature, even the PRON ecological movement and the individual circles within these two organizations, saw themselves as social forces struggling against state bureaucracies for resources or policy outcomes. Furthermore, the arenas in which environmental groups operated were so varied that often it was futile for the regime to address "the environmental movement." While many concentrated on public actions to raise consciousness or worked with the political opposition, others worked within state institutions. Examples include the *Ekos* group in the media, many of the occupational groups, and activists who served on advisory committees or even worked for the various state environmental administrations. Thus, parts of the movement worked for change from within the system. Connected to other activists by norms and goals that differed from those of the regime, as well as by more direct contacts, they weakened the "official" institutions that would counter those norms or goals. A perspective based on confrontation between state and society misses these sorts of influences which society had *in* the state.

Finally, at the individual level, where the "us-them" conflict was mirrored in the self-perceptions of most Poles as "us," citizens made choices about their norms and their activism in any of the public spheres mentioned above. As this study has shown, some crossed the lines between official, independent, and opposition spheres, basing their decisions about political participation on other criteria. Many also chose to remain outside of public life and the process of collective norm formation that bridges private and public spheres.

At the same time that the perceptions of "us" at all of these levels united society in Poland, they also derived from a wide variety of political interactions that cannot be understood through the prism of "society versus the state" or the confrontation between Solidarity and the regime. Often, it was the more specific political interactions and policy failures in various issue areas that prompted new collective actors to form. The emergence of these new collective actors and the process of norm definition linking private and public life were the development of a "civil society." All of these actors and processes taken together strengthened that civil society and weakened state control of society, eventually undermining the party-state itself. The political opposition may have been the original nucleus of this civil society and an important foil for its further and more heterogeneous development, and the "us" sentiment did serve to unite society, but the evolution of civil society was more complex than the building of united opposition to the regime. The power of civil society's challenge to the communist regime also derived from its penetration of the state and the very complexity that made the challenge hard to identify and control.

Environment and Regime Transformation

Environmental destruction is, in and of itself, a crucial issue for Poland and for industrial society as a whole. The fundamental challenge of environmental values and activism to the assumptions and technological bases of human society respects no political system above others. Although environmental movements may arise in specific political circumstances, they address some issues that are common to all and, in fact, should be considered more basic than political systems themselves. Thus, the political and economic transformation in Poland may mean change in types of environmental activism, but the challenge presented by the movement persists.

In the early stages of transition, the environmental movement was part of the general social challenge to the regime, participating in the development and differentiation of a civil society beyond the regime's control and raising crucial issues that further undermined the legitimacy of communist rule. This was the process studied here. With passage to the second stage of the transition, the building of a new system, issues raised and identities formed primarily on bases other than cooperation with or opposition to the regime existing before the transition may provide more effective foundations for organizing various interests in the developing civil societies of the new democracies than can the identities linked with the old system. Environmentalism is one source of identities not linked to the particular political configuration of the old system.

The environmental movement is undergoing a partial transformation of its own. One new direction for a few activists is party politics. However, as is the case throughout Central and Eastern Europe, environmental parties have not fared well in electoral contests.[4] This does not mean that environmental interests have ceased to be a point around which forces in civil society organize. Rather, in the context of the major political and economic transformation occurring in Poland, most ecologists have found more potential in organizing interest groups to lobby the major political parties and state organs at both national and subnational levels. Some actors are intensifying and institutionalizing the networks of communication among movement participants. We see more internal education about political processes, laws, and the technicalities of environmental protection. This self-education is aimed primarily at being able to engage in the policymaking process. Calling themselves NGOs, at least several of the collective actors in the movement are consciously trying to develop the lobbying and organizing skills required of effective interest groups in the new democratic system. Others have concentrated on the entrepreneurial skills necessary in a market economy, helping to develop the foundations, funds, and grant projects for investment in environmental protection and for sustaining environmental activism. Some of these entrepreneurs are focusing their energies on the opportunities for using international and transnational actors to boost their resources and influence at home, as well as to achieve specific environmental goals. In sum, we are seeing the institutionalization of environmental interests.

Despite their changes to meet new political and economic conditions, environmental interests have not experienced a sharp increase in their effectiveness and may even be losing ground in their visibility and on the political agenda. Most of these difficulties stem from the very fact that activists are functioning in rapidly changing political and economic systems. The targets of lobbying efforts are themselves still weak and the procedures for policymaking are still evolving. Another aspect of the changing context that weakens the visibility of environmental issues is the sheer number of major decisions facing the country. Economic transformation—the flux in ownership, regulations, property rights, market accountability—makes tackling the source of much ecological degradation difficult and makes outcomes far less predictable. The support that ecologists receive from the broader public is also subject to the vagaries of transition. Public concern about ecology and support for environmental values remains quite high. Participation in environmental activism, even awareness of and support for that activism, however, is much weaker. Although this phenomenon needs more investigation, opinion surveys suggest that the experience of economic transformation is dimming citizens' views of the possibility of tackling environmental problems and economic restructuring at the same time. Likewise, the difficulties experienced by activists when they face parts of the ever changing political system intensify public perception of movement ineffectiveness.

For environmental activism, the positive side of all of these difficulties associated with transition itself is that they may lessen with the consolidation of political democracy and a market economy. The negative side is that the political and economic transformation may leave the country with all of the environmental problems of Western capitalism, intensified by the nature of Poland's industrial base and its poorer budgets for environmental protection. The chance to build in some ecological soundness during economic restructuring may be lost. The main force working against this fate is the network of interest groups, movements, institutes, and foundations trying to shape policies, procedures and values of political actors and public alike. At the same time, the existence and evolution of these associations and groups is part of the reshaping and expansion of civil society necessary for consolidation of the new democratic polity.

Appendix A
Opposition Press Sources

My survey of the opposition press included an intensive review of the holdings of the Poland Watch Center in Washington, D.C. (now defunct). For additional underground holdings throughout Western Europe and the United States, I consulted the microfiche collection IDC Polish Independent Publications . My use of these collections was supplemented by a review of Biuletyn Informacyjny Solidarności, later titled the Committee in Support of Solidarity Reports, which summarized Solidarity activities and press for distribution abroad, and by summaries of opposition press in Uncensored Poland News Bulletin and Radio Free Europe's Research Reports . While I was in Poland in 1985–86 and 1987–88, I also followed the available opposition press to get a sense of what was reaching the average, nonactivist reader.

The Poland Watch review covers the period from martial law until summer 1987, making use of the center's subject index for all publications received as well as my own survey of the following publications:

Agencja Informacyjna "S" (Warsaw, periodic review of press);

Baza (Warsaw, monthly of the socio-political club "Workers' Thought");

CDN: Głos Wolnego Robotnika (Warsaw, weekly of the Interfactory Workers' Committee);

Dzień (Kraków, bi-weekly of regional Solidarity's Academic Commission for Understanding);

Głos Medyka (Warsaw, bi-monthly of the workers of the Warsaw Health Service in cooperation with the Social Commission for Health);

Informator (Lublin, information bulletin for the East Central region);

KOS (Warsaw, bi-weekly of the Committee for Social Resistance);

Mała Polska (Kraków, weekly);

Niepodległość (Kraków, monthly of the Confederation for an Independent Poland);

Obraz (Szczecin, monthly);

Przegląd Wiadomości Agencyjnych (Warsaw, weekly information review of the Mazowsze Region);

Prześwit (Łódź, bi-monthly);

Samorządna Rzeczpospolita (national, bi-weekly of NSZZ Solidarność);

Sektor (Warsaw, weekly (?) of the regional Committee for Resistance);

Solidarność Chemików (Wrocław, information bulletin of the Solidarity factory committees of "Chemitex," "Polifarb," and "Superfosfat"—three major plants in the chemical industry);

Solidarność Nauczycielska (Lublin, monthly of education workers);

Tygodnik Mazowsze (Warsaw, weekly, main publication of the regional organization of Solidarity);

Wola (Warsaw, weekly of the Inter-factory Coordinating Committee);

Many underground publications sprang up and disappeared during my review period and several issues did not reach Western collections, so it is impossible to get an accurate survey of all articles on the environment. However, this review, supplemented by the Committee in Support of Solidarity, Uncensored Poland and Radio Free Europe summaries from martial law through 1988, provides a clear picture of the pattern of opposition press coverage of environmental issues. A reader of the English language summaries would see this pattern quite clearly—a complete lack of information through 1983, an occasional article in 1984, and steadily increasing coverage of the environment from the second half of 1985 and especially after the Chernobyl accident. Actually, these summaries tend to exaggerate the lack of ecological reporting in the underground press. Concerned primarily with repression and developments inside Solidarity, the Western reviews do not always reflect the richness of issues covered in that press, especially in the nonperiodical underground press from 1985 on. Although the extent of underground press coverage is somewhat underrepresented in Western reviews (with the exception of the Chernobyl accident), the pattern of coverage remains evident.

Appendix B:
Summary of Official Press Review

Articles on the Environment or with Discussions of Environmental
Problems (May - July 1988)

Serial Name and Target Population[a]	Place & Frequency of Publication	No. of Art.'s	Voivodship[a] (New / Old)[b]
Argumenty intelligentsia, economists	Warszawa weekly	4	Stołeczne-Warszawskie
Chłopska Droga farmers, rural population	Warszawa weekly	6	Stołeczne-Warszawskie
Dziennik Bałtycki general regional	Gdańsk daily	28	Gdańskie
Dziennik Ludowy general central, twd rural	Warszawa daily	59	Stołeczne-Warszawskie
Dziennik Łódzki general regional	Łódź daily	11	Łódzkie
Dziennik Pojezierze general regional	Olsztyn daily	28	Olsztyńskie
Dziennik Polski general regional	Kraków daily	24	Krakowskie
Dziennik Wieczorny general regional	Bydgoszcz daily	11	Bydgoskie
Dziennik Zachodni general	Katowice daily	48	Katowickie
Echo Dnia general regional	Kielce daily	19	Kieleckie
Echo Krakowa general regional	Kraków daily	31	Krakowskie
Ekran film-lovers (general)	Warszawa weekly	1	Stołeczne-Warszawskie
Express Ilustrowany general regional	Łódź daily	16	Łódzkie
Express Poznański general regional	Poznań daily	8	Poznańskie

Serial Name and Target Population[a]	Place & Frequency of Publication	No. of Art.'s	Voivodship (New / Old)[b]
Express Wieczorny general central	Warszawa daily	42	Stołeczne-Warszawskie
Fakty socio-cultural, educated	Bydoszcz weekly	5	Bydgoskie
Fundamenty social-economic	Warszawa weekly	4	Stołeczne-Warszawskie
Gazeta Krakowska general regional	Kraków daily	41	Krakowskie
Gazeta Lubuska general regional	Zielona Góra daily	21	Zielonogórskie
Gazeta Młodych central, youth	Warszawa 2x per week	4	Stołeczne-Warszawskie
Gazeta Olsztyńska general regional	Olsztyn daily	16	Olsztyńskie
Gazeta Pomorska general regional	Bydgoszcz daily	29	Bydgoskie
Gazeta Poznańska general regional	Poznań daily	32	Poznańskie
Gazeta Robotnicza general regional	Wrocław daily	51	Wrocławskie
Gazeta Robotnicza - Magazyn general regional	Wrocław weekly	1	Wrocławskie
Gazeta Współczesna general regional	Białysok daily	35	Białostockie
Głos Pomorza general regional	Koszalin daily	32	Koszalińskie
Głos Robotniczy general regional	Łódź daily	26	Łódzkie
Głos Szczeciński general regional	Szczecin daily	34	Szczecińskie
Głos Wielkopolski general regional	Poznań daily	21	Poznańskie
Głos Wybrzeża general regional	Gdańsk daily	26	Gdańskie
Gromada Rolnik Polski central farmers	Warszawa 3x per week	28	Stołeczne-Warszawskie
Ilustrowany Kurier Polski general regional, less educated	Bydgoszcz daily	20	Bydgoskie
ITD central, university students	Warszawa weekly	3	Stołeczne-Warszawskie
Kamena central lit & culture, high ed.	Lublin bi-weekly	2	Lubelskie
Kierunki social-cultural, Catholic (PAX)	Warszawa weekly	8	Stołeczne-Warszawskie
Kobieta i Życie central, women	Warszawa weekly	5	Stołeczne-Warszawskie
Kontrasty socio-cultural, higher ed.	Białystok monthly	3	Białostockie
Kultura central, higher ed, intell'sia	Warszawa weekly	3	Stołeczne-Warszawskie
Kurier Lubelski general regional	Lublin daily	18	Lubelskie
Kurier Podlaski general regional	Białystok daily	22	Białostockie

Serial Name and Target Population[a]	Place & Frequency of Publication	No. of Art.'s	Voivodship (New / Old)[b]
Kurier Polski general central	Warszawa daily	82	Stołeczne-Warszawskie
Kurier Spółdzielczy workers in cooperatives	Warszawa bi-weekly	3	Stołeczne-Warszawskie
Kurier Szczeciński general regional	Szczecin daily	10	Szczecińskie
Ład central Catholic, socio-polit.	Warszawa weekly	6	Stołeczne-Warszawskie
Miesięcznik Literacki central, int'sia in humanities	Warszawa monthly	1	Stołeczne-Warszawskie
Myśl Społeczna social, Catholic	Warszawa weekly	4	Stołeczne-Warszawskie
Na Przełaj general youth, scouts	Warszawa weekly	28	Stołeczne-Warszawskie
Nadodrze regional cultural	Zielona Góra bi-weekly	2	Zielonogórskie
Nowiny general regional	Rzeszów daily	22	Rzeszowskie
Nowości - Dziennik Toruński general regional	Toruń daily	10	Toruńskie Bydgoskie
Nurt teachers, higher educ, culture	Poznań monthly	5	Poznańskie
Odgłosy regional, cultural	Łódź weekly	7	Łódzkie
Odra central, intellectuals, culture	Wroclaw monthly	3	Wrocławskie
Odrodzenie central organ of PRON	Warszawa weekly	8	Stołeczne-Warszawskie
Opole regional	Opole monthly	2	Opolskie
Panorama central general, light features	Katowice weekly	5	Katowickie
Panorama Polska central on nature and tourism	Warszawa monthly	1	Stołeczne-Warszawskie
Perspektywy social, political, cult, h.s.+	Warszawa weekly	5	Stołeczne-Warszawskie
Polityka central political, educated	Warszawa weekly	14	Stołeczne-Warszawskie
Polska Kronika Filmowa texts of doc'ary film clips	Warszawa weekly	1	Short documentary film shown before movies
Prawo i Życie central, lawyers, managers	Warszawa weekly	11	Stołeczne-Warszawskie
Profile regional, cultural	Rzeszów monthly	2	Rzeszowskie
Przegląd Techniczny central, tech int'sia, managers	Warszawa weekly	11	Stołeczne-Warszawskie
Przegląd Tygodniowy central, weekly review	Warszawa weekly	19	Stołeczne-Warszawskie
Przekrój general, emigrees, features	Kraków weekly	8	Krakowskie
Przemiany regional, social-cultural	Kielce monthly	1	Kieleckie
Przyjaciółka central for women	Warszawa weekly	4	Stołeczne-Warszawskie

Serial Name and Target Population[a]	Place & Frequency of Publication	No. of Art.'s	Voivodship (New / Old)[b]
Rada Narodowa central organ, people's council	Warszawa weekly	14	Stołeczne-Warszawskie
Razem central, youth	Warszawa weekly	13	Stołeczne-Warszawskie
Razem Magazyn central, youth	Warszawa monthly	1	Stołeczne-Warszawskie
Rynki Zagraniczne managers, economists	Warszawa 3x per week	1	Stołeczne-Warszawskie
Rzeczpospolita central organ of the gov't	Warszawa daily	70	Stołeczne-Warszawskie
Rzeczywistość general, this edition was new during normaliz.	Warszawa weekly	7	Stołeczne-Warszawskie
Słowo Ludu general regional	Kielce daily	25	Kieleckie
Słowo Polskie general regional	Wrocław daily	16	Wrocławskie
Słowo Powszechne central, official Catholic	Warszawa daily	55	Stołeczne-Warszawskie
Sport central, mostly men	Katowice 5x per week	2	Katowickie
Sportowiec central, mostly men	Warszawa weekly	1	Stołeczne-Warszawskie
Sprawy i Ludzie social issues, higher ed	Wrocław weekly	9	Wrocławskie
Stolica central & reg'l about capital	Warszawa weekly	8	Stołeczne-Warszawskie
Szpilki general humor, h.s. educ +	Warszawa weekly	1	Stołeczne-Warszawskie
Sztandar Ludu general regional	Lublin daily	31	Lubelskie
Sztandar Młodych party organ for youth, students	Warszawa daily	45	Stołeczne-Warszawskie
Świat Młodych central children	Warszawa 3x per week	2	Stołeczne-Warszawskie
Tempo regional, sports	Kraków 3x per week	1	Krakowskie
Teraz TV program on economies	Warszawa ?	3	National TV (Channel 1)
TIM, Tygodnik Ilustrowany Magazyn general features	Warszawa weekly	1	Stołeczne-Warszawskie
TOP, Tygodnik Ogloszen Prasowych general with ads	Warszawa weekly	3	Stołeczne-Warszawskie
Trybuna Ludu central party organ	Warszawa daily	44	Stołeczne-Warszawskie
Trybuna Opolska general regional	Opole daily	19	Opolskie
Trybuna Robotnicza general regional	Katowice daily	50	Katowickie
Tygodnik Demokratyczny organ of Democ Party	Warszawa weekly	16	Stołeczne-Warszawskie
Tygodnik Kulturalny central, culture, h.s. educ +	Warszawa weekly	3	Stołeczne-Warszawskie

Serial Name and Target Population[a]	Place & Frequency of Publication	No. of Art.'s	Voivodship (New / Old)[b]
Tygodnik Polski general central	Warszawa weekly	4	Stołeczne-Warszawskie
Tygodnik Powszechny general organ of Cath Church	Kraków weekly	2	Krakowskie
Tygodnik Tak i Nie socio-cultural, h.s. educ +	Katowice weekly	6	Katowickie
Veto consumers, businessmen	Warszawa weekly	6	Stołeczne-Warszawskie
Walka Młodych young adults, organ of ZSMP	Warszawa weekly	6	Stołeczne-Warszawskie
Warmia i Mazury regional	Olsztyn bi-weekly	1	Olsztyńskie
Widnokręgi central for whole family, broad	Warszawa monthly	1	Stołeczne-Warszawskie
Wieczór general regional	Katowice daily	28	Katowickie
Wieczór Wrocławia general regional	Wrocław daily	20	Wrocławskie
Wieczór Wybrzeża general regional	Gdańsk daily	10	Gdańskie
Za i Przeciw social-political, Catholic	? weekly	4	? ?
Zarzewie central, rural youth	Warszawa weekly	1	Stołeczne-Warszawskie
Zdanie culture, lit., higher educ.	Kraków monthly	2	Krakowskie
Zielony Sztandar organ of Peasant party	Warszawa weekly	11	Stołeczne-Warszawskie
Żołnierz Wolności military, observers of politics	Warszawa daily	13	Stołeczne-Warszawskie
Związkowiec workers, official unions	Warszawa weekly	8	Stołeczne-Warszawskie
Zwierciadło women, general	? weekly	1	Stołeczne-Warszawskie ?
Życie Częstochowy general regional	Częstochowa daily	6	Częstochowskie Katowickie
Życie Gospodarcze managers, economists	Warszawa weekly	3	Stołeczne-Warszawskie
Życie i Zdrowie central family, health	Warszawa ?	1	Stołeczne-Warszawskie
Życie Literackie central literary, int'sia	Kraków weekly	8	Krakowskie
Życie Partii party members and activists	Warszawa bi-weekly	3	Stołeczne-Warszawskie
Życie Radomskie general regional	Radom daily	8	Radomskie Kieleckie
Życie Warszawy general central and regional	Warszawa daily	83	Stołeczne-Warszawskie

Total = 118 serials (116 print, one film documentary, one TV program)

[a]Information on the target population and the nature of the publication is based on my own reading of the articles and/or periodical, any descriptions given in the masthead of the publication, and consultation with educated Poles.

[b]Unless otherwise noted, voivodship is the same, new and old.

Notes

Introduction

1. For this definition and a model of the normalization process, see Zdenek Mlynar's introduction to Brus, Kende and Mlynar 1982, 3–4.

1. Civil Society, Normalization, and Transition

1. The "transitions" literature is voluminous. For Eastern Europe, see especially Bermeo, ed. 1992; Przeworski 1991; Rau, ed. 1991; Ekiert 1991; Welsh 1994. For comparative perspectives, see Rustow 1970; O'Donnell, Schmitter and Whitehead, eds. 1986; Karl 1990; DiPalma 1990; Huntington 1991; Diamond 1991; Mainwaring, O'Donnell and Valenzuela 1992. Helpful reviews of this literature include Bermeo 1990; Karl 1990; Remmer 1991; Lawson 1993.

2. For an extended discussion of the conceptual and substantive origins of civil society, as well as its applications to contemporary societies (including those of East Central Europe), see the contributions in Keane, ed. 1988.

3. See Michnik 1976, especially pp. 273–76. Similar perspectives are evident in the Czechoslovak discussion of "parallel polis" (Benda 1991) and the Hungarian debate about a "second society" (Hankiss 1990, ch.3), as well as the entire East European discussion of "anti-politics" (Konrad 1984). For an illuminating examination of the derivation of the "new evolutionist" strategy see Bernhard 1993, 88–97. Bugajski and Pollack (1989) provide an overview of types of dissent in Eastern Europe. Pelczynski 1988; Rupnik 1988 (217–223); Ost 1990 (ch's.2 and 4); Rau, ed. 1991; Tismaneanu 1992 (chs. 4 and 5); Bernhard 1993 (ch.1); Arato 1981 and Skilling 1991 all discuss the role played by the concept of civil society in East European dissident thought of the 1970s. This emphasis, however, was not unique to Eastern Europe. Perhaps the most striking parallel is provided in the

examination of the role that forces of civil society were playing and the conceptualization of civil society in Brazil's transition (cf. Stepan 1988).

4. Several works have focused on the role of intellectual opposition, in particular the Committee for the Defense of the Workers (KOR), in preparing the ground for Solidarity's successful challenge in 1980. See Lipski 1985; Bernhard 1993; Zuzowski 1992; Ost 1990; Pelczynski 1988; and Lepak 1988. For discussions that emphasize the worker roots of the Solidarity trade union, see Goodwyn 1991; Laba 1986, 1991.

5. This drive toward unity is visible in the sheer size of Solidarity which peaked at a little under 10 million members (from a total population of just over 36 million) in 1981. Moreover, individual farmers in "Rural Solidarity" and the student Solidarity union also sought participation in and the protection of the Solidarity umbrella. For an interesting argument that the language of the Solidarity movement and, after the imposition of martial law, the underground press not only presupposed this unity but also undermined pluralism in society, see Lin 1983. Jan Kubik's (1994) study of Polish public discourse also notes the "oversymbolization" of Solidarity's language and its contribution to developing an almost "monolithic" perception of "us vs. them" in the late 1970s and 1980. He argues that this perception did not reflect the actual differences among its holders. Even Solidarity's emphasis on decentralized, democratic structures faced challenges during the union's legal period as leaders in the National Commission and its Presidium sought to develop effective strategies for dealing with the authorities while trying to control the radicalization of some parts of the membership.

6. In discussing the East European context, for example, Grzegorz Ekiert has suggested replacing "civil society" with a distinction between "political society . . . which embraces the entirety of voluntary associations and social movements in an active political community" and "domestic society . . . the domain of purposeful action restricted to the private sphere and organized in terms of material needs and self-interests" (1991, 300). For him, this is a useful distinction for understanding the relationship between the party-state and the society it ruled. In this framework, we could conceptualize social movements as avenues by which individuals from "domestic society" become collective actors of "political society." Thus social movements would be collective actors who, through their political action to achieve change in the state and public arenas, also seek change in domestic society. Relating Ekiert's two terms back to the concept of "civil society," it is tempting to equate "political" and "civil" society. Yet, the social movement example points out the roots of political society in the norms of domestic society. Indeed, these roots are what gives the concept "civil society" its positive normative power, especially when it is juxtaposed to the "state." Thus, "civil society" must embrace not only the organizations, associations, and social movements of political society, but also the process of social and political norm formation that takes place across the boundaries of domestic and political society.

Ekiert's use of "political society" differs from others who have also sought to put bounds on the concept of civil society. Whereas Ekiert wishes to replace "civil society" with his delineation of domestic and political society, Stepan (1988) uses the term political society to distinguish formal political actors contesting for power over the state from his more informal notion of civil society as an "arena where manifold social movements . . . and civic organizations from all classes . . . attempt to constitute themselves . . . so that they can express themselves and advance their interests (1988, 3–4)." Stepan's distinction between civil and political society is closer to Tocqueville's ([1835 and 1840] 1945) usage of these terms.

7. This distinction between civil society and the economy is not always clear. Examinations of the changing nature of society resulting from economic reform, particularly in the Hungarian and Chinese cases, sometimes identify the "second economy" with civil society.

8. The literal translation of "my-oni," the phrase used in Polish, is "we-they." I favor the "we-they" translation because its captures a stronger sense of agency and active distinction between groups. However, the "us-them" translation captures the somewhat slang usage of the term(s). Both translations are used in the English-language literature on Poland, though increasingly the latter predominates. Hence its use here.

9. For discussion of some of these movements in Poland, see Miształ 1990. Some of the movements he discusses, for example the independent education movement, have been left out of this list because they are more closely associated with the political opposition.

10. For a variety of interpretations of Poland's series of crises and regime strategies for dealing with these crises, see Bielasiak 1984; *Przyczyny, Przebieg i Skutki Kryzysów Społecznych w Dziejach PRL* and *Kalendarium Kryzysów w PRL (lata 1953–1980)* in *Zeszyty Historyczne* 1983, 65:137–77 and 66:144–95, respectively; Taras 1986; and Staniszkis 1984. Kowalski and Malinowski, also stress the exhaustion of political management strategies and all other resources of institutional authority as an explanation for the resort to military force (1982, 24–25).

11. Indeed some authors argue that environmental degradation was central to the downfall of the communist systems. See, for example, Jancar-Webster 1993a, 200 and Feshbach and Friendly 1992. As I argue in chapter 6, Solidarity generally supported the environmental movement but did not place a priority on ecology.

12. See, for example, Brus 1982, 43–45. Jiri Valenta (1984, 128, 144–47), though a little less skeptical, also points out the problems in normalizing Poland.

13. Kolankiewicz (1988) bases his discussion of inclusion in the process of normalization on Kenneth Jowitt's work (1975). Jowitt discusses an earlier period in building the socialist system, the period just after system consolidation when social forces begin to express a plurality of interests. Mobilization of active participation in order to integrate potentially pluralist forces was the main intent of inclusion. In the post-crisis normalization process, inclusion has a slightly different shade of meaning. Here the regime is trying to demobilize participation in general, while bringing those groups who remain active into the policymaking arena, with all of its constraints. For Poland, the main difference in meaning derives from a change in context. While the Polish governments of the late 1960s and early 1970s might have had a chance to build legitimacy using Jowitt's version of inclusion, the Jaruzelski regime of the 1980s was working from the base of a profound rejection of its legitimacy.

14. I am indebted to an anonymous reviewer for this final phrasing of the dilemma.

15. Workers' demands for an independent trade union in 1980, for example, derived from the realization that the government's previous promises of change in policy and procedure after the 1956 and 1970 crises had not been kept.

16. This definition excludes "movements" aimed *solely* at individual change, e.g. self-help movements. If, however, such movements endeavor to change social attitudes or norms, they do fall under this definition. My definition of social movement is similar to those of several authors approaching social movements from a variety of perspectives. It is perhaps closest to Oberschall's view of social movements as "large-scale collective efforts to bring about or resist changes that bear on the lives of many" (1993, 3). We share a focus on change in society, a focus that is also at the heart of the many conceptions of this theoretical term found in the "new social movement" literature. Touraine, for example defines social movements as a "type of social conflict whose stake is the social control of the main cultural patterns, that is of the patterns through which our relationships with the environment are normatively organized" (1985, 754). Melucci sees social movements as a type of collective action characterized by solidarity, which engages in conflict over goods or values and transgresses the boundaries of the existing political or social system (1989, 29–30; cf. 1980, 202). These three elements are essential to most definitions of the term. Zald and McCarthy, working in the resource-mobilization tradition, also maintain a focus on social change in their definition of a social movement as "a set of opinions and beliefs in a population representing preferences for changing some elements of the social structure or reward distribution, or both, of a society (1987, 20, 40n6)." Tarrow defines movements—without using the modifying adjective "social"—as "collective challenges by people with common purposes and solidarity in sustained interaction with elites, opponents and authorities" (1994, 3–4). Again, the emphasis is on common purpose, solidarity, joint action. Tarrow does not make social change (or resistance to it) an explicit target of movement activism, although "challenge" usually implies either direct or indirect pursuit of social change. He has thus defined movement more broadly. Tarrow is also more explicit about the conflictual element in social movements and their sustained challenge to authority. Running through all of the major approaches to social movements is this emphasis on conflict or challenge (to authorities, system boundaries, or other social groups). Although understated, a sense of challenge is also inherent in the definition of social movement adopted here. As social movements attempt to achieve changes in norms, structures, or roles in society, they meet the resistance of those groups and institutions upholding the status quo, and usually this means conflict or, as Tarrow puts it, "sustained interaction." Conversely, if a movement resists change, it is also resisting powerful forces promoting that change, either other groups in society or authorities acting through the state.

17. Obviously the boundaries of "schools" of thought are very porous and individual works vary greatly even within those porous boundaries. Moreover, some of the scholars still working within these traditions have developed their theories to incorporate concerns and critiques of others. Several excellent reviews

discuss the Western social movement literature. See, for example: Tarrow 1988, 1993; Cohen 1983, 1985; Jenkins 1983; McAdam 1982; Kitschelt 1985; Pakulski 1991; Oberschall 1993. A few volumes of collected work are also dedicated to a review of this literature: *International Social Movement Research* Series (Greenwich, CT: JAI Press), see especially Klandermans, Kriesi and Tarrow, eds. 1988, vol.1; Rucht, ed. 1991 also contains several fine discussions of the literature and empirical studies.

18. Mancur Olson's *Logic of Collective Action* (1965) was the point of departure for resource mobilization theory. Leading works include: Zald and McCarthy 1979, 1987; Oberschall 1973; Gamson 1975. Oberschall 1993 extends resource mobilization theory by tackling many of the issues raised by other approaches.

19. See Touraine 1981, 1985; Habermas 1981; Eder 1982, 1985; Offe 1985; Melucci 1980, 1985, 1988, 1989. For more empirical work adopting elements of this general perspective, see: Inglehart 1977, 1990; Kitschelt 1985; Dalton and Kuechler, eds. 1990; Kriesi et al. 1995.

20. For examples of work using this approach see: McAdam 1982 and Kitschelt 1986. McAdam (1982, 36) borrows the term political process from James Rule and Charles Tilly and, while arguing that his model is different, recognizes the earlier contributions that Tilly and William Gamson made in linking social movements to political processes (p. 2).

21. For an interesting attempt to weigh the relative influence of factors emphasized by these different perspectives in West European citizens' attitudes toward environmental activism, see Rohrschneider 1988. An emphasis on national-level opportunity structures is also pronounced in work on protest cycles (see next note for references).

22. For a review of this literature and a discussion of its applicability to the East European "rebellions" in 1989, see Tarrow 1991. Some authors focus on historical patterns of waves of mobilization (Brand 1990); whereas others look more closely at patterns within one wave (Hirschman 1982; Tarrow 1993; Traugott, ed., 1995; Kriesi et al., 1995).

23. See Tarrow 1991, 14–16, for a discussion of the development of this concept and its possible application to the "civil society" literature on Eastern Europe as well as to the 1989 wave of popular mobilization. Stanley Kabala emphasizes the Solidarity roots of the Polish environmental movement in Vari and Tamas 1993, 49–54.

24. For discussion of "social movement sectors," see McCarthy and Zald 1977 and Garner and Zald 1987. McAdam's 1995 discussion of "initiator movements" also describes Solidarity's role in Poland in 1980–81.

25. See especially Barbara Jancar's discussions of environmental agencies and experts in the Soviet Union and Yugoslavia (1987, ch. 3, 6), as well as Ziegler 1979, 1986, Weiner 1988 and Fisher 1993.

26. For two such critiques, see Tucker 1991 and Calhoun 1995. For a defense of the term "new" see Dalton, Kuechler and Bürklin 1990, 10–16.

27. See the discussion of Touraine and Cohen below. Work on post-materialism and the new middle class is very much in this vein as well. Klaus Eder (1993)

has also developed this argument somewhat differently by analyzing these movements and collective actions as parts of *the* new social movement in the development of human society, (see especially chapters 6 and 8).

28. Although these movements eschew a class identity, several studies of new social movements in the West have found that the membership and values of these movements stem predominantly from a "new middle class" of the well-educated and urban post-WWII generation. See, for example, Inglehart (1977) and Dalton and Kuechler, eds. (1990).

29. Cohen's theorizing here (1983, 101) is influenced by Habermas's description of the processes he calls "colonization of the life world."

30. Inglehart and Siemienska (1988) detect post-material values in support for Solidarity. For an argument that Solidarity in 1980–81 was a new social movement see Mason 1989. Given that Solidarity was also a trade union with strong emphasis on workers' material well-being, the picture of values and activism in Poland clearly has to be mixed. Moreover, the labeling of socially oriented values as *post*-materlialist is more dubious than it has been in the West. That a "post-material" or, using Kitschelt's term, "left libertarian" strain existed alongside a class-based materially oriented activism within Solidarity reflects its origins in an intelligentsia-worker alliance and its umbrella role for political opposition from 1980 on; it also presages the movement's split after 1989.

31. Cohen makes this point in distinguishing new movements from older revolutionary or transformative movements. In the former " . . . the slogan 'society vs. the state' means the democratization of social institutions and not dedifferentiation in the name of one total community (1985, 668–69)."

2. Industrial Development, Ideology, and Environmental Destruction

1. Główny Urząd Statystyczny [GUS], *Rocznik Statystyczny, 1989*, p.30.

2. Kozłowski 1985 reports a 1980 study determining that 66.2% of all wells sampled (282,000 village wells) contained water unfit for human consumption. Only 2.5% produced water of high quality; the remaining wells were questionable (p. 104).

3. For further discussion of these regions, see PIOŚ 1986, 148–52.

4. See Kozłowski 1985, pp. 117–25, for more detailed discussion of environmental contamination and health consequences in the seven most devastated areas. Frąckiewicz 1985 examines Upper Silesia (the Katowice area)—the worst of the 27 regions—in greater detail, summarizing the results of several previous environmental and health reports.

5. Under partition, economic development was not only stunted but also shifted. Prussian policy discouraged industrial development in the "Great Poland" area around Poznań (Posen) in favor of agricultural development (Wandycz 1974, 205). As a result 10,000 of the craftsmen in the textile industry moved to the Russian-dominated Kingdom of Poland, establishing Łódź as the center of the Polish textile industry (Topolski 1986, 169). The heart of the old Silesian mining area, long an area of dispute between Poland and Prussia, had been incorporated into Prussia. During partition the Poles developed a mining

and metallurgy center in Dąbrowa, the eastern section of what is now known as Silesia, located just inside the Russian partition (Turnock 1989, 114). This area gradually replaced the old Kielce basin as the heart of Poland's metallurgical industry. Still, the territories of Poland were underdeveloped compared to the more industrialized West. In the 1860s and 1870s, removal of tariff barriers between the Kingdom of Poland and other Russian provinces and the rapid development of railway lines in Russia sparked a more rapid development of industry and its attendant urbanization in that sector of Poland (Wandycz 1974, 201–207). The area left most underdeveloped as a result of Poland's division among its neighbors was the Austrian-controlled region of Galicia. Besides the Silesian area, Łódź, and the old cultural capital of Kraków, Warsaw also became an industrial center and Gdańsk (then part of Prussia) was a ship-building and trade center. All of these cities grew rapidly in the second half of the 19th century.

6. Topolski 1986, 246. Topolski's estimate that Poland lost 38% of all its material resources during the Second World War is typical.

7. See United Nations International Labor Office, *Year Book of Labour Statistics, 1949–89* (Geneva: International Labor Office, 1990), pp. 126–419, and *Year Book of Labour Statistics, 1991*, pp. 52–127. The data are only roughly comparable as Polish statistics include sectors reported separately in ILO data and countries report data for different years.

8. For relevant excerpts from the writings of Marx and Engels and an analysis of them, see Parsons 1977. Grundmann 1991 also examines the contributions and limitations of Marx's thought with regard to ecology, reworking Marx in ways that might be applicable to the contemporary issue of ecology. This type of analysis, however, goes well beyond the canon of Marxism-Leninism. Marx, writing as he was in the early stages of industrial capitalism, did not foresee the global nature of environmental threats or resource scarcity and tended to ascribe local environmental problems to private property and private control of the machinery with which human society acts on nature. Engels' *Dialectics of Nature* likewise cannot serve as a guide to the ideological treatment of ecology in the late twentieth century. For the use and misuse of Marxian conceptions of nature and ecology in Soviet ideology and science, see Weiner 1988, especially pp. 121–48 and 233–35. Although the Soviet system passed through a few different phases of thought on the environment before the Stalinist interpretation of nature as a great resource to be conquered, East European communist states adopted the Stalinist model of development and Stalinist ideology from the beginning. It was against this model that the scholars and activists of the 1970s and 1980s struggled.

9. DeBardeleben is also concerned with how current policy debates shape ideology itself (see, for example, 1985, 17).

10. For DeBardeleben's full argument, see 1985, 35–74. More specific references are given in parentheses where appropriate throughout this summary. Since many of these points are themes developed during the author's discussion, they appear in several places in her book. The references given here indicate the most direct statements of the points cited. For a penetrating account of changing political and ideological limitations on the environmental policy debate in the early phases of Soviet development see Weiner 1988. The policies DeBardeleben analyzes were built largely on this historical base.

11. Bielasiak and Hicks (1990) develop this argument in more detail.

12. This observation is based on a review of the official and opposition press after martial law. For further discussion of the press, see chapters 6 and 7.

13. For some examples of these types of analysis, see the *Eko*[2] series produced by Wydział Nauk Ekonomicznych, Uniwersytet Warszawski, (Warsaw, Poland) starting in 1986. Szymonowicz (1985) reviews earlier studies in this literature in his own study of the economic effects of environmental degradation. Piontek (1988) discusses methods of calculating economic losses due to air pollution. He then calculates the average annual loss to the Katowice voivodship, the most heavily polluted area of the country, to be about 18.6% of the total value of that voivodship's total production. Górka and Poskrobko (1987) examine many of the same issues for ecological degradation more generally (see their chapter 2). After reviewing several studies, including those of the Ministry for Environmental Protection and Natural Resources, they come to the conclusion that the average annual economic losses to the entire country due to ecological degradation (mostly from air pollution) range between 8 and 10 percent of national income and are increasing (p. 89).

14. The censorship laws restricting discussion of the environment remained in force throughout the 1970s and into 1980, i.e. until the Solidarity period. For a partial text of these regulations, see Curry 1984, 218–27.

15. See chapter 7 for a more detailed discussion of this controversy. The reports referred to here are: Pawłowski and Kozak, eds., 1984; Wójcik, ed., 1985; and Oschlies 1986. Oschlies also stresses the point that gaps in even basic information about the environment make it impossible to determined definitively the level of environmental destruction in Poland.

16. This assessment is based primarily on personal observation in Warsaw and the Tatra region at the time of the crisis, as well as a general reading of the opposition and official media.

3. The Structure of Environmental Protection

1. *Słownik języka polskiego*, 1981, 2:1053. Polish also uses the word "*natura*" to denote wild, original nature. Both words translate into English as "nature."

2. "Ustawa z dnia 31 stycznia 1980 r. o ochronie i kształtowaniu środowiska," *Dziennik Ustaw* 1980, no. 3, poz. 6, art. 1, para. 2. See also, Tobera 1988, 6.

3. The one exception to this general rule came in Galicia, the Austrian partition of Poland. After the 1867 *Ausgleich* united the Austrian monarchy with the Kingdom of Hungary, the major regions under their joint dominion gained the right to have a constitution and parliament. One of these regions was the Polish partition of Galicia. Galicia's parliament in Lwów (Lviv) passed a law in 1868 protecting mountain goats and a groundhog species in the Tatra Mountains—one of the first laws of this kind in the world (discounting royal edicts from the middle ages). A project to create a national park in the Tatras, however, was dismissed by the authorities in Vienna. See Szafer et al. 1973, 16.

4. Bolesław Chrobry, the second ruler (and first king) of Poland (992–1025), ordered the protection of beavers. Similarly, other kings limited the cutting down

of certain types of trees and the hunting of certain animal species. See, for example, Łabno and Piontek 1986, 23; Szczęsny, 1982, 9; Jastrzębski 1983, 7.

5. Komitet Obchodów 60-lecia Ligi Ochrony Przyrody 1988, 4. A small "Section for the Protection of Nature" was formed in the Russian partition of Poland in 1906 as part of the Polish Society for Knowledge of the Country, but its existence was short-lived and its activity limited largely to the publication of a nature magazine, (Łabno and Piontek 1986, 24).

6. *Dziennik Ustaw* 1932, no. 29, poz. 277; no. 35, poz. 357; no. 42, poz. 417; no. 67, poz. 625.

7. "Z działalności LOP. Z dziejów Stowarzyszenia," 1988, 25. A voivodship is the formal regional or provincial entity just below the national level. Until the 1975 administrative reform, they were large cultural and geographic regions most closely resembling provinces. The reform broke them down into several smaller administrative units, more closely resembling counties.

8. For membership statistics of these social organizations, see GUS, *Rocznik Statystyczny [RS] 1989*, 36.

9. "Rozporządzenie Rady Ministrów z dnia 20 sierpnia 1968 r. w sprawie uznania ,Ligi Ochrony Przyrody' za stowarzyszenie wyższej użyteczności," *Dziennik Ustaw* 1968, no. 33, poz. 227.

10. The government did pass a water law in 1922. Although the main thrust of the law concerned water rights and usage procedures, not environmental protection, the existence of a general water law provided a base for later environmental measures. "Ustawa wodna z dnia 19 września 1922 r.," *Dziennik Ustaw* 1922, no. 102, poz. 936.

11. "Ustawa z dnia 10 marca 1934 r. o ochronie przyrody," *Dziennik Ustaw* 1934, no. 31, poz. 274.

12. Radecki 1983, 22. "Ustawa z dnia 7 kwietnia 1949 r. o ochronie przyrody," *Dziennik Ustaw*, 1949, no. 25, poz. 180.

13. For a list of these laws, see Jastrzębski 1983, 17. Jastrzębski 1976 discusses the meaning of these laws for the development of norms in environmental protection.

14. "Ustawa z dnia 21 kwietnia 1966 r. o ochronie powietrza atmosferycznego przed zanieczyszczeniem," *Dziennik Ustaw* 1966, no. 14, poz. 87.

15. "Ustawa z dnia 24 października 1974 r. Prawo Wodne," *Dziennik Ustaw* 1974, no. 38, poz. 230.

16. "Ustawa z dnia 24 października 1974 r. Prawo budowlane," *Dziennik Ustaw* 1974, no. 38, poz. 229.

17. See the section on the League for the Protection of Nature for a brief discussion of the development of *social* organizations whose purposes were to support environmental efforts or perform civilian checks on polluters.

18. I could find no direct explanation for placing nature protection under the ministry responsible for religion and education. Given the emphasis on conservation and the role of scientists in that movement, education was probably the most directly related policy area of the government administration at that time.

19. *Dziennik Ustaw* 1934, no. 31, poz. 274, art. 5–14.

20. Szafer et al. 1973, 24. The council members were protesting two specific

decisions: the first was to build a cable line to bring skiers to the top of Kasprowy Wierch and the second was to build a hotel on Kalatówki. Both points are remarkable features of the Polish Tatras and both projects drastically increased the numbers of people trampling the areas, roads and paths cut through woods, and vehicles traveling both in these specific areas and in the Tatras in general.

21. *Dziennik Ustaw* 1949, no. 25, poz. 180, art. 2. This ministry later became the Ministry of Agriculture, Forestry and the Food Industry (*Ministerstwo Rolnictwa, Leśnictwa i Gospodarki Żywnościowej*).

22. The guards were eventually set up at the initiative of the League for the Protection of Nature and have remained a rather secondary force whose rights and powers are quite limited.

23. *Dziennik Ustaw* 1960, no. 29, poz. 163, art.'s 1 and 3.

24. See ibid., art. 2, para.'s 1.1–11 for a more detailed list.

25. Ibid., art. 2, para. 2 and art. 4.

26. *Dziennik Ustaw* 1966, no. 14, poz. 87, art. 10.

27. This ministry has undergone a number of changes in both title and purview in the postwar period. From the interwar period through 1950 it was the Ministry of Agriculture and Land Reform; from 1951 to 1981 the Ministry of Agriculture; from 1981 to 1985 the Ministry of Agriculture and Food Economy; and after 1985 when it was combined with the Ministry of Forestry and the Wood Industry it was titled the Ministry of Agriculture, Forestry, and Food Economy.

28. *Dziennik Ustaw* 1972, no. 11, poz. 77, art. 2.

29. For a more detailed breakdown of these responsibilities, see "Rozporządzenie Rady Ministrów z dnia 23 czerwca 1972 r. w sprawie szczegółowego zakresu działania Ministra Gospodarki Terenowej i Ochrony Środowiska," *Dziennik Ustaw* 1972, no. 28, poz. 22, art. 3, para. 9.

30. *Monitor Polski* 1973, no. 3, poz. 16, art.'s 1–3.

31. *Dziennik Ustaw* 1975, no. 16, poz. 90, art.'s 1 and 2.

32. "Rozporządzenie Rady Ministrów z dnia 9 lipca 1975 r. w sprawie szczegółowego zakresu działania Ministra Administracji, Gospodarki Terenowej i Ochrony Środowiska," *Dziennik Ustaw* 1975, no. 26, poz. 136, art. 2, para. 11. Compare *Dziennik Ustaw* 1972, no. 28, poz. 22, art. 3, para. 9.

33. Szafer et al. 1973, 22. *Monitor Polski* 1939, no. 154, poz. 365.

34. See also special conditions named for individual reserves at the time of their founding in *Monitor Polski*.

35. For the full text, see *Dziennik Ustaw* 1980, no. 3, poz. 6. The most comprehensive commentary on the law is provided in Radziszewski 1987.

36. *Dziennik Ustaw* 1980, no. 3, poz 6, art 2.

37. Ibid., art. 7.

38. "Rozporządzenie Rady Ministrów z dnia 30 września 1980 r. w sprawie szczegółowych zasad i trybu wykonywania przez Ministra Administracji, Gospodarki Terenowej i Ochrony Środowiska koordynacji działalności w dziedzinie ochrony środowiska," *Dziennik Ustaw* 1980, no. 24, poz. 95, art.'s 1–5 and 6, para.'s 1 and 2.

39. Ibid., art. 6, para. 3.

40. "Rozporządzenie Rady Ministrów z dnia 30 września 1980 r. w sprawie

Państwowej Inspekcji Ochrony Środowiska oraz wykonania kontroli w zakresie ochrony środowiska," *Dziennik Ustaw* 1980, no. 24, poz. 96, art.'s 1 and 2.

41. *Dziennik Ustaw* 1980, no. 3, poz. 6, art. 97, para.'s 1–3.

42. "Rozporządzenie Rady Ministrów z dnia 30 września 1980 r. w sprawie organizacji, szczegółowych zasad i zakresu działania Państwowej Rady Ochrony Środowiska," *Dziennik Ustaw* 1980, no. 24, poz. 97, art. 2, para.'s 1.2–4, 1.6, 1.8, and 2.

43. Ibid., art. 3.

44. Ibid., art.'s 4 and 5, and art. 12, para.'s 1 and 2.

45. "Ustawa z dnia 28 lipca 1983 r. o utworzeniu urzędu Ministra Administracji i Gospodarki Przestrzennej" and "Ustawa z dnia 28 lipca 1983 r. o utworzeniu urzędu Ochrony Środowiska i Gospodarki Wodnej," *Dziennik Ustaw* 1983, no. 44, poz. 200 and 201. For the state inspectorate, compare *Dziennik Ustaw* 1983, no. 44, poz. 201, art. 8, para. 2 with *Dziennik Ustaw* 1980, no. 3, poz. 6, art. 94.

46. "Rozporządzenie Rady Ministrów z dnia 16 grudnia 1983 r. w sprawie szczegółwego zakresu działania urzędu Ochrony Środowiska i Gospodarki Wodnej," *Dziennik Ustaw* 1983, no. 73, poz. 321, art. 1, para.'s 7 and 8. See also, *Dziennik Ustaw* 1980, no. 3, poz. 6, art. 71, para. 2.

47. *Dziennik Ustaw* 1983, no. 73, poz. 321, art. 2.

48. For a stimulating discussion and overview of the Jaruzelski regime's administrative reforms from martial law to the mid-1980s, see Kostecki and Mreła, "Institutional Revolt and Institutional Normalization," (unpublished manuscript).

4. The Independent Ecological Movement: Building New Identities

1. Wyka (1988, 60, emphasis in the original) This understanding of deep ecology was confirmed by the positions taken by representatives of the group at a colloquium held on that topic at the Polish Academy of Sciences, Warsaw, 11 June 1988 as part of the Przyroda - Człowiek - Wartości series.

2. Polish Situation Report 1/86, *Radio Free Europe Research*, 11:4 (24 January 1986), p. 15.

3. See, for example, the leaflet calling for action against the localization of a hotel in a particularly important landscape area of Kraków "Ratujmy Błonia!" dated 26 April 1989.

4. For a discussion of the persistence of this ideology even in Soviet environmental studies, see DeBardeleben 1985 (especially pp. 92–94) and Weiner 1988.

5. "Konferencja prasowa dla dziennikarzy zagranicznych," stenogram of the press conference held 3 September 1985, Warsaw, *Rzeczpospolita*, 9 September 1985, p. 4. For ensuing discussion, see "Konferencja prasowa dla dziennikarzy zagranicznych," stenogram of the press conference held 10 September 1985, Warsaw, *Rzeczpospolita*, 17 September 1985, p. 4; "Konferencja prasowa rzecznika rządu," stenogram of the press conference held 19 September 1985, Warsaw, *Rzeczpospolita*, 20 September 1985, p. 5; "Konferencja prasowa dla dzi-

ennikarzy zagranicznych," stenogram of the press conference held 24 September 1985, Warsaw, *Rzeczpospolita*, 30 September 1985, p. 4. For further discussion of the report and ensuing controversy, see chapter 7.

6. Television news coverage and many articles in the Polish press mentioned discussion of the environment as a key issue. For discussion and the reaction of the Minister directing the Office of Environmental Protection and Water Economy, see Witańska (1985).

7. Kossakowski (1988, 11). May 3 is the anniversary of Poland's 1791 constitution, revered as democratic and representing Polish independence. For many Poles, May 3 became an unofficial independence day during the communist period.

8. Międzyrzecz had a population of about 19,000 at the time.

9. "Wolę Być: Wydarzenia, Ogłoszenia" *Na Przełaj*, July 10, 1988, p. 5.

10. My general observations here rely primarily on press accounts in the official and unofficial media, the publications of groups, and interviews with group members. These sources, however, were not systematic in their coverage of group cooperation and, especially, intergroup communication. Since many of the groups were unofficial, they kept few written records. Communication with other unofficial actors, collective and individual, was a particularly sensitive area under communist rule, one in which no records were kept.

Often this overlap in membership would occur at the regional and local level. My information here comes from several interviews with lower level activists conducted in Kraków and Warsaw at various times from early 1986 through early 1988. In some instances, especially when an activist had connections to the political opposition, I was given only the first name of my informant. In other cases, I have a full name but assured them of confidentiality. In any case, this information is not systematic and I have no way of checking its validity. Yet, joint membership appears at least common enough to assure good communication between the PKE and other groups.

5. The Independent Ecological Movement: Organization and Activism

1. Stanisław Juchnowicz, President of the Polish Ecological Club, meeting with environmental delegation from the American Council for International Leadership, Kraków, Poland, June 26, 1989. Almost all of these experts were invited by Solidarity, but a couple did advise government representatives.

2. Hrynkiewicz 1988, 42. Hrynkiewicz goes on to point out that this referral process caused dissension among the regional and local ranks, who felt that the process was cumbersome and dampened initiative. The national level, however, felt that it left the regions a free hand in matters dealing both with their territories and issues left to that level by the club's program. [Meeting with Stanisław Juchnowicz, June 26, 1989.]

3. The exact membership figures were not available except for the 1987 figure of 2,332 and an estimated 200 from regions that had not filed reports by the time of the Second General Conference (Hrynkiewicz 1988, 46). In 1986 Zygmunt Fura, the president of the Małopolska branch of the club, gave the figure of

2,500–3,000 (interview, Kraków, May 1986). The 1989 figure was reported by Stanisław Juchnowicz (Meeting, June 26, 1989). The constant membership between 1985 and 1987 gives some evidence to the activists' claim that, although the Chernobyl accident (April 1986) can be considered a milestone in society's ecological consciousness, it did not lead to an immediate increase in activism. However, it is primarily reflective of the club's policy of not recruiting a mass membership; according to Hrynkiewicz (1988, 47), membership remained constant between the First and Second General Congresses (1983–87).

4. My interviews confirm that this was the general perception inside the club as well.

5. Hrynkiewicz 1988, 47–48; interview with an activist, Kraków, May 1986.

6. Interview with a high-level club activist, Kraków, Poland, May 1986.

7. The movement did not keep full membership lists. This estimate of membership was as of the end of 1987 (Wyka 1988, 58). The movement grew steadily, however, so this estimate is lower than membership figures might have shown by the end of communist rule.

8. Wyka 1988, 81. Comments of a Wolę Być activist at the Przyroda - Człowiek - Wartości colloquium on the ecological education of youth, "Edukacja Ekologiczna Młodzieży: Programy Szkolne i Inne Formy Upowszechniania Wiedzy Ekologicznej," Polish Academy of Sciences, Warsaw, Poland, April 11, 1988. See also, "Wolę Być: Wydarzenia, Ogłoszenia" Na Przełaj, July 10, 1988, p. 5, for an example of a call to participate in green schools.

9. Wyka reports that money raised from selling potted Christmas trees that could be replanted outdoors was used to open two savings accounts for future apartments for orphans (1988, 72–73).

10. Reported by Aleksandrowicz (1988). During the late 1980s, the Minister for Youth Affairs had an office at the level of the Council of Ministers but no ministry. This office was changed during Mazowiecki's reorganization of the cabinet in August and September 1989.

11. Aleksandrowicz 1988, 58. Although Wolę Być did not keep statistics on its members and their backgrounds, evidence from the letters published in Na Przełaj suggests that more members came from urban areas and intellectual families than from other parts of the social structure.

12. By the end of its first year, the group numbered 100 active members. For this figure see: Polish Situation Report 5/86, Radio Free Europe Research 11:13 (March 28, 1986), p. 7. Although it continued to grow until the conscientious objector provisions were introduced, the movement remained small.

13. "RSW Prasa-Książka-Ruch" assumed the costs of publishing and distributing mass periodicals and in turn received all profits. Usually, this was a subsidy since most of these periodicals were priced fairly low and did not earn a profit. The actual printer of this magazine was another Polish newspaper, Słowo Polskie.

14. Unfortunately, the data is not available for detailed discussion of subsidies. This information comes from members of the League.

15. REFA 1988b. The movement's principles, originally published as an undated pamphlet, were reprinted in the first issue of their bulletin (REFA 1988a, 4–6).

16. Jaromi 1988, 18. The Legnica group started meeting in the Fall 1986 and the Łódź circle formed in April of the next year. The Wrocław and Gdańsk circles were started in 1988.

17. That the influence of the Catholic intelligentsia in Polish society should not be underestimated is indicated by the Prime Ministership of Tadeusz Mazowiecki, member of a number of Catholic political associations and one of the original leading group of KIK. For his role in the origins of the group see Markiewicz (1983, 210–11).

18. The first three centered on water treatment and were held in Lublin, Poland in 1976, 1979, and 1981. Due to interest of specialists from all subfields the conferences broadened and adopted the name "Chemistry for Protection of the Environment." The 1983, 1985, and 1987 conferences were held in Western Europe and the September 1989 conference returned to Lublin. Sponsors were the International Committee Chemistry for Protection of the Environment, the Technical University of Lublin, the Polish Chemical Society, the U.S. Department of Energy, and the U.S. Environmental Protection Agency. Source: "7th International Conference 'Chemistry for Protection of the Environment' Lublin, Poland, 4–7 Sept. 1989" announcement and call for papers.

19. Hrynkiewicz 1988, 29. Two (nonactivist) residents of one of the small towns at the edge of the park repeated this thesis to me, as did a couple of environmental activists in Kraków.

20. "Deklaracja Wielkopolskiego Seminarium Ekologicznego," 1987. "Great Poland" is an old term that defines a large geographic area of Western Poland, the principal city of which is Poznań.

21. See, for example, *Wielkopolski Informator Ekologiczny*, no. 1, pp. 2–4.

22. This organization traces its roots in the "flying universities" or underground education in Poland prior to Word War I. It was legally recognized, though it maintained its intellectual and pedagogical independence, which explains its suspension during martial law. Although it offered some help to illegal underground courses after martial law, this organization should not be confused with the Society of Academic Courses (*Towarzystwo Kursów Naukowych* or TKN), the "flying universities" established by the opposition in the 1970s. For more information see "Towarzystwo Wolnej Wszechnicy Polskiej. Czym jest? Jaką przebyło drogę? Ku czemu zmierza?" 1987.

23. Observation based on participation in these colloquia from October 1987 to June 1988.

24. Of the party newspapers *Tygodnik Demokratyczny* covered the environment first and most completely in the mid-1980s with the ecological encyclopedia by Inez Wiatr and regular articles by Ewa Rumińska and Marek Kwiatkowski. See especially *Tygodnik Demokratyczny* 1985–87. The Tenth Congress of United Peasants' Party (ZSL) had a long visible discussion of environmental problems resulting in an overarching resolution, reported on the television news "Dziennik Telewizyjny," March 23, 1988, Polish Television Program 1, and in the English-language daily news release of Polska Agencja Prasowa of March 25. Ecology then became a main topic at the International Conference of Peasants' Parties and Organizations hosted by the ZSL a few days later. Polish Television Program 1, 26 March 1988; see also, *Życie Warszawy*, March 26–27, 1988, p. 1.

25. The name "green movement" has a short history in Poland. In 1981 Wierzbicki and other activists formed an association under the same name. This association, however, was not a political party and was disbanded a few months later by martial law. ["Dokumenty Stowarzyszenia Ochrony Człowieka i Środowiska 'Ruch Zielonych,'" pamphlet printed in Warsaw, 1981] There was no relation between the two organizations.

26. Interview with Zbigniew Wierzbicki, founding member of "Ruch Zielonych," Warsaw, Poland, June 27, 1989.

27. Interview with an environmental activist present at the meeting of PRON's National Council responsible for this movement's creation, July 29, 1988, Warsaw, Poland.

28. See, for example, "Nowa inicjatywa PRON: społeczny ruch ekologiczny" 1986.

29. Hrynkiewicz 1988, 38; see also, Kossakowski 1988, 10–11,48–49.

30. I am excluding the League for the Protection of Nature in this statement as it was a special case of an extensive state-controlled organization with many detailed plans and tasks. To concentrate on these activities would skew the portrayal of *movement* activism.

31. Evidence confirming this conflict was gained from interviews with activists on different sides of the arguments in spring 1986. It is also related in Hrynkiewicz (1988, 39–40). Written evidence of the resulting emphasis on expertise includes PKE (1989a, 1989b); Fura (n.d.).

32. PKE (1989b, 37). The "notebook" format, the standard for instructional material in Poland's independent education movement, has been used at various times in history, so the use of this term tapped a cultural understanding which produces an image of Polish society seeking and circulating knowledge generated within and for itself.

33. The precise data on religious beliefs during the communist period are not available. Estimates of the portion of the population which considered itself Catholic range from 90% to 95%. Surveys since the transition have tended toward the 95% mark; official statistics note 90.4% of the population as baptized Roman Catholic at the end of 1993 (*RS 1994*, 69).

34. Information on topics gained from fliers given to the author by club officials, posters in Kraków and attendance at meetings.

35. See section on "Chernobyl's Repercussions for Poland," especially pp. 16–17, in Polish Situation Report 10/86, Radio Free Europe *Research* 11:27 (27 June 1986).

36. Interview with Zbigniew Wierzbicki, October 22, 1989.

6. The Opposition and Ecology

1. *Konstytucja Polskiej Rzeczpospolitej Ludowej* (1987), roz. 8, art. 71, p. 46.
2. Ibid.
3. For a summary of the development of this controversy see Polish Situation Report 2/81 in Radio Free Europe *Research* 6:6 (January 30, 1981), pp. 26–30.
4. Ibid.
5. See also Kabala 1993, 54. It is interesting that labor activists supported

plant closure. Beyond the cooperation Solidarity could elicit and the concerns about fluoride poisoning, must have lay the expectation that the socialist government would have to support laid off workers or find them other jobs.

6. "Program NSZZ 'Solidarność' uchwalony przez I Krajowy Zjazd Delegatów," Roździał V, Teza 16. Reprinted in *Tygodnik Solidarność* no. 29, 16 October 1981, supplement, p. 6.

7. Hrynkiewicz 1988, 55. Hrynkiewicz was one of the "expert" participants (advisers) in the program working group charged with developing proposals for social policies, among them environmental policies. For a list of participants, see "Spotkania Zespołów Tematycznych" in Agencja Solidarność 1981b, p. 611.

8. For the text of the group's original report to the Congress, see Agencja Solidarność 1981a, 23–24.

9. For English-language documentation of the course of debate at the Solidarity Congress, see Sanford 1990. The congress daily newspaper, *Głos Wolny*, did not report any floor debate on the environment during the entire congress. (*Głos Wolny*, no's 1–24, September 5–October 8, 1981, entire). Even the more extensive published records of congress materials put out by Agencja Solidarność, *Biuletyn Pism Związkowych i Zakładowych* (no's 36–43, September 5 - October 7, 1981), showed no floor debate on ecology.

10. The material discussed in the second session included that of the following groups, (5) economic stabilization, economic reform, working self-management; (6) market, prices, cost of living; (7) work and employment, wages, job security, labor law; (8) man and his environment, social policies. The debate on this whole section of the program took place on October 1 and the morning of October 2. For the text of the debate, see Sanford, ed., pp. 174–209. For descriptions of the groups' assignments, see *Tygodnik Solidarność* no. 26, pp. 4–5.

11. Sanford 1990, 198. (His references are to the draft documents where "teza 15" focused on protection of the environment and "teza 13" was concerned mostly with working conditions.)

12. A typical example of such articles would be: "Wstęp grozi śmiercią lub kalectwem" in *Tygodnik Mazowsze* 54, June 2, 1983, p. 4.

13. See Appendix A for a discussion of opposition press sources.

14. For discussion of the variety and circulation of underground publications in the mid 1980s (i.e., when the ecology movement really started to expand), see Kaminski 1987. Kaminski reports that of the close to 1,000 different newspapers or periodicals that appeared between martial law and early 1986, about 500 had sustained publication, the largest, *Tygodnik Mazowsze*, with a normal circulation of 50,000 (1987, 318–20). The microfiche index of the archives held by Radio Free Europe and a few other Western centers contains 848 underground publications for martial law and the subsequent period (*IDC: Polish Independent Press, 1976+*). Access is difficult to estimate as clandestine publications were circulated heavily from hand to hand. Kaminski reports government and opposition estimates of 3 million *regular* readers (more than 8% of the total population of the country). Approximately 15% of the working class had regular access to this press (1987, 320). Occasional readers would have been much more numerous.

15. See, for example, "Wstęp grozi śmiercią lub kalectwem," *Tygodnik Mazowsze* no. 54, June 2, 1983, p. 4; "O Regionie Śląsko-Dąbrowskim—z prasy

związkowej" reprinted from *Regionalny Informator Solidarności Śląskiej-Dąbrowskiej* in *Tygodnik Mazowsze* no. 59, 11 August 1983, p. 3.

16. "Dodatek ekologiczny. Uwaga: Trują!" *KOS* no. 44/45, December 4, 1983, pp. 5, 6.

17. See "Raport o stanie Środowiska (1)" *Życie Gospodarcze* no. 16 (1643), June 17, 1983, p. 3; and "Raport o stanie Środowiska (2)" *Życie Gospodarcze* no. 17 (1644), June 24, 1983, p. 3. This series exemplifies the differences in Polish censorship practices depending on the target population of the publication. Publications for specialists or elites were allowed more liberties in analysis and criticism than were mass-circulation publications. Equally critical articles did not start appearing in the mass-circulation press for at least another year.

18. See, for example, "Zagrożenia" about Silesia reprinted in *Agencja Informacyjna "S"* no. 2, April 28, 1984, pp. 20–21, from *Wolny Robotnik*, as well as the *KOS* series begun with the 1983 special supplement on ecology, including "Uwaga Trują!" *KOS* no. 47, January 16, 1984, p. 6; "Uwaga Trują! Zagrożenia," *KOS* no. 49, February 13, 1984, pp. 5, 6; and "Uwaga police," *KOS* no. 58, August 13, 1984, pp. 11–12. Other articles in this period include: "Achtung! Achtung! Police!" *Obraz* no. 1(8), January 1984, pp. 16–17; "System wrogi naturze: problemy ochrony środowiska," *KOS* nr. 59, 3 September 1984, pp. 3, 7; "Trują!" *Metrum* no. 19, September 5, 1984, p. 2; "Stan klęski ekologicznej," *Tygodnik Mazowsze* no. 107, November 22, 1984, p. 3.

19. See, for example, the column "W państwie realnego socjalizmu" in *Tygodnik Mazowsze*, especially September 13, 1984 and August 8, 1985; "Za rubieża," *CDN* no. 83, September 18, 1984, p. 2.; note on Grodzisk factory emissions in Untitled, *Sektor* no. 65, September 30, 1984, p. 4; "Dobrodziejstwo XX wieku?" *Solidarność Chemików* no. 5, January 22, 1985.

20. This controversy is discussed at more length in the following chapter.

21. "The State of the Ecological Disaster" translated from *Tygodnik Mazowsze*, no. 107, and reprinted in *Uncensored Poland News Bulletin*, no. 1/85, January 3, 1985, pp. 43–44.

22. *Zeszyty Niezależnej Myśli Lekarskiej*. 1986. Quarterly of the Social Commission for Health, no. 7 (March). (Available in *IDC: Polish Independent Publications 1976+*)

23. "Komitety Ochrony Środowiska" in *Przegląd Wiadomości Agencyjnych* 19, 11 May 1986, p. 2.

24. These ecologists favoring the development of nuclear energy included ministers and a few Polish Ecological Club members.

25. Radio Free Europe. 1986. *Research* 11:27 (June 27). Polish Situation Report 10/86, p. 17.

26. For English language translations of some of these bulletins, see "Chernobyl Viewed from East-Central Europe," *East European Reporter* 2:1 (Spring 1986), pp. 52–59; and "Poland after the Chernobyl Disaster," Committee in Support of Solidarity *Reports* no. 43 (July 30, 1986), pp. 22–25.

27. See, for example, *Tygodnik Mazowsze* no. 169, May 8, 1986, and no. 170, May 15, 1986; and *KOS* no. 94A, May 4, 1986.

28. Reprinted as "Z komunikat TKK NSZZ 'Solidarność - 13.05.86r." in *Przegląd Wiadomości Agencyjnych* 20, May 18, 1986, p. 1.

29. *Wielkopolski Informator Ekologiczny* no. 1, March 1987. Note especially the publication information on the back page.

30. One review of the data from which official statistics were generated found that only 5% of the data derived from actual monitoring of the environment, while 1% came from academic studies. A full 94% came from reports by the enterprises and administrations whose activities were being studied. The authors of this review claim that a truly reliable study should derive half of its data from well-organized monitoring. See, Kozłowski and Lenart 1988, 198.

31. Those parties were: the Independent Party "Green Movement," the Polish Ecological Party, the Polish Green Party. A fourth party, the Federation of Greens, focusing on local activism and grass-roots democracy formed after the Round Table.

32. The political success of the compromise was achieved at a fairly general level of agreement on principles and directions. Once questions of specific issues, resources and guarantees were raised, differences emerged. For a critique of the Round-Table talks on ecology emphasizing this point, see *Serwis Ochrony Środowiska* 7 (March-April 1989), pp. 1–2 and 6 (February 1989), pp. 1, 15.

7. *Official Environmentalism: The Failure of Normalization*

1. For a discussion of environmental administration, see chapter 3.

2. This was very visibly the case with the premier expert body, the State Council for Environmental Protection (*Państwowa Rada Ochrony Środowiska*), which advised the Council of Ministers, but was also true of advisory bodies within various institutions. See chapter 3 for further discussion.

3. Curry 1984, 220–27. See, for example, the discussion of a censored article on water shortages in Upper Silesia. Had the full article been published public pressure might have been brought to bear on the policymakers not to continue locating water-intensive industry in the region (pp. 220–22).

4. See report of results on these individual issues in Ośrodek Badania Opinii Publicznej i Studiów Programowych 1975.

5. This theme came up again in the 1989 "revolutions." Demands for an end to communist rule were also expressed as demands for the development of "normal" political and economic systems.

6. Western and East European scholars studying these processes have generally kept the term normalization. For one who has not, see Gitelman 1981.

7. A partial exception to this rule came in the mining sector. The coal mines were militarized, but the miners continued to have access to better food and consumer goods.

8. Meeting with ACIL Environmental Delegation, Kraków, Poland, June 26, 1989.

9. Interview with an activist, May 1986. After the fall of communist rule, this pattern was reversed, with the more politically minded leaving the club to form and participate in new parties.

10. For further discussion, see Hrynkiewicz 1988, 28–38.

11. Reported to me by Krzysztof Jasiewicz, whose colleague attended the

meeting. Unbeknownst to Rakowski, some of those in attendance were part of the opposition at the time.

12. Interview with Przemysław Wójcik, Deputy Director, Instytut Badań Klasy Robotniczej, Akademii Nauk Społecznych, Warsaw, Poland, April 25, 1988.

13. For an account of the history of this institute and its series "The Situation of the Working Class in Poland," including the controversy surrounding the report on ecological threats, see Wójcik 1990.

14. Minister Urban was forced to back off from this position in a series of questions at the next two press conferences. For further details, see the discussion of the press below.

15. See, for example, the following Życie Warszawy articles: Walczak 1985, 3; "Wyborcy—kandydaci. Rejestr spraw do załatwienia" 1985, 1–2; and a concrete local example in "Wyborcy—kandydaci. Z dedykacją przyszłemu Sejmowi" 1985, 1–2.

16. The Political Bureau was the executive committee of the communist party, the Polish equivalent of the Soviet Politburo. No transcripts of Political Bureau meetings were published. Moreover, the minutes of the 1982–1989 Political Bureau meetings have since been destroyed. This information was corroborated by Przemysław Wójcik, the report's editor and Deputy Director of the institute (interview, June 5, 1996; cf. Wójcik 1990).

17. Interview with Przemysław Wójcik, April 25, 1988; Wójcik 1990.

18. Dziennik Ustaw 1983, no. 44, poz. 201, art. 1.

19. Dziennik Ustaw 1985, no. 50, poz. 262, art. 3.

20. See Jowitt 1975 for the original discussion of inclusion of nonofficial sectors into the decisionmaking process as a key task of Leninist regimes.

21. Jaruzelski 1986, 28–29, 32. See also Messner 1986, especially pp. 126–128 and the final resolution of the Congress, reprinted in X Zjazd Polskiej Zjednoczonej Partii Robotniczej, 29 czerwca–3 lipca 1986r.: Podstawowe dokumenty i materiały, 1986, pp. 225–27.

22. For a discussion of this movement see Hrynkiewicz 1988, 36–38. The announcement of its creation can be found in "Nowa Inicjatywa PRON: Społeczny Ruch Ekologiczny" 1986, pp. 1–2. An unfettered description of PRON's intentions for the movement was gained from an interview with an environmental activist, (Warsaw, Poland, July 19, 1988), invited to the founding meeting.

23. For example, one of the key activists in the PRON ecological movement, Zofia Odechowska, was also active in the Polish Ecological Club and the Warsaw-based group Krajobrazy Mazowieckie. On the group level the independent youth movement Wolę Być and the opposition group Freedom and Peace also worked with the local council of PRON on the Międzyrzecz controversy.

24. So, for example, the Episcopate's environmental representative on the Social Consultative Council, Zbigniew Wierzbicki, continued to lead the Green Cross Seminar and participate in other environmental initiatives, while using the council as yet another forum in which to advance ecological views. He did not see the role of the council or his position on it as sufficiently meaningful to change his other patterns of activism. [Interview, July 7, 1988].

25. See, Kolankiewicz 1988, 153–55 for a discussion of the regime's inclusion policy and validation.

26. This program was certainly ambitious. (Meeting of an Environmental Delegation from the American Council for International Leadership with ministry officials, Ministry of Environmental Protection and Natural Resources, Warsaw, Poland, June 28, 1989.) Official and nonofficial environmentalists have expended a great deal of effort to attract the foreign investment and technical assistance necessary to implement it. However, economic conditions in Poland, privatization of the industrial plant and marketization raise many problems and doubts that the program can be implemented.

27. See Panek 1988, p. 5 for a summary of the government's position on the environment and the environmental ministry's draft program for a comprehensive approach to environmental protection to the year 2010.

28. The official trade unions also carved out a maverick independent position for themselves during these talks. Their argument was that since Solidarity had originally formed as a trade union and still identified itself as such, the official trade unions should have their own representatives.

29. Observations in this section are based upon a nonquantitative review of a few major serials (see bibliography) throughout the 1980s and a quantitative review (discussed below) of the entire central and regional press during a three-month period in 1988. Non-print press review was more episodic and concentrated in the years 1985–86 and 1987–88.

30. "Raport o Stanie Środowiska (1)," *Życie Gospodarcze*, no. 16, April 17, 1983, p. 3. and "Raport o Stanie Środowiska (2)," *Życie Gospodarcze*, no. 17, April 24, 1983, p. 3.

31. A selective list of these *Życie Warszawy* articles show the breadth of topics covered: Walczak 1984e, dust emissions; Jacyna 1984d, water shortages; Walczak 1984c, contamination of the Baltic Sea; Walczak 1984a, ecology in education; Jacyna 1984b and 1984c, forest devastation; Walczak 1984d, industry and (lack of) environmental controls; Jacyna 1984a, noise and vibration; Walczak 1984f, various environmental data; Walczak 1984b, water pollution and drinking water; Jacyna 1985c, facing up to environmental protection, potential programs and their costs; Jacyna 1985a and 1985b, insufficient action to protect the environment, especially air and water, respectively; Jacyna 1986, overlapping and ineffective administration of environmental protection. The heavy emphasis on earlier articles in this list is not meant to imply a slowdown of the pace of Jacyna's and Walczak's coverage, which remained steady throughout the normalization period. Rather it demonstrates the extent of their coverage early in that period. For evidence of censorship of Jacyna's articles in the 1970s, see Curry 1984, 220–22.

32. A number of authors have discussed Poland's "propaganda of success" during the second half of the 1970s. See, Curry 1984, pp. 19–24, for a discussion of the role of censorship in this propaganda. For a more detailed account of the leadership's own optimism standing behind this propaganda, see Lepak 1988.

33. See "Konferencja prasowa dla dziennikarzy zagranicznych" 1985a, for use of the economic argument to justify lackluster performance in environmental protection.

34. See, for example, Szymonowicz 1985, 248. Szymonowicz's review of other attempts to estimate the costs of environmental degradation show his estimate to be fairly moderate. The upper bound of these estimates is slightly over 20% of national income.

35. "Konferencja prasowa dla dziennikarzy zagranicznych" 1985a, 4.

36. "Konferencja prasowa dla dziennikarzy zagranicznych" 1985b, 4.

37. "Konferencja prasowa dla dziennikarzy zagranicznych" 1985c, 4.

38. Viewership of these conferences was high since, in asking their questions, foreign journalists imparted information not officially published.

39. CBOS 1986c, question #1. This poll surveyed a representative sample of the adult population of those fourteen counties. (This polling center is the official one created in 1983 and discussed above. If there was a bias in its polls, as alleged by many Polish scholars, it was toward approval of government policy.) A Radio Free Europe study showed that 56% of the Polish population had first heard of the accident by radio (79% of them from Western broadcasts, for a total of 44% of the population), 34% heard by word of mouth, and 9% heard from television or newspapers. In sum, only 21% first heard of the accident from official Polish news sources. Moreover, a full 85% disagreed with the way the Polish media handled information on Chernobyl (8% agreed; 7% had no opinion). See Radio Free Europe 1986a, pp. 6, 8, and 15. Given that the sample was taken from Poles visiting in the West after the accident, however, the Radio Free Europe results cannot be considered representative of the entire population.

40. The first printed source of this information was an underground publication by "KOS," the Committee for Social Resistance. For a summary of this publication see "Underground KOS on Chernobyl, 4th May 1986 . . . ," *East European Reporter* 2:1 (Spring 1986), pp. 55–56. Comments on popular reaction are based on personal observation.

41. See, for example, "Konferencja prasowa rzecznika rządu," *Życie Warszawy*, May 7, 1986, pp. 1–2; Mojkowski 1986, 8.

42. See, for example, "Nowa Inicjatywa PRON: Społeczny Ruch Ekologiczny," *Życie Warszawy*, September 23, 1986, pp. 1–2.

43. For a list of these serials, see Appendix B. During this period I subscribed to a review service run by the central distributor of the Polish official press, RSW Prasa. Controlling its performance with my own review of four serials, I found the service to be thorough. Nevertheless, this total understates the actual number of articles and references printed, since the reviewers did miss a few shorter articles and references in the serials I controlled. I assume this happened with other serials as well. The total does include wire stories picked up by various newspapers. Since the importance of press coverage turns around readership—i.e. how many readers encounter items about the environment—it is necessary to count wire stories in all their outlets. Overlapping coverage is not mere repetition since different newspapers distributed in any given locality are reaching different audiences.

44. A precise comparison between press coverage and environmental degradation is impossible because publication and distribution of the press remained along the networks of the older, larger counties after the 1975 administrative reorganization, while environmental data was reported by new county. The 17

old counties were not merely broken down into 49 new counties; rather most borders were redrawn. Only three of the new counties had newspapers; two of them are old cultural centers and the other is a major new industrial center. An approximate comparison of press coverage and environmental damage can be made, however, by assigning the new counties to old counties on the basis of where the new county seat was before the reorganization and summing the environmental data. The assumption behind this reassignment is that the current county seat influences the distribution of the press more than do the precise locations of the old county lines.

45. The status of Warsaw presents a problem. Not only is Warsaw the center of the national press, but, as the capital, even its local newspapers are distributed throughout the country. If, however, we count just the serials targeting Warsaw with local information, Warsaw's "regional" press produced more articles on the environment than Kraków and fewer than Katowice. The three totals (149, 133, 117) are close, followed by the third most devastated county (Wrocław, 100).

8. *The Environmental Movement in Transition*

1. See, for example, Taras 1995, Connor and Płoszajski, eds., 1992; Mason 1993; Millard 1994a,b; Sanford, ed. and trans, 1992; Starr, ed., 1993.

2. Two sets of local and regional elections were also held in 1990 and 1994.

3. The Sejm had neglected to name a new prime minister in passing a vote of no confidence in the Suchocka government. This left the President the option of dismissing the government or the parliament. Wałęsa chose the latter.

4. For further discussion, see Howard 1993 and Vinton 1992.

5. The ministers have been: Bronisław Kamiński in Mazowiecki's government, Mariej Nowicki in the Bielecki government, Stefan Kozłowski in the Olszewski government, Zygmunt Hortmanowicz in Suchocka's government, and Stanisław Zelichowski in the governments of Pawlak, Oleksy, and Cimoszewicz. Even the last minister under the communist regime, Józef Kozioł, enjoyed a short tenure in office as he was appointed in fall 1988, less than a year before the regime change.

6. For an example of such efforts and the problems they face, see Roger Manser's discussion of an emission permit scheme in Chorzów, (1993, 120–22). For further discussion of the challenges facing environmentalists during marketization and privatization, see both Manser 1993 and Georgieva 1993.

7. According to Duncan Fisher, this lowering of ecology on the political agenda is a region-wide trend (1993, 107).

8. Interviews with Przemysław Czajkowski, Warsaw, July 29, 1993; Piotr Gliński, Warsaw, July 16, 1993; Jolanta Pawlak, Warsaw, August 5, 1993; Eugeniusz Pudlis, Warsaw, July 28, 1993; Zbigniew Wierzbicki, Warsaw, August 3, 1993; as well as more informal conversations with movement activists.

9. Interview with Eugeniusz Pudlis, Vice President of PKE, Warsaw, July 28, 1993.

10. Interview with Eugeniusz Pudlis. Pudlis, who is organizing this series, reported that the PKE is finding that the change of system has not changed the level of environmental knowledge in parliament, even among commission members.

11. For example, the Mazowiecki Okręg (Warsaw area) now has a kindergarten group. The national organization in Kraków has translated and issued a German ecology text for grammar school, and a high school level text went to print in late 1993.

12. Interview with Eugeniusz Pudlis.

13. This information about BORE comes mainly from the Bureau's own publications and two interviews, one with BORE Director Jolanta Pawlak and one with Board Member Piotr Gliński.

14. This sentiment was voiced by every activist I interviewed or met in the summer of 1993, regardless of their views or group memberships.

15. Interview with Eugeniusz Pudlis. These new centers were set up after the III General Congress in 1990, when regional branches of the club were granted the right to become legal entities and develop contacts and cooperation with partners abroad. The Swedish Secretariat for Acid Rain supported the Katowice center and the Coalition for a Clean Baltic financed the centers in Gdańsk and Szczecin. See PKE 1993a, 7.

16. This trend has been noted by other observers as well. Public-opinion studies in Poland show that the shift is visible to the general public, even though the public does not appear to be well-informed about specific local groups and the overall visibility of ecological activism has declined. See CBOS 1993b.

17. For a similar assessment, see Szacki et al. 1993, 23–24.

18. For discussion of these changes early in the transition, see Bochniarz 1992.

19. Jancar-Webster 1993a, 216; interviews with Przemysław Czajkowski and Jolanta Pawlak. The World Wildlife Fund, for example, has been particularly active in this region of the world.

20. Information about the founding and operation of the office is largely based on an interview with Teresa Orłoś, Specialist in charge of Contacts with Society, Ministry of Environmental Protection, Natural Resources and Forestry, Warsaw, July 27, 1993.

21. Szacki et al. point, for example, to ineffective attempts to build a "green" caucus in parliament and maintain that many legislators who ran in 1991 with environmentally conscious slogans have not pursued these goals once in parliament (1993, 20).

22. Manser (1993, 92–94) describes the weakening of environmental provisions in a law on foreign investment, as well as other obstacles encountered by those pressing for stronger attention to ecology.

23. OBOP 1993b, (1.8%); CBOS 1993c, (2%).

24. CBOS 1993b, 2–3. Of the 16%, 32%, and 34% who had heard of local, national and international groups respectively, only 55%, 50% and 60% could remember hearing of concrete efforts in the last year.

25. Only one third of those who had heard of groups (21% at the local level, 29% at the regional level and 64% at the national level) thought that these groups' primary focus was on action to improve the environment itself (CBOS 1992a, 2,4).

26. CBOS 1993a, 8. Allowed to choose two actors from among local authorities, county (regional) authorities, central authorities, citizen action at the local

level, local industrial managers, ecological parties and "ecological associations and social organizations," only 9% and 6% of the respondents chose the last two categories, respectively.

27. For accounts of other countries, see: Fisher et al., eds., 1992; Jancar-Webster, ed., 1993; Manser 1993; Vari and Tamas, eds., 1993.

9. Conclusions

1. See Tarrow 1988 and discussion of this theme in chapter 1.

2. See Rohrschneider 1988, discussed in chapter 1, n.21.

3. See, for example, Arato 1981. Although this article tackles the question outright, many other works written on Poland in the 1980s adopt this perspective.

4. See Kitschelt 1992, 41–42 for the argument that the combination of environmentalists' political and economic platforms are off of the main axis of party competition, hence not attracting voters. Barbara Jancar-Webster points out that the only cases where environmental parties have enjoyed some support in Central and Eastern Europe are the cases where they have served as vehicles for national interests—Slovakia and Slovenia (1993a, 216).

Selected Bibliography

Serials

Polish Official and Academic

Aura, a monthly published by the Naczelna Organizacja Techniczna.
Dziennik Ustaw, official report of laws enacted by the Sejm (parliament) and the Council of Ministers.
Eko², a series of economic studies of environmental issues by the Warsaw University, Department of Economic Sciences.
Monitor Polski, administrative bulletin of the Council of Ministers containing major regulations.
Na Przełaj, youth weekly.
Polityka, weekly political review.
Przegląd Tygodniowy, general weekly review.
Przyrody Polska, a monthly published by the Central Office of the League for Protection of Nature.
RS [*Rocznik Statystyczny*], Statistical Yearbook published by the Główny Urząd Statystyczny [GUS].
Rzeczpospolita, the official government daily newspaper.
Trybuna Ludu, daily of the Polish United Workers' Party.
Tygodnik Demokratyczny, weekly published by Stronnictwo Demokratyczne, one of the two political parties allied to the Polish United Workers' Party.
Życie Gospodarcze, weekly published for economic managers.
Życie Warszawy, Warsaw Daily.

Polish Unofficial

Agencja Informacyjna "S", Warsaw, periodic review of press.
Baza, Warsaw, monthly of the socio-political club "Workers' Thought."

CDN: Głos Wolnego Robotnika, Warsaw, weekly of the Interfactory Workers' Committee.

Dzień, Kraków, bi-weekly of regional Solidarity's Academic Commission for Understanding.

Głos Medyka, Warsaw, bi-monthly of the workers of the Warsaw Health Service in cooperation with the Social Commission for Health.

Głos Wolny, Gdańsk, daily review of the Solidarity's Congress in 1981.

Informator, Lublin, information bulletin for the East Central region.

KOS, Warsaw, bi-weekly of the Committee for Social Resistance.

Mała Polska, Kraków, weekly.

Niepodległość, Kraków, monthly of the Confederation for an Independent Poland.

Obraz, Szczecin, monthly.

Przegląd Wiadomości Agencyjnych, Warsaw, weekly information review of the Mazowsze Region.

Prześwit, Łódź, bi-monthly.

Samorządna Rzeczpospolita, national, bi-weekly of NSZZ Solidarność.

Sektor, Warsaw, weekly of the regional Committee for Resistance.

Serwis Ochrony Środowiska (SOS), Warsaw monthly ecological bulletin starting in September 1988.

Solidarność Chemików, Wrocław, information bulletin of the Solidarity factory committees of "Chemitex" "Polifarb" and "Superfosfat"—three major plants in the chemical industry.

Solidarność Nauczycielska, Lublin, monthly of education workers.

Tygodnik Mazowsze, Warsaw, weekly, main publication of the regional organization of Solidarity.

Wola, Warsaw, weekly of the Inter-factory Coordinating Committee.

Zielone Brygady, Kraków, monthly ecological bulletin starting in May 1989.

Western

Biuletyn Informacyjny Solidarności, later titled the Committee in Support of Solidarity *Reports*.

IDC Polish Independent Publications.

Radio Free Europe. *Research* Reports.

Uncensored Poland News Bulletin.

Books, Articles, and Documents

"7th International Conference 'Chemistry for Protection of the Environment' Lublin, Poland, Sept. 4–7, 1989" announcement and call for papers.

"I Krajowy Zjazd Delegatów." 1981. *Tygodnik Solidarność*, September 25: 5.

X Zjazd Polskiej Zjednoczonej Partii Robotniczej, 29 czerwca 3 lipca 1986r.: Podstawowe dokumenty i materiały. 1986. Warsaw: Książka i Wiedza.

"Achtung! Achtung! Police!" 1984. *Obraz* nr 1(8), January: 16–17.

Agencja Solidarność. 1981a. *Biuletyn Pism Związkowych i Zakładowych* no. 38, special issue on "Zespoły Programowe," 14–September 20: 23–24.

———. 1981b. *Biuletyn Pism Związkowych i Zakładowych* (no's 36–43, September 5–October 7).

Aleksandrowicz, Anna. 1988. "Alternatwne ruchy młodzieżowe: 'Wolę Być!' " *Kurier Szczeciński*, July 27.

Alves, Maria Helena Moriera. 1989. "Interclass Alliances in the Opposition to the Military in Brazil: Consequences for the Transition Period." Susan Eckstein, ed., *Power and Popular Protest: Latin American Social Movements.* Berkely and Los Angeles: University of California Press.

Arato, Andrew. 1981. "Civil Society vs. the State." *Telos* 47: 217–28.

———. 1985. "Some Perspectives of Democratization in East Central Europe." *Journal of International Affairs* 38 (Winter): 321–35.

——— and Jean Cohen. 1984. "Social Movements, Civil Society, and the Problem of Sovereignty." *Praxis International* 4:3 (October): 266–83.

Benda, Vaclav. 1991. "The Parallel '*Polis*' " originally printed unofficially in May 1978. Reprinted in H. Gordon Skilling and Paul Wilson, eds., *Civic Freedom in Central Europe: Voices from Czechoslovakia.* New York: St. Martin's Press.

Bermeo, Nancy. 1990. "Rethinking Regime Change." *Comparative Politics* 22: 359–377.

——— ed. 1992. *Liberalization and Democratization: Change in the Soviet Union and Eastern Europe.* Baltimore and London: Johns Hopkins University Press.

Bernhard, Michael H. 1993. *The Origins of Democratization in Poland: Workers, Intellectuals and Oppositional Politics, 1976–1980.* New York: Columbia University Press.

Bielasiak, Jack. 1984. "The Evolution of Crises in Poland." Jack Bielasiak and Maurice Simon, eds., *Polish Politics on the Edge of the Abyss.* New York: Praeger Publishers.

——— and Barbara Hicks. 1990. "Solidarity's Self-Organization: The Crisis of Rationality and Legitimacy in Poland, 1980–81." *East European Politics and Societies* 4:3 (Fall): 489–512.

Brand, Karl-Werner. 1990. "Cyclical Aspects of New Social Movements: Waves of Cultural Criticism and Mobilization Cycles of New Middle-Class Radicalism." Russell J. Dalton and Manfred Kuechler, eds. *Challenging the Political Order: New Social and Political Movements in Western Democracies.* New York: Oxford University Press.

Brecht, Bertolt. 1976. "The Solution" [Die Lösung], trans. Derek Bowman. *Bertolt Brecht Poems 1913–1956*, ed. John Willett and Ralph Manheim. New York: Methuen.

Bochniarz, Zbigniew. 1992. "The Ecological Disaster in Eastern Europe: Background, Current Aspects and Suggestions for the Future." *The Polish Review* 37(1): 5–25.

Bojar, Anna. 1992. "Group Identity, Group Interests and Democratic Procedures." *The Polish Sociological Bulletin* 2: 159–66.

Bora, Gyula. 1986. "Environmental protection in centrally planned economies: the case of Hungary," *International Social Science Journal* 38(3): 429–38.

Brumberg, Abraham. 1987. "A New Deal in Poland?" *The New York Review of Books*, 33:21–22 (January 15): 32–36.

Brus, Włodzimierz. 1982. "The Prospect of 'Normalization' in Poland." W. Brus, P. Kende and Z Mlynar, *'Normalization' Processes in Soviet-Dominated Central Europe: Hungary, Czechoslovakia, Poland*, Research Project in Crises in Soviet-Type Systems, Study no. 1. Vienna.

——— Pierre Kende and Zdenek Mlynar. 1982. *"Normalization Processes in Soviet-Dominated Central Europe: Hungary, Czechoslovakia, Poland*. Research Project in Crises in Soviet-type Systems, study no. 1. Vienna.

Budinkowski, Adam, Maria J. Welfens and Stanisław Sitnicki. 1987. *Rozwój Gospodarczy a Ochrona Środowiska w Krajach RWPG*. Warsaw: Państwowe Wydawnictwo Ekonomiczne.

Bugajski, Janusz and Maxine Pollack. 1989. *East European Fault Lines: Dissent, Opposition and Social Activism*. Boulder: Westview Press, Inc.

Bujak, Zbigniew. 1986. Interview. "'We Have to Hold On': A Conversation with Zbigniew Bujak" trans. and intro. Franek Michalski. *Across Frontiers* 3:1–2 (Fall): 12–14,40–42.

Calhoun, Craig. 1995. "'New Social Movements' of the Early Nineteenth Century." Mark Traugott, ed. *Repertoires & Cycles of Collective Action*. Durham and London: Duke University Press.

Carden, Maren Lockwood. 1989. "The Institutionalization of Social Movements in Voluntary Organizations." *Research in Social Movements, Conflict and Change*, Volume 11, Greenwich, CT: JAI Press Inc.: 143–61.

CBOS [Centrum Badania Opinii Społecznej]. 1986a. "Jak minął rok 1986?" study no. T206, November 28 - December 4.

———. 1986b. "Polityka informacyjna," study no. T046, March 3–12.

———. 1986c. Untitled—Study of public opinion regarding the accident in Chernobyl. Study no. T116, May.

———. 1986/1987. "Opinie o gospodarce," study no. T196, December 1986 - January 1987.

———. 1987a. "Dziennikarze o sobie i polityce informacyjnej," study no. T167, September 1–16.

———. 1987b. "Środowiska inteligenckie o społeczeństwie i sobie," pilot study no. T147, August 20–September 15.

———. 1992a. "Aktywność Władz i Społeczeństwa na rzecz Ochrony Środowiska w Miejscu Zamieszkania," komunikat z badań BS/160/17/92. Warsaw, March.

———. 1992b. "Opinia Publiczna o Stanie Środowiska Naturalnego Polski," komunikat z badań BS 135/16/92. Warsaw, March.

———. 1993a. "Ochrona Środowiska Naturalnego—Problem Bliski czy Daleki?," komunikat z badań BS/36/28/93. Warsaw, March.

———. 1993b. "Społeczeństwo wobec działalności Organizacji Ekologicznych," komunikat z badań BS/44/34/93. Warsaw, March.

———. 1993c. "Społeczna Gotowość do Proekologicznych Zachowań," komunikat z badań BS/40/31/93. Warsaw, March.

"Charter 77 on Chernobyl." 1986. *Across Frontiers* 3(1–2) (Fall): 35.

"Chernobyl in Poland." 1986. *Across Frontiers* 3(1–2) (Fall): 15–17. Texts reprinted from *Uncensored Poland*, no.'s 11, 15 (1986).

"Chernobyl is Everywhere!" 1986. *Across Frontiers* 3(1–2) (Fall): 10–11, 39.

"Chernobyl Viewed from East-Central Europe." 1986. *East European Reporter* 2(1) (Spring): 52–59.

— Charter 77 Letter to the Czechoslovak Government.

— TKK Statement, May 13, 1986.

— Krakow Region Statement, Solidarity, May 4, 1986.

— Letter to the Polish Bishops' Conference by Women Workers from the Roza Luksemburg Factory in Warsaw.

— Underground KOS on Chernobyl, May 4, 1986.

— "Freedom and Peace" Declaration, Warsaw, May 14, 1986

— Declaration of Support to the "Freedom and Peace" Movement from The Ljubljana Peace Group, May 9, 1986.

— Declaration of Support to the Ljubljana Peace Group from the "Freedom and Peace" Movement, May 9, 1986.

"Chernobyl's Repercussions for Poland." 1986. in Polish Situation Report 10/86, *Radio Free Europe Research* 11:27 (June 27).

Cigler, Allan J. 1986. "From Protest Group to Interest Group: The Making of American Agriculture Movement, Inc.," in Allan J. Cigler and Burdett A. Loomis, eds., *Interest Group Politics*, 2nd ed. Washington, D.C.: Congressional Quarterly Press: 46–69.

Cloward, Richard A. and Frances Fox Piven. 1984. "Disruption and Organization: A Rejoinder." *Theory and Society: Renewal and Critique in Social Theory* 13(4) (July): 587–99.

Cohen, Jean L. 1982. "Between Crisis Management and Social Movements: The Place of Institutional Reform." *Telos* 52 (Summer): 21–40.

———. 1982. *Class and Civil Society: The Limits of Marxian Critical Theory.* Amherst: The University of Massachusetts Press.

———. 1983. "Rethinking Social Movements." *Berkeley Journal of Sociology* 28: 97–113.

———. 1985. "Strategy or Identity: New Theoretical Paradigms and Contemporary Social Movements." *Social Research* 52(4) (Winter): 663–716.

Committee for Social Resistance [KOS]. 1986. Address to the Congress of Intellectuals, Warsaw.

"The Conditions and Effects of the Development of the Danube in Hungary." 1993. Excerpts of a February 1983 Report of the Interdisciplinary Problems Commission of the Presidency of the Hungarian Academy of Sciences.

Connor, Walter D. and Piotr Płoszajski, eds. 1992. *The Polish Road from Socialism: The Economics, Sociology and Politics of Transition.* Armonk, NY and London: M.E. Sharpe.

Csepel, Andrew. 1985. "Marxism and Ecological Crisis." *East European Reporter* 1(2) (Summer): 41–43.

Curry, Jane Leftwich, trans and ed. 1984. *The Black Book of Polish Censorship,* [compiled from *Rules and Recommendations from the Main Office for Control of Press, Publications and Public Performances* and *Report on Materials Censored*]. New York: Vintage Books (Random House).

Czajkowski, Przemysław, ed. 1990. *Ruchy i Organizacje Ekologiczne w Polsce.* Warsaw: Ośrodek Spraw Międzynarodowych PAX, Studium Ekologiczne.

Dalton, Russell J. and Manfred Kuechler, eds. 1990. *Challenging the Political*

Order: *New Social and Political Movements in Western Democracies.* New York and Oxford: Oxford University Press.

Dalton, Russell J., Manfred Kuechler and Wilhelm Bürklin. 1990. "The Challenge of New Movements." Russell J. Dalton and Manfred Kuechler, eds. *Challenging the Political Order*: *New Social and Political Movements in Western Democracies.* New York and Oxford: Oxford University Press.

Danube Circle. 1985. "Danube Circle Appeal to Czechoslovak Public." *East European Reporter* 1(3) (Autumn): 32.

"Danube Blues." 1986. *East European Reporter* 2(2) (Summer): 5–7.

DeBardeleben, Joan. 1985. *The Environment and Marxism-Leninism: The Soviet and East German Experiences.* Boulder and London: Westview Press.

———, ed. 1991. *To Breathe Free: Eastern Europe's Environmental Crisis.* Baltimore: The Johns Hopkins University Press.

"Deklaracja Wielkopolskiego Seminarium Ekologicznego." 1987. *Wielkopolski Informator Ekologiczny* no. 1 (March): 6.

Denes, Gyula. 1986. "The Politics of Environmental Protection." *East European Reporter* 2(2) (Summer): 4–5.

Diamond, Larry, ed. 1991. *The Democratic Revolution: Struggles for Freedom and Pluralism in the Developing World.* New York: Freedom House.

DiPalma, Giuseppi. 1990. *To Craft Democracies.* Berkeley: University of California Press.

———. 1991. "Legitimation From the Top to Civil Society: Politico-Cultural Change in Eastern Europe." *World Politics* 44: 49–80.

"Dobrodziejstwo XX wieku?" 1985. *Solidarność Chemików* no. 5, January 22.

"Dodatek ekologiczny. Uwaga: Trują!" 1983. *KOS* no. 44/45, December 4: 5, 6.

"Dokumenty Stowarzyszenia Ochrony Człowieka i Środowiska 'Ruch Zielonych.'" 1981. Pamphlet printed in Warsaw.

Drewniak, Stanisław. 1988. "Liga jest Wielką Siłą Społeczną," discussion with Henryk Zimny, President of the Zarząd Główny of Liga Ochrony Przyrody. *Przyroda Polska* 1/373 (January): 3–4.

"Dziennik Telewizyjny." 1988a. Polish Television Program 1, March 23.

"Dziennik Telewizyjny." 1988b. Polish Television Program 1, March. 26

"An Ecological Alarm." 1986. *East European Reporter* 1(4) (Winter): 15–16.

Eder, Klaus, "A New Social Movement?" 1982. *Telos* 52 (Summer): 5–20.

———. 1985. "The 'New Social Movement': Moral Crusades, Political Pressure Groups, or Social Movements?" *Social Research* 52(4) (Winter): 869–90.

———. 1993. *The New Politics of Class: Social Movements and Cultural Dynamics in Advanced Societies.* London: Sage Publications.

Ekiert, Grzegorz. 1991. "Democratization Processes in East Central Europe: A Theoretical Reconsideration." *British Journal of Political Science* 21(3) (July): 285–313.

Engels, Friedrich. 1954. *Dialectics of Nature.* Moscow: Foreign Language Publishing House.

Enloe, Cynthia H. 1975. *The Politics of Pollution in Comparative Perspective*: *Ecology and Power in Four Nations.* New York: Longman, Inc.

Environment: Stockholm. 1972. Summary of United Nations' Conference on the

Human Environment, Stockholm, Sweden June 5–26, 1972. Geneva: Centre for Economic and Social Information, United Nations' European Headquarters.

Feher, Ferenc and Andrew Arato, eds. 1991. *Crisis and Reform in Eastern Europe.* New Brunswick, NJ and London: Transaction Publishers.

Feshbach, Murray and Alfred Friendly, Jr. 1992. *Ecocide in the USSR: Health and Nature under Siege.* New York: Basic Books.

Fisher, Duncan. 1993. "The Emergence of the Environmental Movement in Eastern Europe and its Role in the Revolutions of 1989." Barbara Jancar-Webster, ed. *Environmental Action in Eastern Europe: Responses to Crisis.* Armonk, NY and London: M.E. Sharpe.

——, Clare Davis, Alex Juras, and Vukasin Pavlović. eds. 1992. *Civil Society and the Environment in Central and Eastern Europe.* London: Ecological Studies Institute, (May).

Frąckiewicz, Lucyna. 1985. "Środowisko naturalne i Zagrożenia społeczne Górnośląskiego Okręgu Przemysłowego." Przemysław Wójcik, ed., *Zagrożenia ekologiczne.* Instytut Badań Klasy Robotniczej of the Akademia Nauk Społecznych series on Położenie Klasy Robotniczej w Polsce, vol. 5. Warsaw: Komitet Centralny Polskiej Zjednoczonej Partii Robotniczej.

French, Hilary F. 1990. "Green Revolutions: Environmental Reconstruction in Eastern Europe and the Soviet Union." Worldwatch Paper 99, November.

Friedheim, Daniel. 1993. "Bringing Society Back into Democratic Transition Theory after 1989: Pact Making and Regime Collapse." *East European Politics and Societies* 7:3 (Fall): 482–512.

Fullenbach, Josef. 1981. *European Environmental Policy: East and West.* Boston: Butterworth's.

Fura, Zygmunt. 1985. "Institutions: The Polish Ecological Club." *Environment,* 27(9) (November): 4–5, 43.

——. n.d. "New Green Activism: The Polish Ecological Club," (unpublished manuscript).

"Gabcikovo-Nagymaros Project: Hungarian Misgivings." 1985. *East European Reporter* 1:1 (Spring): 9–10.

Gamson, William A. 1975. *The Strategy of Social Protest.* Homewood, IL: Dorsey Press.

—— and Emilie Schmeidler. 1984 "Organizing the Poor." *Theory and Society: Renewal and Critique in Social Theory* 13(4) (July): 567–85.

Garner, Roberta Ash and Mayer N. Zald. 1987. "The Political Economy of Social Movement Sectors." Mayer N. Zald and John D. McCarthy, eds., *Social Movements in an Organizational Society.* New Brunswick and London: Transaction Publishers.

Garścia , Edward. 1988. "Jubileuszowe wyzwanie." *Aura* 2/88 (February): 2.

Georgieva, Kristalina. 1993. "Environmental Policy in a Transition Economy: The Bulgarian Example." Anna Vari and Pal Tamas, eds., *Environment and Democratic Transition: Policy and Politics in Central and Eastern Europe,* Series on Technology, Risk and Society, vol. 7. Dordrecht: Kluwer Academic Publishers: 67–87.

Gieysztor, Aleksander, Stefan Kieniewicz, Emanuel Rostworowski, Janusz Tazbir, and Henryk Wereszycki, 1979. *History of Poland*, 2nd ed. Warsaw: PWN—Polish Scientific Publishers.

Ginsbert-Gebert, Adam, ed. 1985. *Ekonomiczne i Socjologiczne Problemy Ochrony Środowiska*. Wrocław: Ossolineum.

———, ed. 1988. *Ekonomiczne i Socjologiczne Problemy Ochrony Środowiska*, Tom II. Wrocław: Ossolineum.

Gitelman, Zvi. 1981. "The Politics of Socialist Restoration in Hungary and Czechoslovakia." *Comparative Politics* 13(2) (January): 187–210.

Gliński, Piotr. n.d. "Cooperation between NGO's and government in Poland." (photocopy)

———. n.d. "The Environmental Movement in Poland." (photocopy)

———. 1988. "Świadomość ekologiczna społeczeństwa polskiego—Dotychczasowe wyniki badań." *Kultura i Społeczeństwo* 3: 183–96.

———. 1989. "Ruch ekologiczny w Polsce—stan obecny." *Prace Komitetu Obywatelskiego przy Przewodniczącym NSZZ Solidarność*, no. 2 (June): 31–77.

———. n.d. [1992?]. "Zieloni w wyborach parlamentarnych, 1991." (photocopy)

Goldman, Marshall I.. 1970. "The Convergence of Environmental Disruption." *Science* 170 (October 2): 37–42.

Godzik, Stefan and Przemysław Wójcik, eds. 1990. *Ekologiczne Uwarunkowania Zdrowia i Życia Społeczeństwa Polskiego*. Warsaw: Wydawnictwo SGGW-AR.

Goodwyn, Lawrence. 1991. *Breaking the Barrier: The Rise of Solidarity in Poland*. New York and Oxford: Oxford University Press.

Gorajewska, Elżbieta. 1987a. *Jak minął rok 1987*. Centrum Badania Opinii Społecznej Study no. T217, November 16–19.

———. 1987b. *Młodzież o przyszłości*. Centrum Badania Opinii Społecznej Study no. T097, April 14–May 6.

Górka, Kazimierz and Bazyli Poskrobko. 1987. *Ekonomika Ochrony Środowiska*. Warsaw: Państwowe Wydawnictwo Ekonomiczne.

Grabowski, Andrzej. 1985. *Spacerkiem po Oikosie, czyli co to jest ekologia?* Warsaw: Państwowe Wydawnictwo Rolnicze i Lesne.

Grundmann, Reiner. 1991. *Marxism and Ecology*. Oxford: Clarendon Press.

Habermas, Jurgen. 1981. "New Social Movements." *Telos* 49 (Fall): 33–37.

Hajba, Eva. 1993. "Negotiated Rule-Making: The Case of Hungarian Environmental Protection," Budapest Papers on Democratic Transition, no. 52.

———. 1992. "Environmental Policy and the Democratic Transition," Budapest Papers on Democratic Transition, no. 30.

———. 1991. "The Green Social Movement in an 'Overweight' Political System," Budapest Papers on Democratic Transition, no. 3.

Hankiss, Elemer. 1990. *East European Alternatives*. Oxford: Clarendon Press, 1990.

Hardi, Peter, Alexander Juras and Magda Tóth Nagy, eds. 1993. *New Horizons? Possibilities for Cooperation between Environmental NGOs and Govern-*

ments in Central and Eastern Europe. Budapest: Regional Environmental Center for Central and Eastern Europe.

Hardin, Garrett and John Badin, eds. 1977. *Managing the Commons.* San Francisco: W.H. Freeman and Company.

Hegel, G.W.F. [1820] 1967. *The Philosophy of Right,* trans. and ed. T.N. Knox. New York: Oxford University Press.

Hinrichsen, Don. 1986. "Waldsterben: Forest Death Syndrome." *The Amicus Journal* 7(4) (Spring): 23–27.

Hirschman, Alfred. 1982. *Shifting Involvements: Private Interest and Public Action.* Princeton: Princeton University Press.

Howard, A.E. Dick. 1993. "Constitutional Reform." Richard F. Staar, ed., *Transition to Democracy in Poland.* New York: St. Martin's Press: 97–100.

Hrynkiewicz, Józefina. 1988. "Ruchy ekologiczne." *Państwo i Kultura Polityczna* 4: 23–57.

Huntington, Samuel P. 1991. *The Third Wave: Democratization in the Late Twentieth Century.* Norman, OK and London: University of Oklahoma Press.

Hutchings, Robert L. 1983. *Soviet-East European Relations: Consolidation and Conflict 1968–80.* Madison: University of Wisconsin Press.

Inglehart, Ronald. 1977. *The Silent Revolution: Changing Values and Political Styles among Western Publics,* Princeton: Princeton University Press.

———. 1990. *Culture Shift in Advanced Industrial Societies.* Princeton: Princeton University Press.

——— and Jacques-Rene Rabier. 1986. "Political Realignment in Advanced Industrial Society: From Class-Based Politics to Quality-of-Life Politics." *Government and Opposition* 21(4) (Autumn): 456–79.

——— and Renata Siemieńska. 1988. "Changing Values and Political Dissatisfaction in Poland and the West: A Comparative Analysis." *Government and Opposition* 23:4 (Autumn): 440–57.

Instytut na rzecz Ekorozwoju. 1992. *Raporty Ruchów Ekologicznych "Brazylia 92" (Świat i Polska).* Warsaw: Instytut na rzecz Ekorozwoju.

Iwaszkiewicz, Joanna. 1983. *Samozagłada?* Warsaw: Ludowa Spółdzielnia Wydawnicza.

Jacyna, Iwona. 1984a. "Hałas i wibracje—coraz bardziej uciążliwe: Obrady Państwowej Rady Ochrony Środowiska." *Życie Warszawy,* October 5.

———. 1984b. "Ratujmy lasy: Grzechy Główne," *Życie Warszawy,* June 6.

———. 1984c. "Ratujmy lasy (2): Czy nie jest za późno?" *Życie Warszawy,* June 12.

———. 1984d. "Woda na Kartki." *Życie Warszawy,* March 5.

———. 1985a. "Brak woli działania: Optymizm i rzeczywistość." *Życie Warszawy,* May 29.

———. 1985b. "Brak woli działania: Tydzień czystości wód'?" *Życie Warszawy,* April 15.

———. 1985c. "Początek dyskusji: Schody w dół." *Życie Warszawy,* 9 January.

———. 1986. "Szkodliwa dwuwładza: Pojedynku nie było." *Życie Warszawy,* 27 March.

Jancar, Barbara. 1987. *Environmental Management in the Soviet Union and*

Yugoslavia: Structure and Regulation in Federal Communist States. Durham, NC: Duke University Press.

Jancar-Webster, Barbara. 1993a. "Eastern Europe and the Former Soviet Union." Sheldon Kamieniecki, ed. *Environmental Politics in the International Arena: Movements, Parties, Organizations, and Policy.* Albany: State University of New York Press.

————, ed. 1993b. *Environmental Action in Eastern Europe: Responses to Crisis.* Armonk, N.Y: M. E. Sharpe, Inc.

Jaromi, Br. Stanisław. 1988. "Franciszkanie w służbie ekologii." *Święty Franciszek z Asyżu Patronem Ekologów* (Kraków) 1: 12–18.

Jaruzelski, Wojciech. 1986. "Zadania Partii w Socjalistycznym Rozwoju i Umacnianiu Polskiej Rzeczpospolitej Ludowej." Referat Komitetu Central-nego na X Zjazd PZPR wygłoszony przez I sekretarza KC PZPR Wojciecha Jaruzelskiego, reprinted in *X Zjazd Polskiej Zjednoczonej Partii Robotniczej, 29 czerwca–3 lipca 1986r.: Podstawowe dokumenty i materiały.* Warsaw: Książka i Wiedza.

Jarzębski, Stefan. 1986. Letter from the Minister of Environmental Protection and Natural Resources to Jarema Maciszewski, the Rector of the Academy of Social Sciences, reprinted in Stefan Godzik and Przemysław Wójcik, eds. 1990. *Ekologiczne Uwarunkowania Zdrowia i Życia Społeczeństwa Polskiego.* Warsaw: Wydawnictwo SGGW-AR.

Jasiewicz, Krzysztof. 1993. "Structures of Representation." Stephen White, Judy Batt and Paul G. Lewis, eds., *Developments in East European Politics.* Durham, NC: Duke University Press: 124–46.

Jastrzębski, Ludwik. 1976. "Normy prawne regulujące ochronę środowiska nat-uralnego w systemie prawa." *Państwo i Prawo* 31:11(169) November: 68–77.

————. 1983. *Ochrona Środowiska w PRL. Zagadnienia Administracyjne.* Warsaw: Państwowe Wydawnictwo Naukowe.

Jenkins, J. Craig. 1983. "Resources Mobilization Theory and the Study of Social Movements," *Annual Review of Sociology* 9: 527–53.

———— and Bert Klandermans, eds. 1995. *The Politics of Social Protest: Compar-ative Perspectives on States and Social Movements,* series on Social Movements, Protest & Contention, vol 3. Minneapolis: University of Minnesota Press.

Jones, Ellen and Benjamin L. Woodbury, II. 1986. "Consequences of Chernobyl': Chernobyl' and Glasnost.'" *Problems of Communism* 35 (November-December): 28–39.

Jowitt, Kenneth. 1975. "Inclusion and Mobilization in European Leninist Regimes," *World Politics* 28(1) (October): 69–96.

Kabala, Stanley. 1985. "Poland: Facing the Hidden Costs of Development." *Environment,* 27(9) (November): 6–13, 37–42.

————. 1993. "Environmental Affairs and the Emergence of Pluralism in Poland: A Case Study of Political Symbiosis." Anna Vari and Pal Tamas, eds., *Environ-ment and Democratic Transition: Policy and Politics in Central and Eastern Europe,* Series on Technology, Risk and Society, vol. 7. Dordrecht: Kluwer Academic Publishers.

Kalendarium Kryzysów PRL (lata 1953–1980). 1983. Addendum to *Przyczyny,*

Przebieg i Skutki Kryzysów Społecznych w Dziejach PRL. Reprinted in *Zeszyty Historyczne* 66 (Paris: Instytut Literacki): 144–95.

Kamieniecki, Sheldon, ed. 1993. *Environmental Politics in the International Arena: Movements, Parties, Organizations and Policies.* Albany: State University of New York Press.

Kaminski, Ted. 1987. "Underground Publishing in Poland." *Orbis* 31 (Fall): 313–29.

Karl, Terry Lynn. 1990. "Dilemmas of Democratization in Latin America." *Comparative Politics* 23: 1–21.

Karl, Terry Lynn and Phillippe C. Schmitter. 1991. "Modes of Transition in Latin America, Southern and Eastern Europe." *International Social Science Journal* 43: 269–284.

Kastrofy, Bożena. 1985. "Raport o zagrożeniu ekologicznym: Środowisko i My." *Życie Warszawy*, August 30: 3.

Kavan, Jan. 1986. "Ecology as Deviance: The Case of Pavel Krivka." *Across Frontiers* 2(3–4) (Spring-Summer): 15–16.

Keane, John, ed. 1988. *Civil Society and the State: New European Perspectives.* London and New York: Verso.

Kelley, Donald R., Kenneth R. Stunkel and Richard R. Wescott. 1976. *The Economic Superpowers and the Environment.* San Francisco: W.H. Freeman and Co.

Khozin, G. 1979. *The Biosphere and Politics.* Moscow: Progress Publishers, 1976 (English translation, 1979).

Kis, Janos. 1986. "Democratic Opposition in Hungary Today," interview. *Across Frontiers* 3(1–2) (Fall): 21–22, 43–45.

Kitschelt, Herbert. 1985. "New Social Movements in West Germany and the United States." Maurice Zeitlin, ed. *Political Power and Social Theory 5.* Greenwich, CT: JAI Press.

———. 1986. "Political Opportunity Structures and Political Protest: Anti-Nuclear Movements in Four Democracies." *British Journal of Political Science* 16(1) (January): 57–85.

———. 1991. "Resource Mobilization Theory: A Critique." Dieter Rucht, ed. *Research on Social Movements: The State of the Art in Western Europe and the USA.* Frankfurt am Main: Campus Verlag; Boulder, CO: Westview Press.

———. 1992. "The Formation of Party Systems in Eastern Europe." *Politics and Society* 20(1) (March): 7–50.

Klandermans, Bert. 1991. "New Social Movements and Resource Mobilization: The European and the American Approach Revisited." Dieter Rucht, ed. *Research on Social Movements: The State of the Art in Western Europe and the USA.* Frankfurt am Main: Campus Verlag; Boulder, CO: Westview Press.

———, Hanspeter Kriesi and Sidney Tarrow, eds. 1988. *From Structure to Action: Comparing Social Movement Research Across Cultures.* Series on International Social Movement Research, vol. 1. Greenwich, CT: JAI Press.

Kolankiewicz, George. 1988. "Poland and the Politics of Permissible Pluralism," *Eastern European Politics and Societies* 2(1) (Winter): 152–83.

Komitet Obchodów 60-lecia Ligi Ochrony Przyrody. 1988. "60 lat Ligi Ochrony

Przyrody w Służbie Społeczeństwa i Kraju." *Przyroda Polska*, no. 1 (373), (January): 4–5.

"Komitety Ochrony Środowiska." 1986. *Przegląd Wiadomości Agencyjnych* 19, May 11: 2.

"Konferencja prasowa dla dziennikarzy zagranicznych." 1985a. Stenogram of the press conference held September 3, 1985, Warsaw. *Rzeczpospolita*, September 9: 4.

"Konferencja prasowa dla dziennikarzy zagranicznych." 1985b. Stenogram of the press conference held September 10, 1985, Warsaw. *Rzeczpospolita*, September 17: 4.

"Konferencja prasowa dla dziennikarzy zagranicznych." 1985c. Stenogram of the press conference held September 24, 1985, Warsaw. *Rzeczpospolita*, September 30: 4.

"Konferencja prasowa rzecznika rządu." 1985. Stenogram of the press conference held September 19, 1985, Warsaw. *Rzeczpospolita*, September 20: 5.

"Konferencja prasowa rzecznika rządu." 1986. *Życie Warszawy*, May 7: 1–2.

"Konferencja w SGPiS: Ekologizm, czyli ile tracimy." 1985. *Życie Warszawy*, April 17: 6.

Konrad, George. 1984. *Antipolitics*. New York and San Diego: Harcourt Brace Jovanovich.

Konstytucja Polskiej Rzeczypospolitej Ludowej. 1987. Uchwalona przez Sejm Ustawodawczy w dniu 22 lipca 1952 r. Warsaw: Książka i Wiedza.

Konstytucja Rzeczypospolitej Polskiej. 1992. Wybór źródeł, stan prawny na dzień 1 grudnia 1992, opracowany przez Dariusza Dudka. Lublin: Lubelskie Wydawnictwa Prawnicze.

Kossawski, Marek. 1998. "Leave the Bunkers to the Bats." *Across Frontiers* 4(2–3) (Spring-Summer): 10–11, 48–49.

Kostecki, Marian J. and Krzysztof Mreła, "Institutional Revolt and Institutional Normalization," (unpublished manuscript).

Kowalski, Jan and Andrzej Malinowski [Henryk Szlajfer]. 1982. "Pod wojskową dyktaturą: między 'zamrożeniem' a 'restauracją.'" *Krytyka* 12:23–77.

Kozłowski, Stefan. 1985. "Regiony szczególnie zagrożone." Przemysław Wójcik, ed., *Zagrożenia ekologiczne*. Instytut Badań Klasy Robotniczej of the Akademia Nauk Społecznych series on Położenie Klasy Robotniczej w Polsce, vol. 5. Warsaw: Komitet Centralny Polskiej Zjednoczonej Partii Robotniczej.

—— and Witold Lenart. 1988. "Ocena materiałów statystycznych GUS w zakresie ochrony środowiska i gospodarki wodnej." *Problemy Rozwoju Społeczno-Gospodarczego z Poszanowaniem Dóbr Przyrody*, Biuletyn 3 (1988), Polska Akademia Nauk, Komitet Inżynierii Środowiska. Wrocław: Ossolineum.

Kramer, John M. 1983. "The Environmental Crisis in Eastern Europe: The Price of Progress." *Slavic Review* 42(2) (Summer): 204–20.

——. 1986. "Consequences of Chernobyl': Chernobyl' and Eastern Europe." *Problems of Communism* 35 (November-December): 40–58.

Kriesi, Hanspeter, Ruud Koopmans, Jan Willem Duyrendak, and Marco G. Giugni. 1995. *New Social Movements in Western Europe: A Comparative Analysis*, series on Social Movements, Protest, and Contention, vol 5. Minneapolis: University of Minnesota Press.

———. 1995. "The Political Opportunity Structure of New Social Movements: Its Impact on their Mobilization." J. Craig Jenkins and Bert Klandermans, eds. 1995. *The Politics of Social Protest: Comparative Perspectives on States and Social Movements*, series on Social Movements, Protest & Contention, vol 3. Minneapolis: University of Minnesota Press.

Kubik, Jan. 1994. *The Power of Symbols against the Symbols of Power: The Rise of Solidarity and the Fall of State Socialism in Poland*. University Park, PA: The Pennsylvania State University Press.

Laba, Roman. 1986. "Worker Roots of Solidarity." *Problems of Communism* 35(4).

———. 1991. *The Roots of Solidarity: A Political Sociology of Poland's Working-Class Democratization*. Princeton: Princeton University Press.

Łabno, Zbigniew and Franciszek Piontek. 1986. "Istota i zakres polityki sozologicznej." Franciszek Piontek, ed., *Zarys polityki sozologicznej*. Wrocław: Ossolineum: 11–30.

Lawson, Stephanie. 1993. "Conceptual Issues in the Comparative Study of Regime Change and Democratization." *Comparative Politics* 25: 183–205.

Lepak, Keith John. 1988. *Prelude to Solidarity: Poland and the Politics of the Gierek Regime*. New York: Columbia University Press.

Lin, Gustaw [Marek Beylin]. 1983. "Język a Pluralizm." *Krytyka* 16: 72–77.

Lipski, Jan Józef. 1985. *KOR: A History of the Workers' Defense Committee in Poland, 1976–81*. Berkeley: University of California Press.

Locke, John. [1960] 1965. "The Second Treatise of Government: An Essay Concerning the True Original, Extent, and End of Civil Government." *Two Treatises of Government* with introduction and notes by Peter Laslett. New York: New American Library, Inc.

Lowe, Philip D. and Wolfgang Rüdig. 1986. "Review Article: Political Ecology and the Social Sciences—The State of the Art." *British Journal of Political Science* 16(4) (October): 513–50.

Mainwaring, Scott, Guillermo O'Donnell and J. Samuel Valenzuela, eds. 1992. *Issues in Democratic Consolidation: The New South American Democracies in Comparative Perspective*. Notre Dame: University of Notre Dame Press.

Majda, Tomasz. 1987. *Ochrona Środowiska: Wybór Podstawowych Aktów Prawnych*. Warsaw: Instytut Wydawniczy Związków Zawodowych.

"Manifesto Ekologiczne." 1989. *Przekrój*, February 26: 4.

Manser, Roger. 1993. *Failed Transitions: The Eastern European Economy and Environment Since the Fall of Communism*. New York: The New Press.

Markiewicz, Stanisław. 1983. *Współdziałanie Kościoła i Państwa w Świetle Teorii i Praktyki*. Warsaw: Książka i Wiedza.

Marples, David R. 1986. "Work and Safety in Ukraine's Nuclear Power Industry." *Across Frontiers* 3(1–2) (Fall): 1–4, 37–38.

———. 1986. "Consequences of Chernobyl': Chernobyl' and Ukraine." *Problems of Communism* 35 (November-Decmeber): 17–27.

Mason, David. 1989. "Solidarity as a New Social Movement," *Political Science Quarterly* 104(1) (Spring): 41–58.

———. 1993. "Poland." Stephen White, Judy Batt and Paul G. Lewis, eds., *Developments in East European Politics*. Durham, NC: Duke University Press: 36–50.

McAdam, Doug. 1982. *Political Process and the Development of Black Insurgency, 1930–1970*. Chicago: The University of Chicago Press.

Meadows, Donella H, Dennis L. Meadows, Jorgen Randers and William W. Behrens. 1974. *The Limits to Growth*, 2nd ed. A Report for the Club of Rome's Project on the Predicament of Mankind. New York: The New American Library.

Melucci, Alberto. 1980. "The New Social Movements: A Theoretical Approach." *Social Science Information* 19(2): 199–226.

———. 1985. "The Symbolic Challenge of Contemporary Movements." *Social Research* 52(4) (Winter): 789–816.

———. 1988. "Getting Involved: Identity and Mobilization in Social Movements." Bert Klandermans, Hanspeter Kriesi, and Sidney Tarrow, eds. *From Structure to Action: Comparing Social Movement Research Across Cultures*, series on International Social Movement Research, vol. 1. Greenwich, CT: JAI Press.

———. 1989. *Nomads of the Present: Social Movements and Individual Needs in Contemporary Society*. Philadelphia: Temple University Press.

Messner, Zbigniew. 1986. "Założenia Społeczno-Gospodarczego Rozwoju Kraju w Latach 1986–1990 i do Roku 1995." Referat Rady Minstrów PRL wygłoszony przez premiera Zbigniewa Messnera, reprinted in *X Zjazd Polskiej Zjednoczonej Partii Robotniczej, 29 czerwca–3 lipca 1986r.: Podstawowe dokumenty i materiały*. Warsaw: Książka i Wiedza.

Michajłow, Włodzimierz. 1976. *Środowisko i Polityka*. Wrocław: Zakład Narodowy imienia Ossolińskich—Wydawnictwo Polskiej Akademii Nauk (Ossolineum).

Michnik, Adam. 1976. "The New Evolutionism." *Survey* 22(3/4) (Summer-Autumn): 267–77.

Millard, Frances. 1992. "The Polish Parliamentary Elections of October 1991." *Soviet Studies* 44: 837–855.

———. 1994a. *The Anatomy of the New Poland*. Aldershot, UK: Edward Alger.

———. 1994b. "The Shaping of the Polish Party System, 1989–93." *East European Politics and Societies* 8: 467–494.

Ministerstwo Ochrony Środowiska i Zasobów Naturalnych. 1988. *Informacja o Realizacji Ustawy o Ochronie i Kształtowaniu Środowiska*. Warsaw: March.

Miształ, Bronisław. 1990. "Alternative Social Movements in Contemporary Poland." Louis Kriesberg, ed., *Research in Social Movements: Conflict and Change*, vol. 12. Greenwich, CT: JAI Press.

——— and J. Craig Jenkins. 1995. "Starting from Scratch is not Always the Same: The Politics of Protest and the Postcommunist Tranistions in Poland and Hungary." J. Craig Jenkins and Bert Klandermans, eds. 1995. *The Politics of Social Protest: Comparative Perspectives on States and Social Movements*, series on Social Movements, Protest & Contention, vol 3. Minneapolis: University of Minnesota Press.

Mojkowski, Jacek. 1986 "Po Katastrofie w Czernobylu: Porady Praktyczne." *Polityka*, 17 May: 8.

Mlynar, Zdenek. 1982. "Introduction." W. Brus, P. Kende and Z. Mlynar, *'Normalization' Processes in Soviet-Dominated Central Europe: Hungary, Czechoslovakia, Poland*, Research Project in Crises in Soviet-Type Systems, Study no. 1. Vienna: 3–4.

Nikorow, Maksym. 1985. "Żywność." Przemysław Wójcik, ed., *Zagrożenia ekologiczne*. Instytut Badań Klasy Robotniczej of the Akademia Nauk Społecznych series on Położenie Klasy Robotniczej w Polsce, vol. 5. Warsaw: Komitet Centralny Polskiej Zjednoczonej Partii Robotniczej.

"Nowa Inicjatywa PRON: Społeczny Ruch Ekologiczny." 1986. *Życie Warsawy*, September 23: 1–2.

"O Regionie Śląsko-Dąbrowskim—z prasy związkowej." 1983. Reprinted from *Regionalny Informator Solidarności Śląśkiej-Dąbrowskiej* in *Tygodnik Mazowsze* nr 59, 11 August: 3.

Oberschall, Anthony. 1973. *Social Conflict and Social Movements*. Englewood Cliffs, NJ: Prentice-Hall, Inc.

———. 1993. *Social Movements: Ideologies, Interests, and Identities*. New Brunswick, NJ and London: Transaction Publishers.

"Obłok Przyjaźni." 1986a. *Solidarność: Biuletyn Informacyjny* (Paris), no. 142–144 (June 20): 5–9.

"Obłok Przyjaźni." 1986b. *Solidarność: Biuletyn Informacyjny* (Paris), no. 145–146 (June 25): 22–25.

OBOP [Ośrodek Badania Opinii Publicznej]. 1989. "O wyborach i telewizji," badanie panelowe 21/C/89, May 22–23.

———. 1990a. "Bieżące sprawy z życia kraju," badanie panelowe 9/A/90, January 26–27.

———. 1990b. "Opinie o programie telewizyjnym i innych sprawach," badanie panelowe 8/D/90, February 19–20.

———. 1990c. "Różne wartości w życiu," badanie panelowe 19/C/90, May 7–8.

———. 1992a. "Sprawy Środowiska naturalnego," badanie panelowe 19/C/92, May 4–5.

———. 1992b. "Życie codzienne i problemy mieszkaniowe," badanie panelowe 26/B/92, June 22–23.

———. 1993a. "O zagadnieniach prawa i przestępczości," badanie panelowe 24/D/93, June 14–15.

———. 1993b. "Stowarzyszenia, Uczestnictwo w Organizacjach Społecznych a Demokracja," badanie panelowe 26/B/93, June 28–29.

"Odezwa programowa do cytelników 'Wolę Być.'" 1984. *Na Przelaj*, July 27. Reproduced in Anna Wyka, "Ruch 'Wolę Być'" (unpublished manuscript).

O'Donnell, Guillermo, Phillippe C. Schmitter and Lawrence Whitehead, eds. 1986. *Transitions from Authoritarian Rule: Prospects for Democracy*. Baltimore and London: Johns Hopkins University Press.

Offe, Claus. 1985. "New Social Movements: Challenging the Boundaries of Institutional Politics." *Social Research* 52(4) (Winter): 817–68.

Olson, Mancur, Jr. 1965. *The Logic of Collective Action*. Cambridge: Harvard University Press.

Olszewski, Dariusz, Waldemar Bielański and Mariola Kamińska. 1987. "Economic Pressure on the Environment in the European CMEA Countries: Statistical Tables." EKO^2 Series no. 8716. Warsaw: Wydział Nauk Ekonomicznych, Uniwersytet Warszawski.

Oschlies, Wolf. 1986. *"Europas ökologisch meistbedrohtes Land?" Umweltzerstörung in Polen*. Berichte des Bundesinstituts für ostwissenschaftliche und internationale Studien, 45–1986. Köln: Bundesinstitut für ostwissenschaftliche und internationale Studien.

Ost, David. 1990. *Solidarity and the Politics of Anti-Politics*. Philadelphia: Temple University Press.

Ośrodek Badania Opinii Publicznej i Studiów Programowych (OBOPiSP). 1975. "Problemy Zagrożenia i Ochrony Środowiska Naturalnego w Opinii Publicznej," study no. 22/63, July.

"Ósme posiedzenie Rady Konsultacyjnej przy Przewodniczącym Rady Państwa nad Programem Ochrony Środowiska." 1988. *Rada Narodowa*, special edition 8/3/88, October 11.

Pakulski, Jan. 1991. *Social Movements: The Politics of Moral Protest*. Melbourne: Longman Cheshire.

Panek, Krystyna. 1988. "Ekologiczna strategia." *Trybuna Ludu*, November 21: 5.

Parsons, Howard L. 1977. *Marx and Engels on Ecology*. Series on Contributions in Philosophy, no. 8. Westport, CT: Greenwood Press.

Pawłowski, L. and Kozak, Z., eds. 1984. "Chemiczne Zagrożenia Środowiska w Polsce." *Wiadomości Chemiczne* 38: 451–95.

Pelczynski, Zbigniew. 1988. "Solidarity and the 'Rebirth of Civil Society' in Poland, 1976–81." John Keane, ed., *Civil Society and the State: New European Perspectives*. London and New York: Verso: 361–80.

Petracca, Mark P., ed. 1992. *The Politics of Interests: Interest Groups Transformed*. Boulder: Westview Press.

Piontek, Franciszek. 1988. "Ocena Wartości Ekonomicznych Strat Spowodowanych Brakiem Skutecznej Ochrony Powietrza w Województwie Katowickim." *Problemy Rozwoju Społeczno-Gospodarczego z Poszanowaniem Dóbr Przyrody*, Biuletyn 3, Polska Akademia Nauk, Komitet Inżynierii Środowiska. Wrocław: Ossolineum.

Piontek, Franciszek, Stanisław Dziadek, Jerzy Kusztal and Zbigniew Łabno. 1986. *Zarys polityki sozologicznej*. Wrocław: Ossolineum.

Piven, Frances Fox and Richard A. Cloward. 1979. *Poor People's Movements: Why They Succeed, How They Fail*. New York: Vintage Books.

PKE [Polski Klub Ekologiczny]. 1985. *Rola edukacji ekologicznej w kształtowaniu świadomości ekologicznej społeczeństwa*. Kraków: Akademia Górniczo-Hutnicza im. Staszica.

———. 1986. *Ekorozwój Szansą Przetrwania Cywilizacji*, materials from the conference of the Polish Ecological Club, June 4–5, 1985, Prace Naukowe Okręgu Małopolska, vol. 3. Kraków: Akademia Górniczo-Hutnicza im. Staszica.

———. 1989a. "Deklaracja Ideowa Polskiego Klubu Ekologicznego." *Deklaracja Ideowa i Tezy Programowe Polskiego Klubu Ekologicznego*. Krakow: Uniwersytet Jagiellonski.

———. 1989b. "Ku Cywilizacji Ekorozwoju: Tezy Programowe Polskiego Klubu Ekologicznego." *Deklaracja Ideowa i Tezy Programowe Polskiego Klubu Ekologicznego*. Krakow: Uniwersytet Jagiellonski.

———. 1993a. "Protokoł z Obrad IV Walnego Zjazdu Delegatów Polskiego Klubu Ekologicznego w dniach 5 i 6 czerwca 1993r." (photocopy)

———. 1993b. Zarząd Główny. *Sprawozdanie z działalności Zarządu Głównego*

Polskiego Klubu Ekologicznego w okresie 3.VI. 1990 do 4.VI. 1993, prepared for the National Congress of PKE Delegates. Kraków: Polski Klub Ekologiczny, May.

"Poland after the Chernobyl Disaster." 1986. Committee in Support of Solidarity *Reports* no. 43 (30 July): 22–25.

Polska Akademia Nauk Komitet Ochrony Przyrody. 1988. *Problemy Ochrony Polskiej Przyrody*, eds. Romauld Olaczek and Kazimierz Zarzycki. Warsaw: Państwowe Wydawnictwo Naukowe.

"Program NSZZ 'Solidarność'" uchwalony przez I Krajowy Zjazd. 1981. *Tygodnik Solidarność*, October 16.

"Program Theses of the 'Future Times' ('Czas Przyszły') Group." 1989. Trans. by Franek Michalski. *Across Frontiers* 5:2 (Summer): 24.

Protokoł Podzespołu do Spraw Ekologii Okrągłego Stołu. 1989. Warsaw, March.

"Protokoł Rozbieżności w Sprawie Rozwóju Energetyki." 1989. Appended to *Protokoł Podzespołu do Spraw Ekologii Okrągłego Stołu.* Warsaw, March.

Przeworski, Adam. 1991. *Democracy and the Market: Political and Economic Reforms in Eastern Europe.* Cambridge: Cambridge University Press.

Przyczyny, Przebieg i Skutki Kryzysów Społecznych w Dziejach PRL. 1983. Projekt opracowania syntetycznego Komisji Komitetu Centralnego PZPR dla wyjaśnienia okoliczności, faktów i przyczyn konfliktów społecznych w dziejach Polskiej Ludowej. Reprinted in *Zeszyty Historyczne* 65 (Paris: Instytut Literacki): 137–77.

Rada Ekologiczna przy Prezydencie RP. 1993a. *Sprawozdanie z inauguracyjnego posiedzenia Rady Ekologicznej przy Prezydencie Rzeczypospolitej Polskiej.* Warsaw, February 16.

———. 1993b. *Tezy programowe* (written by Stefan Kozłowski, Chair). Warsaw: Belweder, January.

Radecki, Wojciech. 1983. *Odpowiedzialność Karna w Ochronie Środowiska.* Wrocław: Ossolineum.

———. 1985. *Odpowiedzialność Administracyjna w Ochronie Środowiska.* Wrocław: Ossolineum.

———. 1987. *Odpowiedzialność Cywilna w Ochronie Środowiska.* Wrocław: Ossolineum.

Radio Free Europe. 1981. *Research.* Polish Situation Report 2/81, 30 January.

———. 1986a. "East Europeans and the Chernobyl Events: Awareness, Primary Sources of Information and Attitudes towards Soviet and Home Media Handling of Information." *East European Area Audience and Opinion Research*, no. 732, December.

———. 1986b. *Research.* Polish Situation Report 1/86, January 24.

———. 1986c. *Research.* Polish Situation Report 5/86, March 28.

———. 1986d. *Research.* Polish Situation Report 10/86, June 27.

———. 1986e. *Research.* Polish Situation Report 13/86, August 29.

———. 1988. *Research.* Polish Situation Report 23/86, December 2, 1988.

Radziszewski, Edward. 1987. *Ustawa o ochronie i kształtowaniu Środowiska. Komentarz. Przepisy wykonawcze.* Warsaw: Wydawnictwo Prawnicze.

"Raport o Stanie Środowiska (1)," 1983. *Życie Gospodarcze*, April 17: 3.

"Raport o Stanie Środowiska (2)." 1983. *Życie Gospodarcze*, April 24: 3.

"Ratujmy Błonia!" 1989. Leaflet, April 26.

Rau, Zbigniew, ed. 1991. *The Reemergence of Civil Society in Eastern Europe and the Soviet Union*. Boulder: Westview Press.

REFA [Ruch Ekologiczny Św. Franciszka z Asyżu]. 1988a. *Święty Franciszek z Asyżu Patronem Ekologów*, no. 1, (Kraków).

———. 1988b. "Zasady Ideowe Ruchu Ekologicznego Św. Franciszka z Asyżu (REFA)," (undated pamphlet) reprinted in *Święty Franciszek z Asyżu Patronem Ekologów*, no. 1, Kraków.

Regulska, Joanna. 1993. "Democratic Elections and Political Restructuring in Poland, 1989–91." In *The New Political Geography of Eastern Europe*, eds. John O'Loughlin and Herman van der Wusten. London: Belhaven Press.

Remmer, Karen. 1990. "New Wine in Old Bottlenecks? The Study of Latin American Democracy." *Comparative Politics* 23: 479–495.

Richter, Edelbert. 1986. "Domestic Sources of Bloc Confrontation in Eastern Europe." *Across Frontiers* 3(1–2) (Fall): 8–9.

"Rivers of Pollution." 1985. *East European Reporter* 1:1 (Spring): 54. Reprinted from *Tygodnik Mazowsze* 107, November 22, 1984.

Rohrschneider, Robert. 1988. "Citizens' Attitudes Toward Environmental Issues: Selfish of Selfless?" *Comparative Political Studies* 21:3 (October): 347–67.

"Rozporządzenie Rady Ministrów z dnia 20 sierpnia 1968 r. w sprawie uznania ‚Ligi Ochrony Przrody' za stowarzyszenie wyższej użyteczności." *Dziennik Ustaw* 1968, nr 33, poz. 227.

"Rozporządzenie Rady Ministrów z dnia 23 czerwca 1972 r. w sprawie szczegółowego zakresu działania Ministra Gospodarki Terenowej i Ochrony Środowiska." *Dziennik Ustaw* 1972, nr 28, poz. 22.

"Rozporządzenie Rady Ministrów z dnia 9 lipca 1975 r. w sprawie szczegółowego zakresu działania Ministra Administracji, Gospodarki Terenowej i Ochrony środowiska." *Dziennik Ustaw* 1975, nr 26, poz. 136.

"Rozporządzenie Rady Ministrów z dnia 30 września 1980 r. w sprawie szczegółowych zasad i trybu wykonywania przez Ministra Administracji, Gospodarki Terenowej i Ochrony Środowiska koordynacji działalności w dziedzinie ochrony środowiska." *Dziennik Ustaw* 1980, nr 24, poz. 95.

"Rozporządzenie Rady Ministrów z dnia 30 września 1980 r. w sprawie Państwowej Inspekcji Ochrony Środowiska oraz wykonania kontroli w zakresie ochrony Środowiska." *Dziennik Ustaw* 1980, nr 24, poz. 96.

"Rozporządzenie Rady Ministrów z dnia 30 września 1980 r. w sprawie organizacji, szczegółowych zasad i zakresu działania Państwowej Rady Ochrony Środowiska." *Dziennik Ustaw* 1980, nr 24, poz. 97.

"Rozporządzenie Rady Ministrów z dnia 16 grudnia 1983 r. w sprawie szczegółowego zakresu działania urzędu Ochrony Środowiska i Gospodarki Wodnej." *Dziennik Ustaw* 1983, nr 73, poz. 321.

Rucht, Dieter, ed. 1991. *Research on Social Movements: The State of the Art in Western Europe and the USA*. Boulder, CO: Westview Press.

Rupnik, Jacques. 1988. *The Other Europe*. London: Weidenfeld and Nicolson.

Rustow, Dankart. 1970. "Transitions to Democracy." *Comparative Politics*. 2(3): 337–63.

Sabatowski, Andrzej. 1988. "Nie jest aż tak dobrze . . . " *Życie Literackie*, July 17.
Sanford, George, ed. 1990. *The Solidarity Congress, 1981: The Great Debate.* Houndmills, Baskingstoke, Hampshire and London: The MacMillan Press Ltd.
————, ed. and trans. 1992. *Democratization in Poland, 1988–90: Polish Voices.* New York: St. Martins Press.
Shain, Yossi and Juan J. Linz. 1995. *Between States: Interim Governments and Democratic Transitions.* Cambridge: Cambridge University Press.
Short, Andrew. 1986. "Cooperation Among the Democratic Oppositions of Poland, Hungary and Czechoslovakia." *East European Reporter* 1(4) (Winter): 24–26.
Singleton, Fred. 1985 "Ecological Crisis in Eastern Europe: Do the Greens Threaten the Reds?" *Across Frontiers* 2(1) (Summer): 5–10.
Skilling, H. Gordon. 1991. "Introductory Essay." H. Gordon Skilling and Paul Wilson, eds., *Civic Freedom in Central Europe: Voices from Czechoslovakia.* New York: St. Martin's Press.
Sklar, Richard L. 1988. "Beyond Capitalism and Socialism in Africa." *The Journal of Modern African Societies* 26(1): 1–21.
Słownik języka polskiego. 1981. 3 vols. Warsaw: Państwowe Wydawnictwo Naukowe.
Solidarity, Małopolska Regional Commission. 1986. "On Radioactivity in the Krakow Area and Proper Preventative Measures: Statement of the Małopolska Regional Solidarity Commission of May 4, 1986." Committee in Support of Solidarity *Reports*, no. 43, July 30: 24–25.
Solidarity, Temporary Coordinating Commission. 1986. "Poland after the Czernobyl Disaster: Statement of the Temporary Coordinating Commission, May 13, 1986." Committee in Support of Solidarity *Reports*, no. 43, July 30: 22–23.
"Spotkania Zespołów Tematycznych." 1981. Agencja Solidarność, *Biuletyn Pism Związkowych i Zakładowych* no. 36, September 5–10: 611.
"Stan klęski ekologicznej." 1984. *Tygodnik Mazowsze* nr 107, 22 November: 3.
"Stan Środowiska Naturalnego w Polsce." 1986. *Solidarność: Biuletyn Informacyjny* (Paris), no. 141 (June 11): 3–16.
Staniszkis, Jadwiga. 1984. *Poland's Self-Limiting Revolution*, ed. Jan T. Gross. Princeton: Princeton University Press.
Starr, Richard F., ed. 1993. *Transition to Democracy in Poland.* New York: St. Martin's Press.
Stasiak, Jadwiga and Krzysztof Stasiak. 1983. *Problemy Środowiska Przyrodniczego.* Warsaw: Państwowe Wydawnictwo Naukowe.
"The State of the Ecological Disaster." 1985. Translated from *Tygodnik Mazowsze*, no. 107, and reprinted in *Uncensored Poland News Bulletin*, no. 1/85, 3 January: 43–44.
Stepan, Alfred. 1988. *Rethinking Militray Politics: Brazil and the Southern Cone.* Princeton: Princeton University Press.
Stępniak, Mirosław, "I o co tym młodym znowu chodzi?! Zagazowanie województwa" 1988. *Na Przełaj*, 12 June: 11–13.
Surowiec, Stanisław, Wacław Tarasiewicz and Teresa Zwięglińska. 1981. *Prawo*

Wodne. Komentarz. Przepisy wykonawcze. Warsaw: Wydawnictwo Prawnicze.

"System wrogi naturze: Problemy ochrony Środowiska." 1984. *KOS* nr. 59, 3 September: 3, 7.

Szacki, Jakub, Irmina Głowacka, Anna Liro and Barbara Szulczewska. 1993. "Political and Social Changes in Poland: An Environmental Perspective." Barbara Jancar-Webster, ed. *Environmental Action in Eastern Europe: Responses to Crisis.* Armonk, NY and London.

Szafer, Władysław and Włodzimierz Michajłow, eds. 1973. *Ochrona Przyrodniczego Środowiska Człowieka.* Warsaw: Państwowe Wydawnictwo Naukowe.

Szczęsny, Tadeusz. 1982. *Ochrona Przyrody i Krajobrazu* (Wydanie IV zmienione i uzupełnione). Warsaw: Państwowe Wydawnictwo Naukowe.

Szmak, Andrzej. 1988. "Niepotrzebne skreślić: Trzy szczęścia w nieszczęściu." *Przegląd Tygodniowy,* July 17.

Szymonowicz, Antoni. 1985. "Społeczne i Ekonomiczne Skutki Degradacji Środowiska Naturalnego." Przemysław Wójcik, ed., *Zagrożenia ekologiczne.* Instytut Badań Klasy Robotniczej of the Akademia Nauk Społecznych series on Położenie Klasy Robotniczej w Polsce, vol. 5. Warsaw: Komitet Centralny Polskiej Zjednoczonej Partii Robotniczej.

Taras, Ray. 1986. "Official Etiologies of Polish Crises: Changing Historiographies and Factional Struggles." *Soviet Studies* 38(1) (January): 53–68.

———. 1995. *Consolidating Democracy in Poland.* Boulder: Westview Press.

Tarrow, Sidney. 1988. "National Politics and Collective Action: Recent Theory and Research in Western Europe and the United States." *Annual Review of Sociology* 14: 421–40.

———. 1991. "'Aiming at a Moving Target': Social Science and the Recent Rebellions in Eastern Europe." *PS: Political Science and Politics* 24(1) (March): 12–20.

———. 1994. *Power in Movement: Social Movements, Collective Action and Politics.* Cambridge: Cambridge University Press.

"Text of the Indictment Against Pavel Krivka and Pavel Skoda." 1986. *Across Frontiers* 2(3–4) (Spring-Summer): 17–18.

Thornton, Judith. 1986. "Consequences of Chernobyl': Chernobyl' and Soviet Energy." *Problems of Communism* 35 (November-December): 1–16.

Tilly, Charles. 1985. "Models and Realities of Popular Collective Action." *Social Research* 52(4) (Winter): 717–48.

Tismaneanu, Vladimir. 1992. *Reinventing Politics: Eastern Europe from Stalin to Havel.* New York: The Free Press.

Tobera, Piotr. 1988. *Kryzys Środowiska—Kryzys Społeczeństwa.* Warsaw: Ludowa Spółdzielnia Wydawnicza.

Tocqueville, Alexis de. [1835 and 1840] 1945. *Democracy in America.* New York: Random House (Vintage Books).

Topolski, Jerzy. 1986. *An Outline history of Poland,* trans Olgierd Wojtasiewicz. Warsaw: Interpress Publishers.

Touraine, Alain. 1981 [1978]. *The Voice and the Eye: An Analysis of Social Movements.* Cambridge: Cambridge University Press.

———. 1985. "An Introduction to the Study of Social Movements." *Social Research* 52:4 (Winter): 749–87.

"Towarzystwo Wolnej Wszechnicy Polskiej. Czym jest? Jaką przebyło drogę? Ku czemu zmierza?" 1987. (Warsaw, December).

Traugott, Mark, ed. 1995. *Repertoires & Cycles of Collective Action.* Durham and London: Duke University Press.

"Trują!" 1984. *Metrum* nr 19, 5 September: 2.

Tucker, Kenneth. 1991. "How New are the New Social Movements?" *Theory, Culture and Society* 8(2) (May): 75–98.

Turnock, David. 1989. *Eastern Europe: An Historical Geography, 1815–1945.* London and New York: Routledge.

"Underground KOS on Chernobyl, 4th May 1986 . . . " 1986. *East European Reporter* 2:1 (Spring): 55–56.

"Unfinished Past: The Gabcikovo-Nagymaros Project: 1953 and Now." 1985. *East European Reporter* 1:3 (Autumn): 25–28.

— Minutes of the Meeting Held on the 18th April 1953 in the Office of Comrade Gero (Subj: The Danube Hydroelectric Project).

— The Hungarian Council of Ministers on the Gabcikovo-Nagymaros Hydro-electric Barrage Project.

— Situation Report on the Bos (Gabcikovo)-Nagymaros Barrage, *Nepsza-badsag*, August 16, 1985.

United Nations. 1990. *Year Book of Labour Statistics, 1945–1989.* Geneva: International Labour Office.

———. 1991. *Year Book of Labour Statistics, 1990.* Geneva: International Labour Office.

Urząd Rady Ministrów. 1992. *Polityka Ekologiczna Państwa*, prepared by the Ministry of Environmental Protection, Natural Resources and Forestry. Warsaw: February.

Urząd Wojewódzki [Płocki]. 1985. Wydział Ochrony Środowiska, Gospodarki Wodnej i Geologii and Ośrodek Badań i Kontroli Środowiska. *Ochrona i Kształtowanie Środowiska*, pamphlet. Płock.

"Ustawa wodna z dnia 19 września 1922 r." *Dziennik Ustaw* 1922, nr 102, poz. 936.

"Ustawa z dnia 10 marca 1934 r. o ochronie przyrody." *Dziennik Ustaw* 1934, nr 31, poz. 274.

"Ustawa z dnia 7 kwietnia 1949 r. o ochronie przyrody." *Dziennik Ustaw* 1949, nr 25, poz. 180.

"Ustawa z dnia 21 kwietnia 1966 r. o ochronie powietrza atmosferycznego przed zanieczyszczeniem." *Dziennik Ustaw* 1966, nr 14, poz. 87.

"Ustawa z dnia 24 października 1974 r. Prawo budowlane." *Dziennik Ustaw* 1974, nr 38, poz. 229.

"Ustawa z dnia 24 października 1974 r. Prawo Wodne." *Dziennik Ustaw* 1974, nr 38, poz. 230.

"Ustawa z dnia 31 stycznia 1980 r. o ochronie i kształtowaniu środowiska." *Dziennik Ustaw* 1980, no. 3, poz. 6.

"Ustawa z dnia 28 lipca 1983 r. o utworzeniu urzędu Ministra Administracji i Gospodarki Przestrzennej." *Dziennik Ustaw* 1983, nr 44, poz. 200.

"Ustawa z dnia 28 lipca 1983 r. o utworzeniu urzędu Ochrony Środowiska i Gospodarki Wodnej." *Dziennik Ustaw* 1983, nr 44, poz. 201.

"Uwaga Trują!" 1984. *KOS* nr 47, 16 January: 6.

"Uwaga Trują! Zagrożenia," 1984. *KOS* nr 49, 13 February: 5–6.

"Uwaga police," 1984. *KOS* nr 58, 13 August: 12.

Valenta, Jiri. 1984. "Revolutionary Change, Soviet Intervention and 'Normalization' in East-Central Europe." *Comparative Politics* 16(2) (January): 127–51.

Vari, Anna and Pal Tamas, eds. 1993. *Environment and Democratic Transition: Policy and Politics in Central and Eastern Europe.* Series on Technology, Risk, and Society, vol. 7. Nordrecht, Netherlands: Kluwer Academic Publishers.

Vinton, Louisa. 1992. "Poland's 'Little Constitution' Clarifies Wałęsa's Powers." *RFE/RL Research Report* 1:35, September 4: 19–26.

Volgyes, Ivan, ed. 1974. *Environmental Deterioration in the Soviet Union and Eastern Europe.* New York: Praeger Publishers.

"W państwie realnego socjalizmu." 1984. *Tygodnik Mazowsze*, September 13.

"W państwie realnego socjalizmu." 1985. *Tygodnik Mazowsze*, August 8.

Walczak, Krzysztof. 1984a. "Ekologiczny elementarz: Matura z sozologii." *Życie Warszawy*, May 23.

———. 1984b. "Herbata z wody niepewnej." *Życie Warszawy*, November 8.

———. 1984c. "Na Bałtyku bez Zmian." *Życie Warszawy*, March 12.

———. 1984d. "Przemysł i Środowisko: Samorządni, nieobecni . . . " *Życie Warszawy*, June 19.

———. 1984e. "Pyłów mniej, ale tylko pozornie: Alarmujące sygnały NIK." *Życie Warszawy*, February 9: 2.

———. 1984f. "Ubywa ziemi, Rzeka ścieków, Gaz w powietrzu: GUS o ochronie Środowiska." *Życie Warszawy*, November 6.

———. 1985. "Czas wyborów. Ekologia na miejscu punktowym." *Życie Warszawy*, September 4: 3.

———. 1987. "Ekologiczny Ruch Społeczny: Presja Zespolona." *Życie Warszawy*, May 5: 3.

———. 1988. "Porozumienie podpisane—czas na konkrety: 'Zielone Płuca Polski.'" *Życie Warszawy*, 14–15 May: 1–2.

Waller, Michael and Frances Millard. 1992. "Environmental Politics in Eastern Europe." *Environmental Politics* 1:2 (Summer): 159–185.

Wandycz, Piotr S. 1974. *The Lands of Partitioned Poland, 1795–1918.* Series on A History of East Central Europe, vol. 7. Seattle and London: University of Washington Press.

Weigle, Marcia A. and Jim Butterfield. 1992. "Civil Society in Reforming Communist Regimes: The Logic of Emergence." *Comparative Politics* 25:1 (October): 1–23.

Weiner, Douglas R. 1988. *Models of Nature: Ecolocy, Conservation and Cultural Revolution in Soviet Russia.* Bloomington and Indianapolis: Indiana University Press.

Welsh, Helga A. 1994. "Political Transition Processes in Central and Eastern Europe," *Comparative Politics* 26:4 (July):379–94.

Wereszycki, Henryk. 1979. "Poland 1918–1939" in Aleksander Gieysztor et al., eds. 1979. *History of Poland*, 2nd ed. Warsaw: PWN-Polish Scientific Publishers: 541–604.

Wiatr, Inez. "Encyklopedia ekologicznya." Column in *Tygodnik Demokratyczny*, 1985–88.

Wielkopolski Informator Ekologiczn, no. 1, (March 1987).

Wierzbicki, Zbigniew. 1987. Open letter to potential participants in the Green Cross Seminar, January 5.

Witańska, Irena. 1985. "Wnioski ze spotkań przedwyborczych. Jak chronić środowisko naturalne," rozmowa ze Stefanem Jarzębskim, Ministrem-Kierownikiem Urzędu Ochrony Środowiska i Gospodarki Wodnej. *Rzeczpospolita*, September 21–22: 3.

Wojciechowski, Iwo. 1987. *Ekologiczne Podstawy Kształtowania Środowiska*. Warsaw: Państwowe Wydawnictwo Naukowe.

"Wolę Być: Wydarzenia, Ogłoszenia." 1988. *Na Przełaj*, July 10: 5.

Wójcik, Przemysław, ed. 1985. *Zagrożenia Ekologiczne*. Instytut Badań Klasy Robotniczej of the Akademia Nauk Społecznych series on Położenie Klasy Robotniczej w Polsce, vol. 5. Warsaw: Komitet Centralny Polskiej Zjednoczonej Partii Robotniczej.

———. 1990. "Aneks," in Stefan Godzik and Przemysław Wójcik, eds. 1990. *Ekologiczne Uwarunkowania Zdrowia i Życia Społeczeństwa Polskiego*. Warsaw: Wydawnictwo SGGW-AR.

"Wstęp grozi śmiercią lub kalectwem." 1983. *Tygodnik Mazowsze* 54, June 2: 4.

"Wyborcy—kandydaci. Rejestr spraw do załatwienia." 1985. *Życie Warszawy*, 26 August: 1–2.

"Wyborcy—kandydaci. Z dedykacją przyszłemu Sejmowi." 1985. *Życie Warszawy*, 24–25 August: 1–2.

Wyka, Anna. 1988. "Ruch 'Wolę Być.'" *Państwo i Kultura Polityczna* 4: 58–95.

———. "Ruch 'Wolę Być'" (unpublished manuscript). Contains early documents and letters of the movement.

"Wykaz organizacji i inicjatyw proekologicznych." 1989. *Prace Komitetu Obywatelskiego przy Przewodniczącym NSZZ Solidarność*, no. 2 (June): 78–89.

"Z działalności LOP. Z dziejów Stowarzyszenia." 1988. *Przyroda Polska*, no. 5 (377), (May): 25.

"Z komunikatu TKK NSZZ 'Solidarność - 13.05.86r." 1986. *Przegląd Wiadomości Agencyjnych* 20, 18 May: 1.

"Za rubieżą." 1984. *CDN nr 83*, 18 September: 2.

Zacłona, R. 1987. "Sprawy Polski i Polaków," Centrum Badania Opinii Społecznej Study no. T207, December 9–12.

"Zagrożenia." 1984. Reprinted in *Agencja Informacyjna "S"* nr 2, 28 April: 20–21, from *Wolny Robotnik*.

Zald, Mayer N. and John D. McCarthy, eds. 1979. *The Dynamics of Social Movements: Resource Mobilization, Social Control, and Tactics*. Cambridge, MA: Winthrop Publishers.

———. 1987. *Social Movements in an Organizational Society*. New Brunswick, NJ: Transaction Publishers.

Zarzycki, Kazimierz. 1988. "Problemy ochrony przyrody," (speech delivered at the III Congress of Polish Science). Polska Akademia Nauk Komitet Ochrony Przyrody, *Problemy Ochrony Polskiej Przyrody*, ed. Romuald Olaczek and Kazimierz Zarzycki. Warsaw: Państwowe Wydawnictwo Naukowe.

Zeszyty Niezależnej Myśli Lekarskiej. 1986. Quarterly of the Social Commission for Health, no. 7, March. (Available in *IDC: Polish Independent Publications 1976+*)

Ziegler, Charles E. 1979. "Disaggregated Pluralism in a Socialist System: Environmental Policy in the USSR." Ph.D. Dissertation, University of Illinois at Urbana-Champaign.

———. 1982. "Centrally Planned Economies and Environmental Information: A Rejoinder." *Soviet Studies* 34(2) (April): 296–99.

———. 1985. "Soviet Images of the Environment." *British Journal of Political Science* 15(3) (July): 365–80.

———. 1986. "Issue Creation and Interest Groups in Soviet Environmental Policy: The Applicability of the State Corporatist Model." *Comparative Politics* 18(2) (January): 171–92.

Zuzowski, Robert. 1992. *Political Dissent and Opposition in Poland: The Workers' Defense Committee "KOR"*. Westport, CT: Praeger.

Zvosec, Christine L. 1984. "Environmental Deterioration in Eastern Europe." *World Affairs* 147(2) (Fall): 97–126.

Żylicz, Tomasz. 1987. "Możliwosci Stosowania Rynkowych Instrumentów Ochrony Środowiska w Polsce (Podsumowanie Badań 1986–87)." *EKO*^{2} Series no. 8722. Warsaw: Wydział Nauk Ekonomicznych, Uniwersytet Warszawski.

Cited Interviews, Meetings and Seminars

Activist, Polish Ecological Club. Kraków, Poland, May 1986.

Activist (high-level), Polish Ecological Club. Kraków, Poland, May 1986.

Czjakowski, Przemysław. Founding Member of the Polish Ecological Club, Board Member of Center for Environment and Development, MSc in Geography and in Ecology. Warsaw, 29 July 1993.

Environmentalist present at the formation of the PRON ecological movement ERS. Warsaw, Poland, 19 July 1988.

Former Solidarity activist in the Polish Ecological Club. Kraków, Poland, May 1986.

Fura, Zygmunt. Kraków, Poland, May 1986; Washington, D.C., June 16, 1987; Kraków, Poland, April 14, 1988.

Gliński, Piotr. Board member of Service Bureau for the Environmental Movement, Ph.D. in Sociology, Researcher at the Institute of Philosophy and Sociology, Polish Academy of Sciences. Warsaw, Poland, July 16, 1993.

Juchnowicz, Stanisław. Meeting with an environmental delegation from the American Council for International Leadership. Kraków, Poland, 26 June 1989.

Ministry of Environmental Protection and Natural Resources Delegation. Meeting with an environmental delegation from the American Council for International Leadership. Warsaw, Poland, June 28, 1989.

Orłoś, Teresa. Specialist in charge of Contacts with Society, Ministry of Environmental Protection, Natural Resources, and Forestry. Warsaw, Poland, July 27, 1993.

Pawlak, Jolanta. Member of the National Chamber of Commerce's Committee on Environmental Protection, President of the Social Ecological Institute, Director of the Service Bureau for the Ecological Movement. Warsaw, Poland, August 5, 1993.

Pudlis, Eugeniusz. Vice-President of the Polish Ecological Club, Editor of "Green Voice," monthly insert to "Warsaw Voice," Founder, first President and current Vice President of EKOS. Warsaw, Poland, July 28, 1993.

Przyrody - Człowiek - Wartości. Colloquia, Polish Academy of Sciences. Warsaw, Poland, October 1987–June 1988.

Wierzbicki, Zbigniew. Member of the President's Ecological Council, founding member of Polish Ecological Club, founder of "Green Cross" Seminar, member of former Social Consultative Council, activist in several other organizations. Warsaw, Poland: July 7, 1988; August 16, 1988; June 27, 1988; October 22, 1989 (by telephone); August 3, 1993.

Wójcik, Przemysław. Deputy Director, Institute for Research on the Working Class, Academy of Social Sciences. Warsaw, Poland, April 25, 1988; June 5, 1996 (by telephone).

Index

Academy of Social Sciences. *See* Institute for the Study of the Working Class; Polish United Workers' Party

Activism, 83; components of, 24; in electoral politics, 109–10; human rights, 5; and movement formation, 76, 183; networking in, 183; opportunity-based, 25; political identity in, 88, 94, 162, 170; post-communist, 26; of Roman Catholic Church, 24, 76, 103–4, 107, 108, 116; under Solidarity, 7, 84–85; sources of, 2; types of, 113–14, 119; nonofficial, 140. *See also* Organizations; Social movements

Activism, environmental, 1, 3; decline in visibility, 219n16; "expert," 113, 167, 173; of groups, table 5.1; influence on decisionmaking, 169; local, 169, 184; public awareness of, 175–76, 219–20n24–26; weakness under regime transition, 172, 173, 177, 188. *See also* Environmental movement, Polish

Actors: autonomy of, 14, 112; in civil society, 7–9, 93–94, 180; connections among, 86; external, 112, 171; identity of, 82, 162; in social movements, 16, 20, 25. *See also* Environmentalists; Organizations

Administration, environmental, 46–47, 58–65, 74–75; under Gierek regime, 62–63; legislation for, 53–55, 56, 70; under normalization, 145; weakness in, 53–54, 65

Agriculture, 35; biodynamic, 108, 117; collectivization of, 36; run-off from, 31

Air pollution, 12; administration of, 62; damage to national parks, 69; economic effects of, 204n13; legislation, 54, 55; press coverage of, 157; public opinion on, 136; regulation under martial law, 33

All-Poland Committee for Peasant Resistance "Rural Solidarity." *See* "Rural Solidarity"

Andrzejewski, Roman, 88

Animal species: legislation for, 52; protection of, 50, 67, 204n4

Anti-nuclear movements, 44, 89; following Chernobyl, 129–33; in Klempicz, 107; in underground press, 128; in Żarnowiec, 104, 118. *See also* Freedom and Peace

Anti-politics, 197n3

Anti-state movements, 23–24

Association of Urbanists of Poland, 106

Authoritarianism: challenges to, 200n16; effect of civil society on, 6; effect of networks on, 184

Autonomy: of actors, 14, 112; within envi-